DATE DUE

DEMCO 38-297

A NEW DEAL FOR SOCIAL SECURITY

A NEW DEAL FOR SOCIAL SECURITY

Peter J. Ferrara and Michael Tanner

CATO INSTITUTE
Washington, D.C.

Library of Congress Cataloging-in-Publication Data

Ferrara, Peter J., 1956–
    A new deal for social security / Peter J. Ferrara and Michael Tanner.
      p.   cm.
    Includes bibliographical references and index.
    ISBN 1-882577-62-0 (cloth).—ISBN 1-882577-63-9 (pbk.)
    1. Social security—United States. 2. Old age assistance—United
States—Finance. 3. Social security—United States—Finance.
I. Tanner, Michael, 1956– . II. Title.
HD7125.F4679   1998
368.4'3'00973—dc21   98-36656
                                                  CIP

Printed in the United States of America.

CATO INSTITUTE
1000 Massachusetts Ave., N.W.
Washington, D.C. 20001

Contents

Preface

It has been nearly 20 years since the Cato Institute published *Social Security: The Inherent Contradiction* by Peter Ferrara. Back then, Ferrara's warning that Social Security was an unsustainable and deeply flawed program and his call to privatize the retirement program were seen as truly radical.

But much has changed in the years since. The Berlin Wall has fallen and communism has been consigned to the trash heap of history. Socialism has been discredited as a political philosophy and the virtues of the free market are being embraced throughout the world. The United States has seen three presidents, the Republican takeover of Congress, and innumerable commissions to fix Social Security.

Shortly after the publication of *Social Security: The Inherent Contradiction*, the small South American country of Chile privatized its Social Security system. Chile's program was so successful that it has been copied by seven other Latin American countries and is now being considered by other countries from Eastern Europe to China. Other countries, such as Britain and Australia, have also discovered that private capital markets are a better way to provide for a secure retirement than traditional Social Security. A worldwide revolution is under way.

Today, the problems faced by Social Security are even more apparent. The system's finances are unsustainable. Without major tax hikes it will soon be unable to pay promised benefits. But Social Security taxes are already so high that many young workers will receive a negative rate of return on their taxes—less back in benefits than they paid in taxes. Social Security also contains a variety of inequities that penalize the poor, ethnic minorities, working women, and others.

This book provides an alternative. Building on the experience and studies since *Social Security: The Inherent Contradiction*, it lays out the political and economic case for transforming Social Security. It provides the details for a new system of retirement—a system based on individual liberty and private capital.

This is no longer a radical idea. It is a concept built on sound economics and practical experience. It is an idea that is being increasingly embraced across the political spectrum. It is an idea whose time has come.

No book like this can be the effort of just two people. To start with, our efforts merely build on the work of true path breakers such as Milton Friedman, Martin Feldstein, Carolyn Weaver, and José Piñera. Without them, there would be no movement for Social Security privatization. Nor could we have written this book without the support and timely advice of many people, including Lea Abdnor, David Boaz, Ed Crane, Steve Entin, Dan Mitchell, and Grover Norquist. We must also thank Cary Lipps and Gregg Van Helmond for their assistance with research, and Darcy Olsen, who did a little bit of everything and then some. We are also indebted to Elizabeth Kaplan for her editorial help. Finally, Michael Tanner wishes to extend his personal thanks to Ellen for her advice, support, and encouragement.

1. The Worldwide Revolution in Social Security

Social Security turned 62 years old in 1997, the age of early retirement. From modest beginnings, this government-run old-age pension program has grown to be America's most popular social welfare program and the largest single government program in the world. For more than six decades, many Americans have relied on Social Security to enable them to retire with financial dignity. Yet it is a program that was flawed from its initial design, an unsustainable pyramid scheme that places ever heavier burdens on young workers while making promises for the future that it cannot keep.

Now the flaws are beginning to show. Young workers have lost faith in the system. A famous poll shows that twice as many young workers believe in flying saucers as believe they will receive a Social Security check when they retire.[1] While their belief in extraterrestrial life is problematic, their estimation for the future of Social Security is not far off the mark. Social Security is on the brink of financial crisis and soon will no longer be able to pay the benefits it has promised. Without drastic reform, young workers face the prospect of higher and higher taxes in exchange for fewer and fewer benefits.

The need for Social Security reform is well known to the political leaders in Washington. It has been apparent for years. But until now, politicians have been afraid to make the necessary reforms, intimidated by Tip O'Neill's famous dictum that Social Security is the "third rail" of American politics—touch it and your career dies.

That is changing now. In America and around the world a revolution in Social Security thinking is taking place—a revolution that promises a new Social Security system based on private markets and individual control.

The Revolution Begins

The revolution began in 1981 in the South American nation of Chile. Chile had been the first nation in the Western Hemisphere to

1

adopt a traditional social security system. But in 1981, the Chilean government allowed workers a choice: they could stay in the government-run system or, instead, choose a new system based on private savings and investment in the free market. Workers were allowed to divert their social security payroll taxes to individually owned accounts that were invested in private capital markets, through such instruments as stocks and bonds.[2]

Today, more than 90 percent of Chilean workers have chosen the private option. The payments into the new system are only about half of the total payroll taxes under the government-run system. Yet retirees are receiving benefits 200 percent higher than under the old system. Already, average Chilean workers, well on their way to achieving the socialist dream of owning the nation's business and industry, in fact have more savings than average U.S. workers, even though average U.S. workers earn seven times more than average Chilean workers.

Chile's experience was recognized as such a great economic and political success that other countries around the world began adopting similar reforms. Today, seven other Latin American countries have enacted private social security options on the Chilean model: Argentina, Mexico, Peru, Colombia, Bolivia, Uruguay, and El Salvador.[3]

The trend is now spreading beyond Latin America. Great Britain has adopted a two-tier social security system, with workers allowed to opt out of a portion of the program. Nearly 80 percent of British workers have now opted out of half the government-run system.[4] Moreover, the current Labour government of Prime Minister Tony Blair is discussing extending the private option to the other half of the public system.

Australia, Singapore, and many other countries have also adopted some form of a privatized social security system.[5] More recently, the trend has spread to Eastern Europe. Hungary adopted a private option for its workers in 1997, and Poland will soon also. Kazakhstan, a newly independent state of the old Soviet Union, adopted a private option in 1997 as well.[6] The idea is now spreading throughout all of the nearby independent former Soviet states, as well as other Eastern European countries.[7]

Perhaps most remarkable of all, at a Cato Institute conference in Shanghai in 1997, a senior official of the People's Republic of China announced that his country would be moving to a private system as well.[8] And, near the end of 1997, Russia announced that new workers in that country would soon be paying into new, private savings and investment accounts instead of a traditional social security program.[9] Today, workers in that country pay half their retirement payments into an individual investment account system, and half into a traditional public social security system.

The World Bank endorsed this trend in its 1994 report, *Averting the Old-Age Crisis*.[10] The 400-page report concludes that Chile's reforms have been a success and urges other countries to consider private alternatives as a way of dealing with the worldwide crisis in social security and as a way to stimulate economic growth. The worldwide popularity of privatizing social security has spread to such a degree that delegates from 38 countries met at a 1997 conference in London, sponsored by the Cato Institute and *The Economist*, to discuss how and why to privatize social security.[11]

The Revolution Comes to America

In the annual Ely Lecture to the American Economics Association in 1996, Harvard economics professor Martin Feldstein, president of the National Bureau of Economic Research, called for privatization of Social Security in the United States. Feldstein estimated that the present value of the future benefits of such reform would be a truly astounding $10 trillion to $20 trillion.[12] Such reform also has been endorsed by Nobel laureates Gary Becker, James Buchanan, and Milton Friedman, as well as former American Economics Association president Arnold Harberger, among others.

Longtime anti-poverty activist Sam Beard is now popularizing the benefits of such reform with his book, *Restoring Hope in America: The Social Security Solution*.[13] A former aide to Senator Robert Kennedy, Beard has dedicated his life to bringing economic growth to the inner city, most notably through his National Development Council. In his book, Beard shows that with a private, invested system, the middle class would retire as millionaires. Most important, he argues that giving lower income workers control over some capital through such a private system is the key to breaking the cycle of poverty in inner city areas. Beard is now on a long-term national campaign conducting regular conferences in inner city areas across the country to explain and promote the idea among the nation's poor and minorities, who he believes will be helped the most.

Marshall Carter and William Shipman of State Street Global Advisors, the largest pension investment management firm in the country, have also written a new book on the subject, *Promises to Keep: Saving Social Security's Dream*.[14] Drawing on their years of experience in the investment field, they show that through a private, invested system, workers would get three to six times the benefits promised by Social Security. This includes low-income workers as well as others. The same conclusion is reached in a book by economist Robert Genetski, appropriately entitled *A Nation of Millionaires*.[15]

In January 1997, the usually staid Advisory Council on Social Security surprised the public policy community. The president appoints council members every five years to review Social Security, identify problems, and recommend changes. Usually the council insists everything is fine with Social Security and recommends only minor changes.

But this council, appointed by President Clinton in 1995, was different. Its report was more than a year late and the subject of bitter infighting, but eventually the panel unanimously agreed that some sort of new, invested system was necessary. Although the panel split three ways over what form such a system should take, 5 of the council's 13 members supported allowing workers an option to choose a private invested system for almost half of their Social Security taxes.[16]

Early in 1997, still another unexpected development arose. The Oregon state legislature passed a resolution calling on the federal government to give the state permission to adopt its own private, invested plan in place of Social Security for all workers in the state. The resolution is based on a precedent in federal welfare programs, by which states can ask the federal government for a waiver to adopt their own welfare experiments and reforms. Highly successfully innovations have resulted from this waiver process. The resolution asked Congress to adopt a similar waiver system for Social Security, so states can try their own Social Security reforms.[17] Several other states are considering similar resolutions.

The United States has, in fact, already tried its own small experiment on how privatization would work here. At about the same time that Chile adopted its reforms in 1981, three counties near

Galveston, Texas, switched to a private, invested system rather than Social Security for their county government workers.[18] (At that time the law allowed state and local workers to make such a choice. The law was changed in 1983 to prohibit further switches.)

The system for those county workers operates much like the Chilean system. Workers pay into private individual investment accounts. The funds, which are managed by private companies, are invested in stocks, bonds, and other private capital investments. At retirement, the accumulated funds are used to purchase annuities that guarantee workers a specified monthly income for the rest of their lives. The plan also includes private life insurance and disability benefits, replacing Social Security's survivors' and disability benefits. Today, those workers who retire after 20 years under this private plan will receive benefits three to four times greater than Social Security would pay. Not surprisingly, the survivors and disability benefits are higher too.

In 1995, the Cato Institute launched what has become a highly successful project to advance a private, invested, alternative system to Social Security. The project is chaired by José Piñera, architect of Chile's successful reform, and its Board of Advisors includes top economists Becker and Harberger, as well as Dorcas Hardy, a former commissioner of Social Security, and Tim Penny, a former Democratic congressman. Americans for Tax Reform, an influential grassroots taxpayers organization, has also recently launched a campaign for a private option for Social Security. The national Jaycees are also conducting highly informative seminars across the country to educate young people on this issue.

All of this activity is building on powerfully favorable grassroots opinion. A 1994 Luntz Research poll found that 82 percent of adults under age 35 supported the idea "of directing a portion of their Social Security taxes into a personal retirement account like an IRA which could be kept at any financial institution they would like, and receiving less in Social Security benefits from the government."[19] A 1995 Luntz poll of all adults, conducted for the seniors organization 60 Plus, found the public supporting such an option by 77 to 14 percent.[20] In 1996, Bill McInturff of Public Opinion Strategies, perhaps the leading polling firm for political campaigns, conducted a nationwide poll for the Cato Institute, which found the public favoring the idea by 68 to 11 percent.[21]

Indeed, a 1994 Gallup Poll found that 54 percent of Americans thought that participation in the Social Security system should be made voluntary, which is actually a more radical change than privatization.[22] Another Gallup Poll, this one in January 1995, found that by 47 to 32 percent, Americans thought that Social Security was not "a good program for today's younger workers."[23] The same poll found that by 53 to 23 percent, those interviewed believed that "most people could make more money by investing their retirement funds in the private sector than they could with Social Security."

Likewise, a poll by GrassRoots Research in November of 1995 found that 38 percent of today's workers would withdraw from Social Security if offered the option, *even if they received nothing in return for the taxes they have already paid*. Among workers ages 30 to 39, 48 percent would choose to leave the current system.[24] A poll for the Democratic Leadership Council, conducted by White House pollster Mark Penn, found 73 percent of Democrats want to be able to privately invest all or part of their Social Security taxes.[25] Most recently, the respected Zogby poll found that 60.8 percent of Americans supported "taking part of the money you now pay into Social Security and investing it for your future as you see fit." Among voters ages 18 to 29, support for privatization reached an astounding 85.9 percent.[26]

Politicians are responding to the shift in public opinion. Reps. Jim Kolbe (R-Ariz.) and Charles Stenholm (D-Tex.) have launched a bipartisan caucus group in the House of Representatives to promote discussion of Social Security reform, including privatization. Approximately 80 members from both parties have joined. Reps. Nick Smith (R-Mich.), Mark Sanford Jr. (R-S.C.), and John Porter (R-Ill.) have introduced bills establishing a fully private alternative to Social Security. In the Senate, Sens. Robert Kerrey (D-Neb.) and Judd Gregg (R-N.H.) have introduced legislation calling for partial privatization of the system, while Sen. Phil Gramm (R-Tex.) is also developing privatization legislation.

Republican presidential hopeful Steve Forbes made Social Security privatization a key element of his campaign and has remained outspoken since then. President Clinton has also promised to push for Social Security reform. Recently, Alan Greenspan warned that Social Security reform must come "sooner rather than later," and suggested that privatization was a viable solution to the system's problems.[27]

A private option for Social Security is now a viable political issue in the United States. It enjoys broad public support, with strong intensity among young voters under age 40. And it has earned the support of establishment institutions and leading intellectual figures.

The Basis for Reform

There are five main reasons that a private option for Social Security should be adopted. Briefly, they are as follows:

Bankruptcy

Social Security is going bankrupt. The federal government's largest spending program, accounting for nearly 22 percent of all federal spending, faces irresistible demographic and fiscal pressures that threaten the future retirement security of today's young workers. According to the 1998 report of the Social Security system's Board of Trustees, in 2013, just 15 years from now, the Social Security system will begin to run a deficit.[28] That is, it will begin to spend more on benefits than it brings in through taxes. Anyone who has ever run a business—or balanced a checkbook—understands that when you are spending more than you bring in, something has to give—you need to start either earning more money or spending less to keep things balanced. For Social Security, that means either higher taxes or lower benefits.

In theory, Social Security is supposed to continue paying benefits after 2013 by drawing on the Social Security trust funds. These trust funds are supposed to provide enough money to guarantee benefits until 2032, when they will be exhausted. But one of Washington's dirty little secrets is that there really are no trust funds. The government spent that money long ago to finance general government spending, hiding the true size of the federal budget deficit. The trust funds now consist only of government bonds, essentially IOUs—a promise that at some time in the future the government will replace that money, which can be done only through collecting more taxes or issuing even more debt.

Even if Congress can find a way to redeem the bonds, the trust funds surplus will be completely exhausted by 2032. At that point, Social Security will have to rely solely on revenue from payroll taxes. But such revenues will not be sufficient to pay all promised benefits.

Moreover, after that point, the financial gulf in Social Security becomes huge. Based on the government's own latest projections, paying all promised Social Security benefits to young workers entering the workforce today would probably require a payroll tax increase of 50 to 100 percent, 6 to 12 percentage points.[29] If we look at all the benefits financed by the 15.3 percent payroll tax today, which includes the hospital insurance benefits of Medicare, paying all the retirement benefits promised to today's young workers would probably require doubling or almost tripling that tax to as much as 30 to 40 percent.[30] That level of taxation is neither economically nor politically feasible. Consequently, there is no prospect that today's young workers will receive their currently promised benefits.

Bad Deal for Young Workers

Even if Social Security did somehow manage to pay all its promised benefits, the taxes for today's young workers are already so high that the benefits would be a bad deal in return for those taxes. Those benefits provide a low, below-market, rate of return, or effective interest rate, on the taxes workers and their employers had to pay into the system throughout their careers. Studies show that investing these tax funds instead in private savings and insurance would likely yield three or more times the benefits Social Security promises to today's young workers.[31]

Investing through the private system and earning modest returns, the average two-earner couple would retire with a trust fund of about $1 million in today's dollars to support their retirement benefits. This trust fund would pay them more than Social Security out of the continuing interest alone, while still allowing the couple to leave almost $1 million to their children or other heirs. Alternatively, they could use the entire trust fund for an annuity that would pay them three times what Social Security promises.

This is a measure of what Social Security is costing average families today—$1 million over their lifetimes, or about three times the benefits of Social Security. Moreover, this financial crisis exists today, not some time in the future. Every year that workers are forced to participate only in Social Security, without the freedom to choose the private alternatives, workers are irreversibly suffering a bigger and bigger portion of this lifetime loss. Roughly, the average two-earner couple is losing $25,000 a year each year they are forced to go without a private option.

The first two problems alone show why privatization is the only solution to Social Security's problems. If taxes are raised or benefits cut to solve the bankruptcy problem, then Social Security will become an even worse deal for today's young workers. Or if taxes are cut or benefits raised to make Social Security a better deal for today's workers, then the system's financial crisis will worsen. The only way to solve both the problems is to turn to the private sector, where the high returns and new income generated by private investments will in fact fully finance even better benefits than Social Security.

Savings and Economic Growth

Social Security operates on a pay-as-you-go basis, with almost all of the funds coming in immediately paid out to current beneficiaries. This system displaces private, fully funded alternatives where the funds coming in would be saved and invested for the future benefits of today's workers. The result is a large net loss of national savings, reducing capital investment, wages, national income, and economic growth. Moreover, by increasing the cost of hiring workers, the payroll tax substantially reduces wages, employment, and economic growth as well.

Shifting to a private system, with hundreds of billions of dollars invested in individual retirement accounts each year, would likely produce a large net increase in national savings, depending on how the government financed the transition. That would increase national investment, productivity, wages, jobs, and economic growth. Replacing the payroll tax with private retirement contributions also would improve economic growth, because the required contributions would be lower and the contributions would be seen as directly part of the worker's compensation, stimulating more employment and output.

Feldstein's estimate that privatization of Social Security would produce $10 trillion to $20 trillion in present value net benefits to America is essentially his estimate of the present value of the improved economic performance resulting from the reform.[32] Most of the net benefit probably would come in the form of the higher returns and benefits earned for retirees through the private investment accounts. But some also would come in the form of higher wages and employment for working people.

Helping the Poor

Low-income workers would be among the biggest winners from a private system.[33] A private, invested system would pay low-income

9

workers at least two to three times the benefits promised by Social Security. And this does not even count the fact that blacks and other minorities, and the poor in general, have below average life expectancies. As a result, they tend to live fewer years in retirement and collect less in Social Security benefits. In a private, invested system, by contrast, they would each retain control over the funds paid in and could pay themselves higher benefits over their fewer retirement years, or leave more to their children or other heirs.

The higher returns and benefits in a private, invested system would be most important to low-income families, as they most need the extra funds. The saved funds in the individual retirement accounts, which could be left to the children of the poor, would also greatly help families break out of the cycle of poverty. Similarly, the improved economic growth, higher wages, and increased jobs that would result from privatization also would be most important to the poor. Moreover, without reform, low-income workers would be hurt the most by the higher taxes or reduced benefits that will be necessary on our current course. Averting this financial crisis and the otherwise inevitable results would consequently again be most important to low-income workers.

In addition, with average- and low-wage workers accumulating huge sums in their own investment accounts, the distribution of wealth throughout society would become far more broad than it is today. That would occur not through the redistribution of existing wealth but through the creation of new wealth, far more equally held. Because privatizing Social Security would turn every worker into a stockowner, the old, senseless division between labor and capital would be eroded. Every laborer would become a capitalist. The socialist dream of the nation's workers owning its business and industry would be effectively achieved. At the same time, as the nation's workers become capitalists, support for free market, pro-growth economic policies would increase among all sectors of society. This social effect is one of the least cited but most important reasons for privatizing Social Security.

Freedom of Choice and Control

After all the economic analysis, however, perhaps the single most important reason for privatizing Social Security is that it would restore to American workers freedom of choice and control over the one-eighth of their earnings that is now consumed by Social Security.

In an ideal world, each of us would be free to make our own decisions over how to provide for our retirement—how much and when to save. A purely voluntary Social Security system would be consistent with human dignity and individual liberty. However, political reality means that a mandatory retirement system is likely to be with us for the conceivable future. Privatization, therefore, becomes the next best option.

Under privatization, workers would gain direct personal control over the thousands and thousands of dollars they and their employers now must pay into Social Security each year. In addition, in the private market, families would be freer to tailor their retirement and insurance benefits to their own personal needs and circumstances. They would have broader freedom to choose their own retirement age, for example, or the level of life and disability insurance protection appropriate for them.

All of these reasons for privatization of Social Security will be discussed in thorough detail in later chapters of this book, after a short history and review of the major features of the program. Then we will discuss how Social Security could be privatized in the United States, and how such reform would work in practice.

Such reform should now be top priority for U.S. policymakers, for perhaps no other single change could do so much to increase the freedom and prosperity of the American people.

2. A Short History of Social Security

On August 14, 1935, in a surprisingly subdued ceremony with no press in attendance, President Franklin Delano Roosevelt signed into law the Social Security Act, capping a year-long political battle and creating what would become the largest government program in the world.[1]

Although Roosevelt had called for the creation of a government-run old-age pension program only a little more than a year earlier, the impetus for a program of this nature goes back much farther. Perhaps the first recorded use of the term "social security" was in a speech by Simón Bolívar in 1819, calling for a government "which produces the most happiness, the most social security, and the most political stability."[2] Bolívar's concept of a government responsible for the economic and social security of its citizens was a continuing theme of 19th century political theory, which found its fruition in the welfare states of this century. In practice, this meant a government responsible for the care of those who were considered unable to care for themselves, particularly children, the disabled, and the elderly.

The idea of state-funded pensions for the elderly was debated in many countries and was finally put into practice by Chancellor Otto von Bismarck in Germany in 1889.[3] A number of historians have suggested that Bismarck was not particularly driven by humanitarian impulses, but rather was seeking to outflank the opposition Social Democrats who were causing problems for his military buildup.[4] Bismarck's program was remarkably similar to the current American Social Security system, social insurance financed through compulsory contributions (i.e., through payroll taxes). Social insurance programs provide defined benefits according to eligibility rules prescribed by law, with the cost being met by mandatory contributions from covered individuals, their employers, or both.[5]

Other countries soon followed Germany's lead. By 1929, 35 countries, mostly in Europe and Latin America, had established old-age pension programs. Most of them took the form of social insurance financed through payroll taxes, although a few countries, such as Italy and France, subsidized private insurance, and a few others, such as Denmark, had noncontributory systems financed out of general tax revenues.[6]

Social Security Comes to America

In the United States support for Social Security was much slower in developing. That was due in part to the belief that a program of this nature was a socialistic European import, at a time when there was a great deal of anti-European sentiment in this country, as well as a long-standing Jeffersonian philosophy of self-reliance and minimal government. There was also opposition because government old-age pensions were considered unnecessary. Many American retirees were already protected by pensions, either public or private.[7] For example, the large number of Civil War veterans were covered through pensions. At the turn of the century, in fact, nearly one-quarter of all men older than 18 in the country, and nearly one-third of all men from Northern states, were covered by Civil War pensions.[8] Civil War pensions were quite generous and were increased regularly by Congresses seeking the powerful veterans' vote. Between 1910 and 1932, veterans' pensions increased fourfold.[9] States, cities, and counties also provided benefits to retired veterans.

Government employees were also generally protected by pensions. State and local pension systems for police, firemen, and teachers first emerged in the 1890s. By 1920, most other state and municipal employees were covered. A 1927 study of states and cities with populations of more than 400,000 found that public retirement systems for police and fire department personnel existed in every city, and teacher retirement systems existed in all but a handful. Six states had statewide programs for all public employees, and 21 states had statewide teacher retirement programs.[10] Federal civil service employees received retirement benefits beginning in 1920. By 1927, retirement benefits for federal employees were equal to 50 percent of the average annual wages earned by those employees during their working years.[11]

Private companies were also beginning to offer pensions, particularly railroads, public utilities, and heavy manufacturing enterprises such as the steel industry.[12] By some estimates, as much as 15 percent of the private-sector workforce was covered by corporate pension programs by 1932.[13] It is important to note, however, that neither the public nor private systems were pension systems in the sense we think of today with assets being accumulated against future liabilities. Public pensions were usually funded directly from current tax revenue.[14] Private pensions were paid out of corporate earnings and often amounted to more of a moral than a legal commitment to retirees.[15] In fact, many company pension plans had provisions allowing benefits to be reduced or eliminated if funding became insufficient.[16] Those provisions would become important factors when the country hit hard economic times.

Finally, several states had established old-age pensions. Those were not contributory social insurance programs; rather they were cash grants to the elderly poor. The first of these was passed by Arizona in 1914. The law was quickly declared unconstitutional, but in 1923 Montana, Nevada, and Pennsylvania passed similar laws. By 1934, 28 states had established old-age pensions. Those programs were not actually statewide programs, but generally stipulated a maximum monthly pension that counties were allowed to provide.[17] Most state old-age pensions were strictly means-tested and were modeled after existing welfare or poor laws, meaning that an elderly person could be denied benefits if the person (1) had financially responsible relatives, (2) failed to work if he was able, (3) had deserted his family, (4) was a "tramp or begger," (5) disposed of property to qualify for the pension, (6) was the recipient of another government pension, or (7) was a prison inmate.[18] Benefits under the programs varied widely from state to state, but they were generally low, ranging from as little as $1 per month in North Dakota to $30 per month in Maryland.[19]

Of course the existence of public and private pensions did not mean that American retirees faced no risks. Most retirees received no pensions and were either self-supporting or dependent on voluntary care from family and friends. For example, a 1929 survey of retirees in the state of New York found that 43 percent were supported by their own earnings and savings. Another 50 percent were supported by other family members.[20] In addition, many seniors worked well beyond today's retirement age. For example, in 1930, more than 58 percent of men over age 65 were still employed, as were 8 percent of women.[21] Surprisingly few elderly were dependent on charity, either public or private, including state old-age pensions.

Poverty among the elderly *was* a problem. But, then, poverty was a problem among all age groups in the United States at that time. The widespread prosperity that followed World War II had not yet come to this country. By some measures at least a third of the U.S. population could have been considered poor.[22] For those retirees who were poor, the evidence suggests that this was not due to their short-sighted failure to make provisions for their old age or the lack of existing insurance or pension programs, but to low incomes during their working years.[23]

The push for social insurance in the United States originated primarily among European immigrants, particularly Germans, who had experience with such systems in their home countries. Among the first to call for the creation of a national government-run social insurance program was the American Association for Labor Legislation, an offshoot of the German-created International Association for Labor Legislation.[24] The émigré groups provided the social insurance movement with much of its intellectual foundation.

Supporters of social insurance explicitly supported government as an agent of "social justice." In particular, they believed that government should redistribute wealth, favoring labor over capital, and should attempt to eliminate what they saw as the primary evil of the industrial age—worker insecurity.[25] As Abraham Epstein, perhaps the leading proponent of social insurance, stated:

> Ever since Adam and Eve were driven from the sheltered Garden of Eden, insecurity has been the bane of mankind. The challenge confronting us in the 20th century is that of economic insecurity, which weighs down our lives, subverts our liberty, and frustrates our pursuit of happiness. The establishment of economic security has become a paramount issue because our modern system of industrial production has rendered our lives insecure to the point of despair. The wage system has made economic security depend entirely on the stability of our jobs. Such utter dependence upon a wage for the necessities of life has never been known before in any society.[26]

The push for social insurance gradually moved to the mainstream labor movement. Initially unions had opposed national social insurance, partly because in its early days American labor was preoccupied by local issues such as organizing, wages, and working conditions. Also, and more important, labor had traditionally supported voluntary efforts to deal with such issues (including union pensions). In its early years, American labor was quite suspicious of government action.[27] In fact, Samuel Gompers denounced social insurance as "in its essence undemocratic."[28] Gompers felt that reliance on government would subvert unions by denying their role in meeting the needs of workers.[29]

As political scientist James Q. Wilson has noted, "For the first 30 or 40 years of its history, the American Federation of Labor (AFL) and most of its affiliated unions opposed . . . certain forms of government intervention in labor management affairs or, indeed, in the economy generally, even when the proposed legislation was aimed at improving the welfare of workers."[30]

Ironically, one of the issues that influenced labor's growing support for social security was the increasing success of company-sponsored pensions. Unions opposed corporate pensions on the practical grounds that they undermined union pensions, and on the ideological grounds that they enabled management to "manipulate" workers. The unions argued that allowing companies to give or withhold pensions at their discretion could be used as a weapon against union organizing. Second, workers were being encouraged to trade current wage increases for future pension benefits that might turn out to be a bad deal if the company collapsed or discontinued promised benefits. Third, unions appealed more to young workers who were concerned about wage and hour issues, while companies used pensions to attract older workers who were less likely to be pro-union. Unions also cited companies that discontinued workers' pension benefits in retaliation for strikes. And, finally, pensions were not portable so workers felt bound to a single employer, limiting their leverage.[31] All this led some labor leaders to call for moving pensions "to the more neutral hands of state and national governments."[32] In 1932, the AFL finally reversed its opposition and called for the creation of federal old-age insurance.[33]

The Great Depression

Perhaps no event was as pivotal in the development of Social Security as the Great Depression, the most economically traumatic event in U.S. history. At its worst point, in 1933, nearly 13 million Americans were unemployed, 24.9 percent of the labor force. Among nonfarm workers, unemployment was even worse, as high as 37.6

percent. The nation's real gross national product declined by one-third between 1929 and 1933. One-third of the nation's banks suspended operations. Businesses went bankrupt and there were widespread mortgage foreclosures, particularly on farms.[34]

The general economic collapse undermined the emerging public and private pension systems. Of 418 large employers offering corporate pension programs in 1929, 45 had dropped them by 1932. Many others had reduced benefits.[35] State and municipal governments had problems meeting their pension commitments as well.

Other traditional means of support for the elderly were also threatened. Bank collapses wiped out the savings of many. Friends and relatives, struggling to support their own immediate families, lacked the resources to provide for the aged. With millions of unemployed, there were fewer jobs for older Americans.[36]

Newly poor seniors swelled the rolls of state old-age pension programs. Authorities in New York and Massachusetts (the two biggest pensioning states) estimated that the Depression was responsible for a 35 percent increase in the number of elderly receiving old-age pension benefits.[37] But, in the face of a shrinking tax base and increased demands, the hard-pressed states were unable to cope with this new burden. Most sharply curtailed benefits, with some refusing to accept any new pensioners. Between January and December of 1934, for example, the average monthly old-age pension fell by nearly 20 percent.[38] In some states the number of elderly on the waiting list for eligibility exceeded the number receiving benefits.[39]

Americans everywhere were frightened and insecure. As a result, the call for government action grew. Leading the fight were Abraham Epstein and the American Association for Old-Age Security (AAOAS), later renamed the American Association for Social Security. He was joined by a cross-section of groups such as the American Association for Labor Legislation and the Fraternal Association of Eagles. The social insurance movement had become a political force to reckon with.[40]

Enter Roosevelt

In 1932, Franklin Roosevelt was elected president, promising a "New Deal for the American people." Although Roosevelt was a champion of activist government, old-age pensions were not at the top of his priorities. His early actions at fighting poverty were directed toward working people, with programs such as public works projects.

But political pressure was building. Upton Sinclair ran for governor of California with a call for a $50 per month pension for everyone over age 65 who had lived in the state for at least three years. Huey Long's "Share Our Wealth" campaign included a call for a $30 per month pension for every American over age 60 with an annual income of less than $1,000. Dr. Francis Townsend attracted national support for his proposal to give every nonworking American over age 60 a pension of $200 per month, provided they spend the money within 30 days.[41]

In 1934, with the cost of state old-age pensions reaching the breaking point, calls for a federal bailout became a major issue in congressional elections.[42] Both the Republican and Democratic National Committees endorsed federal action to assist the elderly poor, and even the U.S. Chamber of Commerce added its voice to the chorus demanding action.[43]

That year Sen. Charles Dill (D-Wash.) and Rep. William Connery (D-Mass.) introduced legislation, drafted by the AAOAS, to provide federal aid to states that enacted old-age pension laws. The federal grant would have equaled approximately 30 percent of the state's expenditures. The legislation had strong bipartisan support and became the first federal old-age pension bill to pass both the House Labor Committee and the Senate Pensions Committee. The legislation would probably have swept to final passage, but President Roosevelt did not yet believe the time was right for action. He told lawmakers that he was developing a more comprehensive social-insurance program and asked them to delay action. Using his clout with the powerful House Rules Committee, Roosevelt was able to prevent the bill from ever coming to a vote.[44]

Despite his opposition to Dill-Connery, Roosevelt was inching toward action on the issue of old-age pensions. In 1934, he signed the Railroad Retirement Act, establishing a retirement pension for railroad workers. However, the program was quickly declared unconstitutional by the Supreme Court for a number of reasons that had nothing to do with the pension program itself.[45] Congress repassed the Railroad Retirement Act in 1935 without the offending provisions, and Roosevelt jawboned railroad owners into an agreement not to challenge the legislation in court. In return for this concession, Roosevelt agreed to have the new retirement system assume all the liabilities of existing railroad pension programs.[46] The provisions of the retirement program would substantially resemble those that would one day be in Social Security: a defined benefit pension plan funded by equal employer and employee contributions.[47]

On June 8, 1934, Roosevelt sent a message to Congress outlining his administration's objectives for dealing with the continuing depression and the poverty it was causing. The message's theme echoed that of social-insurance activists such as Epstein in calling for the elimination of "economic insecurity." According to Roosevelt,

> Among our objectives I place the security of the men, women, and children of the nation first. This security for the individual and for the family concerns itself primarily with three factors. . . . The third factor relates to security against the hazards and vicissitudes of life. . . . Next winter we may well undertake the great task of furthering the security of the citizen and his family through social insurance. . . . Hence, I am looking for a sound means which I can recommend to provide at once security against several of the great disturbing factors in life—especially those which relate to unemployment and old age.[48]

To implement those objectives, Roosevelt created the Committee on Economic Security (CES), chaired by Labor Secretary Frances Perkins and including the Secretaries of the Treasury and Agriculture, the Attorney General, and Harry Hopkins, Roosevelt's close friend and director of the Federal Emergency Relief Administration. Subordinate to the CES were three other organizations: a technical board composed of representatives from various federal departments, an executive director and research staff, and an advisory council selected by the president.[49]

At all levels, the process was heavily stacked in favor of those who favored social insurance. Industrial and business groups known to oppose social insurance, such as the National Association of Manufacturers, were not asked to participate.[50] Although high-profile activists like Epstein were not included, social reformers, progressives, and other advocates of social insurance were prominently featured.

Roosevelt himself vacillated. In a statement to a two-day conference of supporters sponsored by the CES, Roosevelt said that he
did not know "whether now is the time for legislation concerning
old age."[51] That comment caused such an uproar that Secretary
Perkins immediately clarified the president's remarks, assuring supporters that the CES still strongly favored old-age pension legislation.[52] Roosevelt believed that unemployment was the greatest threat
to the nation and devoted most of his political capital to that issue.
Thus, he was much more concerned about the CES's proposals for
unemployment insurance than he was about old-age pensions.
Indeed, even Roosevelt's rationale for old-age insurance was
couched in terms of relieving unemployment. If seniors could be
assured of a secure retirement, they would be more likely to leave
the workforce, freeing up jobs for younger workers.[53] Roosevelt did
not really enthusiastically embrace Social Security until it was introduced in Congress.

The CES issued its final report on January 15, 1935. There were
three central recommendations: (1) the federal government would
partially underwrite the cost of state old-age pension programs;
(2) the federal government would administer a new system of voluntary annuities; and (3) a national system of compulsory old-age
insurance would be established for all workers earning less than
$250 per month.[54] Two days later, legislation based on the report
was introduced by Sen. Robert Wagner (D-N.Y.) and Reps. David
Lewis (D-Md.) and R.L. Doughton (D-N.C.).[55]

The Legislative Debate

Hearings began on January 21 in the House and the next day in
the Senate. The voluntary annuity and subsidy for state old-age
pension components were quickly shunted aside.[56] The focus turned
to the compulsory social insurance component, what we know today
as Social Security. Over the next several months, Congress, the
media, and the public would debate many of the same issues that
are being discussed today.

One of these, of course, was the fundamental question of individual responsibility vs. government coercion. A number of legislators
complained that government should not be put in charge of individual savings and retirement decisions. They saw Social Security as
an enormous expansion of federal government power at the expense

of individual liberties. Senator Hastings, for example, attacked proponents' portrayal of Social Security as a "contract" by pointing out that contracts were voluntary agreements.[57]

Proponents of voluntarism nearly won the day with an amendment by Sen. Bennett Clark (D-Mo.). The Clark amendment would have allowed employers with a private retirement annuity program that required combined premiums at least equal to the federal payroll tax, and that could provide benefits at least as large as those provided under the government program, to opt out of the Social Security system.[58]

But supporters of social insurance staunchly opposed the voluntarism underlying the Clark amendment. As Sen. Robert LaFollette (D-Wisc.) warned, "If we shall adopt this amendment, the government having determined to set up a federal system of old-age insurance will provide, in its own bill creating that system, competition which in the end may destroy the federal system. . . . It would be inviting and encouraging competition with its own plan which ultimately would undermine and destroy it."[59] However, supporters of the Clark amendment argued that if the private sector guaranteed benefits as good as the government, why not allow free choice and competition rather than a government monopoly?[60] The argument was persuasive. Despite a 2 to 1 Democratic majority in the Senate, the Clark amendment passed 51 to 35.

Roosevelt pulled out all the stops in his efforts to defeat the Clark amendment, even threatening to veto the entire Social Security bill.[61] Under intense pressure from the president, a House-Senate conference committee stripped the amendment from the bill, promising a special committee to examine the issue and report back the next year. In reality, the Clark amendment was never reconsidered.[62]

A second major issue was whether the program should be funded out of general revenues or through payroll taxes. Proponents of Social Security saw the program as social insurance and wanted it structured as closely as possible to actual insurance, with individuals paying "contributions" or "premiums" and receiving a "right" to future benefits. This constant allusion to private insurance was deliberate. As Robert Myers, Social Security's chief actuary from 1947 to 1970, and deputy commissioner from 1971 to 1972, has noted, supporters of Social Security "over-stressed the insurance concept in the early days of the program. This was done primarily to build up and maintain public support for the Social Security program—by drawing on the good name and reputation of private insurance." [63]

Roosevelt was explicit in describing Social Security as insurance:

> Get these facts straight. The Act provides for two kinds of insurance for the worker. For that insurance both the employer and the worker pay premiums—just as you pay premiums on any other insurance policy. Those premiums are collected in the form of taxes. The first kind of insurance covers old age. Here the employer contributes one dollar in premium for every dollar of premium contributed by the worker; but both dollars are held by the government solely for the benefit of the worker in his old age.[64]

Moreover, they saw this link between contributions and benefits as making the program inviolable in the future. As Roosevelt himself explained, "We put those payroll contributions there so as to give the contributors a legal, moral, and political right to collect their pensions. . . . With those taxes in there, no damn politician can ever scrap my social security program."[65] Therefore, they strongly supported the use of payroll taxes to fund the program.[66]

Opponents pointed out that any promise of future benefits based on taxes paid was illusory. As Sen. Albert Gore (D-Tenn.) put it, "What guarantee is there? Has the citizen got any constitutional guarantee? Has the citizen got any moral guarantee . . . that some man might not come into power who would take more than he ought from one and give to another?"[67]

Opponents of the payroll tax raised several objections, pointing out that payroll taxes were regressive and might cost jobs, reduce wages, or lead to increased prices and inflation.[68] However, in the end, establishing a presumed link between contributions and benefits was considered more important than economics. As Roosevelt said, "I guess you are right on the economics, but those taxes were never a problem of economics. They are political all the way through."[69]

Finally, there was a major debate over whether the program should be fully funded or should operate on a pay-as-you-go basis. A fully funded pension system invests taxes or contributions, accumulating funds with which to pay future benefits. A pay-as-you-go system uses current taxes to immediately pay current benefits, relying on future taxes to pay future benefits.

It is clear that Roosevelt originally intended the program to be fully funded. In his 1934 message to Congress, he spoke of the federal government's responsibility for "investing, maintaining, and safeguarding the necessary insurance reserves."[70] Again the analogy to private insurance was important—as a social insurance program, the burden of financing should be borne by those receiving the benefits, not be passed on to future generations or possible noncontributors. Moreover, it was suggested that accumulation of funds and their productive investment would substantially lighten the burden on future generations, helping to ensure that benefits would continue to be paid.[71]

The final Social Security bill provided for a fully funded system, but it was a short-lived victory.[72] By 1939, full funding had been abandoned in favor of pay-as-you-go financing.[73]

Social Security was also attacked by those on the left who sought a more comprehensive program of redistributing wealth, most notably supporters of the Townsend proposal for a guaranteed $200 per month pension. Millions of Americans signed petitions urging Congress to pass Townsend's proposal.[74] Although none of the leftist proposals had any real chance for enactment, Roosevelt and his supporters skillfully used the fear of extremists to make their plan look moderate. Indeed, they may have even helped organize attacks from the left.[75]

In the end, on August 5, the Social Security Act passed overwhelmingly. In its final form the legislation[76]

- Imposed a 1 percent tax on employees' wages to be matched by a 1 percent tax on employers. The amount of wages subject to the tax was capped at $3,000, making the maximum tax $60 ($30 by the employee and $30 by the employer). The tax rate was scheduled to rise by 1 percent every three years, reaching a maximum of 6 percent in 1949.
- In return for taxes, beginning January 1, 1942, old-age benefits would be paid to qualified individuals upon their reaching age 65, in the form of monthly benefits payable until death. The size of the annuity would be a function of total covered wages. Individuals who earned more (and therefore paid more in taxes) would receive proportionately higher benefits.
- Individuals who continued to work after age 65 would not be eligible for benefits so long as they were employed.

- Other benefits, including a death benefit, were included.
- The law applied to all workers except agricultural workers, domestic servants, casual laborers, seamen, government workers, and employees of any nonprofit organization, including educational, religious, and scientific organizations.

In signing the legislation on August 14, Roosevelt said, "We can never insure 100 percent of the population against 100 percent of the hazards and vicissitudes of life, but we have tried to frame a law which will give some measure of protection to the average citizen and to his family against. . .poverty-ridden old age."[77]

Social Security vs. the Constitution

Political opposition to Social Security faded following Roosevelt's reelection in 1936.[78] However, the program quickly faced a new and even more formidable threat—the Supreme Court.

Between 1935 and early 1936, the court had found seven out of nine New Deal acts to be unconstitutional.[79] There was ample reason to believe that Social Security would likewise be struck down. Clearly, there was nothing in the Constitution that granted Congress the power to create a national insurance system or to regulate relations between employers and employees.

The Roosevelt administration relied on the "General Welfare" clause (Article I, Section 8) for justification, Roosevelt himself stating that "If our constitution tells us our Federal Government was established among other things 'to promote the general welfare,' it is our plain duty to provide for that security upon which welfare depends."[80] The act itself included language saying it had been enacted "To provide for the general welfare by establishing a system of federal old-age benefits. . . ."[81]

But that clause did not grant Congress the power to pass any law it saw as benefiting the general welfare. It was meant to serve as a brake on the power of Congress to tax and spend *in furtherance of its enumerated powers*, meaning that spending within the exercise of an enumerated power had to be for the general welfare rather than to the benefit of specific individuals or factions.[82] Further, the court had already invalidated efforts to "expropriate from one group for the benefit of another," making it unlikely that taxing employers for the benefit of employees would be upheld.[83]

25

The very emphasis on Social Security as an insurance program that had hastened the legislation's passage dimmed its prospects in court. Court precedents made it extremely unlikely that any form of federal insurance system would be upheld.[84] Therefore, the Roosevelt administration, which had so strongly stressed the insurance aspect of Social Security, now argued that the program was in no way an insurance program. In fact, Edwin Witte, executive director of the CES research staff, told a group of supporters, "The only hope ... is that the Court will find that [the Act] does not, in fact, establish an old-age insurance program."[85] In the same vein, the Social Security Administration issued instructions for its employees to "play down the use of terms such as 'insurance' and not allow, in any official reports or publicity, the coupling of the tax titles with the two insurance titles lest the Court take judicial notice when considering the constitutionality of the Act."[86]

Roosevelt was determined not to allow the Supreme Court to interfere with his programs. Following his reelection, he made an audacious assault on the Court itself. The president launched his assault with a fireside chat on March 9, 1937, denouncing the Court for using the Constitution to "thwart the will of the people."[87] Moreover, Roosevelt claimed, the Court was "casting doubt on the ability of the elected Congress to protect the nation from economic and social catastrophe through legislation."[88]

Roosevelt's response was his infamous "court-packing" plan. He proposed that the president be allowed to appoint 6 new Supreme Court justices, expanding the Court from 9 to 15 members and creating a majority more favorable to government activism.[89] Even some of Roosevelt's supporters thought that he was going too far on this one and Congress eventually defeated the plan—but not before it had accomplished its goal. Several Justices "reconsidered" their previous opposition to New Deal legislation—the famous "switch in time that saved nine."[90]

On May 24, 1937, the Supreme Court upheld Social Security in the case of *Helvering v. Davis*.[91] The 7 to 2 decision accepted both major contentions of the Roosevelt administration—that Social Security was authorized under the General Welfare clause and that it was not an insurance program. Writing for the majority Justice Benjamin Cardozo wrote:

> Congress did not improvise a judgment when it found that
> the award of old-age benefits would be conducive to the

general welfare. The President's Committee on Economic
Security made an investigation and report. . . . With the loss
of savings inevitable in periods of idleness, the fate of workers over 65, when thrown out of work, is little less than
desperate. . . . Moreover laws of the separate states cannot
deal with this effectively. . . . Only a power that is national
can serve the interests of all.[92]

The Court also agreed that Social Security was *not* an insurance
program. The Court noted that "The proceeds of both the employee
and employer taxes are to be paid into the Treasury like any other
internal revenue generally, and are not earmarked in any way."[93]

This is an extremely important point, confirmed 23 years later in
the case of *Fleming v. Nestor.*[94] Although Social Security continues
to call payroll taxes "contributions" and many people believe that
they have an earned right to Social Security benefits based on their
contributions, the courts have made it clear that Social Security taxes
are simply taxes like any other, and individuals have no right to
any benefit based on paying them.[95]

Interestingly, as soon as the Supreme Court's ruling was handed
down, the Social Security Administration began using insurance
terminology again.[96]

Growth and Expansion

With no further political or legal challenges, Social Security was
now free to expand. In fact, the day after the Supreme Court issued
its decision, Arthur Altmeyer, who had become chairman of the
Social Security Board, told a group of social workers:

Passing the law is only, as it were, the "curtain raiser" in
the evolution of such a program. It is already possible to
distinguish at least three phases of this evolution, each with
its own distinctive emphasis—first, the double-barreled job
of setting up the administrative machinery and of getting it
into operation; second, the development and integration of
administration and services within the present framework;
and third, further expansion to liberalize existing provisions.[97]

The first major changes came in 1939. Chief among these was the
abandonment of any pretense of full funding and adoption of an
explicitly pay-as-you-go financing system. As the size of the potential

reserve fund became apparent, the original opponents of full funding were joined by conservatives who were worried over how the government would use and invest so much money. Sen. Arthur Vandenberg (R-Mich.) warned that "it is scarcely conceivable that rational men should propose such an unmanageable accumulation of funds in one place in a democracy."[98] As early as the 1930s, these fiscal conservatives warned that unless private securities were included in the government's portfolio, the trust fund would earn less than market returns. But they also realized that, if the government invested in private securities, it would lead to large-scale government ownership of capital and interference in American business—the de facto socialization of the American economy.[99] They also warned that issuing new government bonds would create a huge burden on future generations who would have to redeem those IOUs.[100]

Therefore, in order to dissipate the surplus, scheduled tax increases were delayed and benefits were increased and accelerated. New benefits were added, including survivors' benefits, all with the express purpose of preventing any trust fund accumulation.

In addition, the benefit formula was adjusted to make it more progressive—that is, more redistributive. Henceforth, lower income workers would receive more back in benefits per dollar paid in taxes than would higher income workers. This moved the program even further from any semblance of being an insurance program.[101]

Ironically, even as the amendments were making it clear that Social Security was not an insurance program, much of the language surrounding the program was changed in the amendments to make it sound more like insurance. For example, the term "old-age benefits" was renamed "old-age insurance benefits." Payroll taxes were renamed "insurance contributions" under the Federal Insurance Contributions Act (FICA).[102]

World War II effectively prevented any major expansion of Social Security during the 1940s, but by 1950 the program was ripe for significant liberalization. Political pressure to expand the program had increased steadily throughout the late 1940s, and President Harry Truman was strongly committed to expanding the program, including extending coverage to more workers, increasing benefits, making benefits payable to women at an earlier age, liberalizing the retirement earnings test, and providing disability insurance.[103]

Although he failed to achieve all his goals, Truman guided through Congress more than 30 major changes to the Social Security Act during 1950 alone. Compulsory coverage was extended to agricultural workers, most self-employed workers, domestic servants, federal workers not covered by federal pensions, and residents of the Virgin Islands and Puerto Rico. Employees of nonprofit organizations and state and local government workers were given the option of joining the system. Survivor's benefits were increased and expanded. Benefits were increased dramatically, as much as 77.5 percent for current beneficiaries, but changes were also made to increase the progressivity of benefits. To partially fund the additional expenditures, the ceiling on taxable earnings was increased to $3,600, and future tax rates were increased.[104]

The floodgates were now open. In 1952, benefits were again increased dramatically. Dwight Eisenhower succeeded Truman, but Social Security continued to grow. In 1954, benefits were again increased and the retirement earnings test was further liberalized. To pay for the new benefits, the taxable earnings ceiling was raised to $4,200. In 1956, Social Security established a disability program with benefits payable to disabled workers at age 50. Increasing Social Security benefits had now become a preelection routine. In 1958, for the fifth consecutive election year, benefits were increased again, and several other parts of the program were expanded.[105]

This dramatic expansion in coverage and benefits was not without cost. In 1959, for the first time in its history, Social Security paid out more in benefits than it brought in through tax receipts.[106] The response was one that was to become typical in future years—the ceiling on taxable income was increased and tax rates were raised.[107] The system's financial problems, of course, did not stop the election-year benefit expansion spree. In 1960, disability benefits were extended to all workers regardless of age, survivors' benefits were hiked, and the retirement earnings test was liberalized yet again.[108]

President John F. Kennedy was the next president to realize the vote-getting potential of increasing Social Security benefits. In 1961, he pushed through Congress a 20 percent increase in benefits and established an early retirement provision, allowing workers to retire at age 62 while receiving partial benefits. Of course, payroll taxes were increased once again.[109]

While not strictly speaking a part of Social Security, the largest ever expansion of the Social Security Act occurred in 1965 with the

29

adoption of Medicare.[110] (Although partially financed through its own payroll tax and enacted as a new title of the Social Security Act, the problems of that troubled program are generally beyond the scope of this book.) President Johnson, of course, did not neglect the traditional route of increasing Social Security benefits. In addition to Medicare, he also raised retirement benefits, extended the length of time that survivors could receive benefits, reduced eligibility requirements for disability benefits, and extended benefits to divorced wives.[111]

Throughout the late 1960s and early 1970s, the rush to increase and expand benefits continued unabated. Benefits were increased again in 1966, 1969, 1970, 1971, and 1972. To fund the increased benefits, tax rates and the ceiling on taxable income were also repeatedly raised.[112]

Whatever problems those constant benefit increases were posing for the future of Social Security, they were to be dwarfed by an especially ill-timed proposal in 1972—to tie future increases in Social Security benefits directly to increases in the consumer price index, the beginning of cost of living adjustments (COLAs).[113] COLAs were originally thought to solve two problems, one real (the inability of Congress to resist increasing benefits in an election year) and the other political (Nixon's resentment that the Democrat-controlled Congress received credit for benefit increases).[114] However, they were to do more damage to Social Security's financial solvency than any other measure. As Carolyn Weaver of the American Enterprise Institute puts it, "In one fell swoop, the new indexing provisions converted a system characterized by ad hoc growth to one of automatic and uncontrolled growth."[115] Moreover, the adoption of COLAs had the spectacularly bad timing of taking place just as America was about to enter an era of rampant inflation.[116]

Congress made the problem even worse through the use of a mistaken computation formula that created a "double indexing" of benefits. This caused a sharp boost in benefits for new retirees just entering the system and caused benefits to rise faster than wages.[117]

The period between Social Security's birth and the mid-1970s was marked by an almost uninterrupted expansion of the program, both in the scope of coverage and benefits provided, as well as the level of the benefits themselves. To finance these increases, taxes were raised repeatedly. Politicians had discovered the advantages of increasing benefits to the large and powerful voting bloc of senior citizens, while passing the cost on to future generations.

But storm clouds were on the horizon.

The Crisis Begins

By the mid-1970s, it was becoming apparent that Social Security could not continue to finance all the benefits it had promised. In 1975, for the first time since 1959, Social Security ran a deficit, spending more on benefits than it brought in through taxes. The same thing happened in 1976 and 1977.[118] Operating deficits were projected to continue in subsequent years and reserves would be exhausted by the early 1980s. Future unfunded liabilities were estimated to be as much as $1 trillion, with nearly 40 percent of promised future benefits unfunded.[119] In 1976, Treasury Secretary William Simon wrote that "the future prospects of the system as we know it are grim."[120]

Congress and President Jimmy Carter responded with the largest tax increase in American history (until that time), more than $227 billion.[121] Social Security payroll tax rates were increased significantly and the earnings ceiling took its biggest jump since the program's inception.[122] The latter was particularly significant because it increased the proportion of American workers whose total wages were below the taxable ceiling, from 85.2 percent to 94.1 percent of the population, the largest percentage since 1940.[123] Promised benefits were also reduced, primarily changes in spousal benefits and tightening the retirement earnings test.[124] Significantly, double indexing was repealed.[125]

In signing the changes, Carter announced that "From 1980 through 2030, the Social Security system will be sound."[126] He was wrong.

In 1980 and 1981, as worries about cash shortfalls again appeared, stop-gap measures were necessary to keep the system afloat for a few more years while Congress studied more comprehensive reforms. These included reductions in survivors' benefits, limits to the death benefit, further changes in the retirement earnings test, and reallocation of funds between the various trust funds, including limited permission for one trust fund to borrow from another.[127]

President Ronald Reagan had proposed more drastic changes in 1981, including a reduction in early retirement benefits and a 50 percent cut in COLAs for the next seven years.[128] The proposals provoked a firestorm from the seniors lobby, organized labor, and Democrats in Congress. The National Council on Aging warned the proposals were "throwing old people to the sharks."[129] The National Council of Senior Citizens called it the "biggest frontal attack on Social Security ever launched."[130] Sen. Edward Kennedy (D-Mass.) called the cuts "devastatingly punitive."[131] The proposals were rejected by the Senate on a vote of 92 to 0 within a week of their being offered.[132]

The Greenspan Commission

Early in 1982, a bipartisan commission began meeting monthly to discuss Social Security reforms. The commission was chaired by Alan Greenspan and included representatives from Congress, business, and labor.[133] With Social Security such a hot political issue, it was not surprising that the commission took no action before the election. But, once the 1982 midterm elections were over, it became increasingly difficult to ignore Social Security's problems. Only days after the election, the commission voted unanimously to accept projections showing that Social Security faced a deficit of $150 billion to $200 billion between 1983 and 1989, with a 75-year shortfall of more than $1.6 trillion.[134] Indeed, by some estimates Social Security would not be able to pay benefits by July 1983.[135]

However, the commission remained deadlocked on what steps to take to correct this situation. Democrats and Republicans spent most of their time attacking each other's proposals, and by December any pretense of cooperation had ended.[136]

With disaster threatening, the White House began direct negotiations with House Speaker Tip O'Neill. A small group of leaders from the commission, including Greenspan, Dole, Moynihan, Conable, and Ball, was brought into the discussions that took place in absolute secrecy.[137] The range of possible fixes was extremely narrow. After the battering they had taken in the last election, President Reagan and congressional Republicans were unwilling to push any reforms that Democrats would not also agree to. As a result, true structural reforms, such as privatization, were never on the table. Likewise, deep benefit cuts were considered unacceptable. That left the usual assortment of minor adjustments in benefits along with hefty tax hikes and other revenue-raising measures.[138]

Once they had reached an agreement, the party leadership relayed it to the commission, which voted 12 to 3 in favor of a set of recommendations that Greenspan predicted would keep Social Security solvent until at least 2068. Indeed, Greenspan called the commission's proposals a "permanent" solution to Social Security's problems.[139] Among the most important recommendations are the following:

- Tax increases that had been scheduled for future years would be accelerated, an effective tax hike of about $40 billion. The FICA tax on self-employed workers was also increased to equal the combined employee-employer payroll taxes paid by other workers.
- The 1983 COLA increase would be delayed for six months.
- Up to 50 percent of Social Security benefits would now be counted as taxable income for higher income retirees. Revenue from taxes on this income, however, would not go into general revenue, but would be recycled into the Social Security program.
- All new state, municipal, and nonprofit workers would be required to participate in the system.
- The normal retirement age would be gradually increased from 65 to 67. However, this provision was agreed to by only a slim margin, setting up a battle in Congress.

Despite opposition from both right and left, President Reagan and the bipartisan congressional leadership were able to push the package through Congress, including the increase in the retirement age.[140] President Reagan signed the bill on April 20, 1983, claiming that the bill would "prevent Social Security from becoming a burden on generations still to come."[141]

Despite assurances from Greenspan and Reagan, Social Security is once again headed for financial disaster. As Figure 2.1 shows, the Greenspan Commission's projections for Social Security's future solvency were not even close to reality.[142] The system will begin to run a deficit by 2013 and has unfunded liabilities of more than $9 trillion.[143]

Social Security Today

Social Security today is the largest program operated by the federal government. Indeed, it is the largest government program in the

Figure 2.1
REVISED INTERMEDIATE PROJECTIONS FOR SOCIAL SECURITY TRUST FUND BALANCES (current dollars)

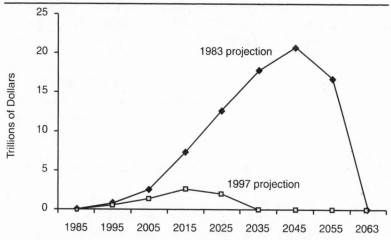

SOURCE: Derived from Social Security Administration data.

world, providing more than $347 billion in benefits to 43.7 million recipients in 1996.[144] Social Security accounts for more than 22 percent of all federal spending, more than the amount that the federal government will spend on all other entitlement programs, except Medicare, combined.[145]

Social Security provides a variety of benefits, the major ones being retirement benefits, including spousal benefits, disability, and survivors benefits.

Retirement Benefits

Social Security has become the primary source of retirement income for most Americans. Approximately 42 percent of all income earned by individuals age 65 or older comes from Social Security benefits.[146] More than half of elderly Americans have no private pension and more than one-third have no income from assets.[147]

In determining an individual's Social Security retirement benefits, the Social Security Administration first calculates that person's Average Indexed Monthly Earnings (AIME). All earnings upon which the person has paid Social Security taxes between 1951 and the year in which the individual reaches age 60 are indexed to account for past inflation and real wage growth. The indexing formula is based on the ratio of the average national wage in the year the individual turns 60 to the year to be indexed. Wages earned after age 60 are not indexed, but left in nominal dollars. The Social Security Administration then selects the 35 years in which wages are highest. The wages for these years are totaled and divided by 420 months. The result is the AIME.[148]

From this amount a progressive formula is used to determine the person's Primary Insurance Amount (PIA). For people turning 65 in 1997, that formula was 90 percent of the first $455 of the AIME, plus 32 percent of the next $2,286 of the AIME, plus 15 percent of the remaining AIME.[149]

In the case of early or late retirement, benefits are adjusted accordingly. For example, if a worker retires at age 62 (the earliest allowable age under Social Security), the worker's benefits will be *permanently* reduced to 80 percent of his or her PIA. If the worker delays retirement until age 67, the benefit will be increased to 109 percent of PIA.[150]

Spousal Benefits

A spouse who has not worked long enough to be eligible for benefits will, at age 65, receive benefits equal to 50 percent of the worker's PIA.

Survivors Benefits

If a worker dies, a surviving spouse over age 65 receives benefits equal to 100 percent of the worker's PIA. If the widowed spouse is under age 65, she is eligible for benefits equal to 75 percent of PIA if she is caring for children under age 16. Minor children of a deceased worker are also eligible for survivors benefits equal to 75 percent of PIA. However, a family's total benefits are capped at between 150 percent and 187.5 percent of PIA, according to a mildly progressive formula.[151]

Disability Benefits

Social Security also provides benefits to disabled workers, defined as someone with a physical or mental impairment that prevents them from performing "substantial" work for at least a year. Generally, earnings of $500 or more per month are considered substantial work. Further, the disability must generally be considered permanent. The program is not intended for temporary conditions, and there is no such thing as "partial" disability under Social Security.[152] Serious medical conditions such as heart disease, terminal cancer, blindness, or the loss of a limb constitute nearly 80 percent of all disability claims awarded.[153]

Disability benefits are generally equal to the individual's PIA, computed as though the person were age 62 at the time of disablement. If the person is receiving worker's compensation or other types of government disability benefits, the Social Security disability payment may be reduced.[154]

Conclusion

In more than 60 years Social Security has grown into the primary source of American retirement income. But, as this venerable program matures, its underlying flaws are beginning to show. Despite more than 30 tax hikes, the program is facing severe financial problems. The coming chapters will examine Social Security's many problems and whether there is a better way to provide a secure retirement for today's young workers.

3. The Financial Crisis

Social Security's financial crisis is both much more severe and more imminent than is commonly believed. According to Social Security's Board of Trustees, the program will most likely begin running a deficit by 2013.[1] Without radical restructuring, the program will not be able to meet its promised obligations in just a few short years.

Workers today pay a Social Security payroll tax of 12.4 percent.[2] This tax burden is supposedly split between the employer and the employee. However, most economists agree that the employer's share of federal payroll taxes is a function of the employee's tax burden that is passed to the employee through a reduced salary and/or benefits.[3]

Many people believe that Social Security payroll taxes are saved and used to pay retirement benefits. Indeed, in describing Social Security, Franklin Roosevelt claimed, "In effect, we have set up a savings account for the old-age of the worker."[4] But that is not what actually happens. As we saw in chapter 1, Social Security operates on a pay-as-you-go basis. That means that taxes paid by workers today are not saved or invested but are immediately used to pay benefits to today's retirees. When today's workers retire in the future, they will have to rely on taxes paid by the next generation of workers.

In many ways, Social Security resembles the type of pyramid or "Ponzi" schemes that are illegal in all 50 states. Charles Ponzi, an Italian immigrant, started the first such scheme in Boston in 1916.[5] He convinced some people to allow him to invest their money, but he never made any real investments. He just took the money from later investors and gave it to the earlier investors, paying them a handsome profit on what they originally paid in. He then used the early investors as advertisement to get more investors, using their money to pay a profit to previous investors, and so on.

In order to keep paying a profit to previous investors, Ponzi had to continue to find more and more new investors. Eventually, he could not expand the number of new investors fast enough and the system collapsed. Since he never made any real investments, there were no funds to pay anything back to those later investors who were still in the system and had not been paid off yet. They lost all of the money they "invested" with Ponzi.

Ponzi was arrested for fraud and sent to prison for two years. When he came out, he returned to Italy, where he became a top economic adviser to Benito Mussolini.

But Ponzi's scheme lives on today in the Social Security system. Just like Ponzi's plan, Social Security does not make any real investments, but just takes the money from the later "investors," or taxpayers, to pay the benefits to the earlier, now retired, taxpayers. Like Ponzi, Social Security will not be able to recruit new "investors" fast enough to continue paying promised benefits to previous investors. Eventually, Social Security must collapse just like Ponzi's scheme.

In 1967, Paul Samuelson, a leading liberal economist and supporter of Social Security, was completely honest—if naively optimistic—about the nature of Social Security funding:

> The beauty about social insurance is that it is actuarially unsound. Everyone who reaches retirement age is given benefit privileges that far exceed anything he has paid in. How is this possible? Always there are more youths than old folks in a growing population. More important, with real incomes growing at some 3 percent per year, the taxable base upon which benefits rest in any period are much greater than the taxes paid historically by the generation now retired.[6]

Demography Is Destiny

Unfortunately, Samuelson was wrong about both demographics and economic growth. The ratio of "youths" to "old folks" is declining. The number of Americans age 65 and over has grown from about 9 million in 1940 to more than 34 million in 1995, and is expected to reach at least 80 million by the middle of the next century. As a share of the total U.S. population, the elderly population grew from 7 percent in 1940 to 13 percent in 1990. By 2030, the elderly will make up more than 20 percent of the American population.[7] To place this in context, 18.4 percent of the population of Florida is over age 65. Early in the next century, the entire United States will resemble Florida today.[8]

In 1940, life expectancy at birth was only 64 years; it is now more than 75 years.[9] However, a more important issue is life expectancy for those who reach age 65. In 1940 men age 65 could have expected to live roughly another 12 years, women another 13. Today, men age 65 can expect to live an additional 15 years; women can expect to live another 19 years.[10]

This increase in life expectancy is accelerating. For example, in the 25 years between 1940 and 1965, life expectancy for men age 65 and over increased from 11.9 years to 12.9 years, an increase of 8.4 percent. But, in the next 25 years, from 1965 to 1990, it increased to 15.0 years, an increase of 16 percent. For women age 65, life expectancy increased by 10.2 percent between 1940 and 1965, and 19 percent between 1965 and 1990.[11]

The future may bring even greater increases in life expectancy. For example, Charles Mullin and Tomas Philipson of the University of Chicago recently examined data from the annuity and life insurance market to make projections about future increases in longevity. They concluded that Americans are likely to live much longer than previously predicted. Indeed, they suggest that longevity could increase as much as 5 percent faster than previously estimated.[12]

Other demographers agree. Eileen Crimmins from the University of Southern California, who headed a panel of expert demographers for the Advisory Council on Social Security, says that it is foolish not to assume that the future will bring major inroads against the diseases that kill us today.[13] Duke University's Kenneth Manton notes that, for instance, people retiring after 1996 will be increasingly less likely to smoke than the rest of the population. Therefore, death rates from cancer will be lower in the future. Manton also sees improving trends in cholesterol and high blood pressure. He thinks there is a 95 percent chance that life expectancies will rise as high as age 96 in the middle of the next century.[14] James Vaupel, a demographer at the National Institute on Aging, goes even further, suggesting that we are on the edge of "a new paradigm of aging," with average life expectancy reaching 100 or more.[15]

This represents a tremendous testimonial on the American health care system, and is good news to those of us who can expect to live to a ripe old age, but it is a ticking time bomb for Social Security—there are more and more people receiving Social Security benefits for longer and longer periods of time.

At the same time, we are having fewer children, meaning there will be fewer workers to support those retirees. To maintain a constant population, the fertility rate must be 2.1 lifetime births per woman. But the U.S. fertility rate has been below this level for 25 years now. In fact, it stabilized at around 1.8–1.9 from 1973 to 1988, before climbing to just over 2.0 for the last eight years. This low fertility rate indeed represents a continuation of a long-term trend of decline over the last 200 years, from a high of 7.0 in Revolutionary War times.[16] There are powerful social, economic, and technological trends behind this long-term decline, including the spread of more effective birth control, and the changing roles of women in the workforce and home. If anything, these trends may well produce further declines in fertility. These forces have lowered fertility rates even more in many Western European countries, to around 1.5, portending substantial workforce declines in future years. Even with immigration, the growth in the U.S. population will slow by 75 percent over the next 50 years.[17]

As a result, the ratio of workers to retirees is falling dramatically. For example, in 1950, there were 16 people working and paying taxes into the system for every person who was retired and taking benefits out of it. Today, there are just 3.3 workers per retiree. By 2025, when the baby boom generation has retired, there will be only two workers per retiree. Beyond 2025, the ratio declines to less than 2:1.[18] (See Figure 3.1.)

A handful of economists argue that the worker-to-retiree ratio is unimportant. Instead they stress the "dependency ratio," that is, the number of workers to nonworkers in society, including children.[19] While the dependency ratio is also declining (it fell from 5.8:1 in 1960 to 4.7:1 in 1995 and will decline to 2.7:1 by 2040[20]), it is not doing so anywhere near as fast as the worker-to-retiree ratio. These economists' point is that while society may have to spend more on the elderly, it will not have to spend as much on, say, education for children. Therefore total spending will average out. However, while this may or may not be true in a macroeconomic sense, within the closed system of Social Security only the worker-to-retiree ratio drives solvency. Moreover, there have been relatively few proposals in recent years to *reduce* spending on children.

Samuelson was also wrong on economic growth. In any pay-as-you-go system, because benefits are paid directly out of current income (usually payroll taxes), the ability to fund those benefits is

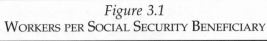

Figure 3.1
WORKERS PER SOCIAL SECURITY BENEFICIARY

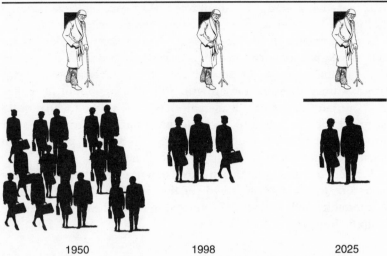

| 1950 | 1998 | 2025 |

SOURCE: *1995 Annual Report of the Board of Trustees of the Federal Old-Age and Survivors Insurance and Disability Insurance Trust Funds* (Government Printing Office, 1995), p. 122.

ultimately tied to the growth rate of labor compensation. The growth rate of labor compensation, in turn, depends on two factors: the growth rate of labor productivity and the size of the working population.[21]

The growth rate of the American workforce is slowing. A combination of the baby boom and the movement of women into the workforce produced an unprecedented growth in the American labor supply between 1960 and 1990.[22] However, with women fully integrated into the workforce, the baby boom about to leave it, and fewer young workers coming along to take their place, the trend will soon begin to reverse.

From 1953 to 1973, American labor productivity grew rapidly, averaging 2.3 percent annually, which was generally sufficient to offset demographic changes. However, between 1973 and 1993, the rate of increase in productivity fell to an annual average of only 0.9 percent.[23] In turn, real wage growth, which averaged a healthy 2.0 percent annually from 1953 to 1973, actually turned negative from 1973 to 1993, declining an average 0.2 percent annually.[24]

Of course there is no reason to believe that America is trapped forever in its current low rate of wage growth. Nevertheless, it is true that savings and investment rates, a key contributor to productivity, are low and continue to decline.[25] Moreover, the failure of our government-run education system has left many workers without the skills necessary for a high technology economy. However, these problems could be turned around by government policies more attuned to economic growth. Still, it is important to realize that our current political leadership has shown little inclination to support the tax cuts and regulatory rollback necessary to spur growth. Nor have most opponents of Social Security privatization been in the forefront of calling for such policies.

Without a dramatic change in government policy, we are unlikely to return to the robust growth of the pre-1973 years. Therefore, economic growth will not be sufficient to offset the negative demographic trends.

The Trust Fund Fraud

In theory, once Social Security begins to run a deficit in 2013, the system will rely on the monies accumulated in the Social Security trust funds to continue to pay benefits until 2032, at which point the trust funds will be exhausted and Social Security will be insolvent. However, this theory fundamentally misrepresents the nature of the trust funds.

Social Security is currently running a surplus. In 1996, for example, Social Security taxes amounted to $385.7 billion, counting both payroll taxes and income taxes on benefits. The system was also credited with $38.7 billion in interest payments, for total revenues of $424.4 billion. Benefit payments and administrative expenses totaled only $353.6 billion, providing a surplus of $70.8 billion.[26] Since 1983, surpluses have totaled $567 billion.[27] By 2013, they will total nearly $2.9 trillion.[28] The accumulation of these surpluses constitutes the Social Security trust funds.

On the surface, this appears to mean that, once Social Security's cash flow turns negative in 2013, there will be $2.9 trillion available to help pay benefits. The reality, however, is far different.

About half of the surplus is attributed to a positive cash flow, that is, the excess of taxes over benefits. By law, this money must be invested solely in U.S. government securities. The securities can be any of three types: government securities purchased on the open market; securities bought at issue, as part of a new offering to the public; or special-issue securities, not traded publicly. In actual practice, virtually all the purchased securities have been special issue.[29]

The other half of the trust fund surplus can be traced to accounting procedures whereby interest owed to the fund on the securities that it holds is credited to the fund, meaning that the fund's actual cash flow, or operating balance, is lower than its reported balance by roughly half.[30] (The interest rate for the special-issue securities is equal to the average market rate yield on all U.S. government securities with at least four years remaining until maturity, rounded to the nearest one-eighth percent.[31])

When the government sells securities to the trust funds, it receives revenue that is used to finance the government's general operating expenses, from roads and bridges to defense spending, from welfare to health care. Therefore, any excess funds received by the Social Security system are not being "saved," but are being lent to the U.S. Treasury in return for IOUs that give the Social Security system authority to spend up to the amount of the trust funds.[32] Strictly speaking, as a matter of law, the Social Security trust funds are nothing more than a statement of the amount that Social Security is legally authorized to draw from general revenues, in addition to payroll tax revenues.

As discussed above, Social Security's cash outflow will exceed the cash inflow from taxes by 2013, forcing the system to begin spending down the trust funds in order to continue paying promised benefits. However, as we have seen, when the government attempts to withdraw the cash surplus that has been accumulating, it will not find any money, only Treasury obligations. In order to draw down trust fund assets and pay Social Security benefits in a timely manner, the government will have no choice but to call in the IOUs.[33]

At that point the federal government faces two very unpleasant realities. First, the absence of cash flow into the trust funds will deprive the government of a source of revenue it has used to meet current operating expenses. More importantly, perhaps, the government will have to find the money to pay off its debt to the Social Security system. It will have several alternatives, most of which are unpalatable, unwise, or both. The government could increase payroll or other taxes to raise money, or it could borrow money by issuing new bonds and using the proceeds to pay off the prior obligations held by the trust funds. It could also decide to monetize the debt (to print more money), but the economic repercussions from monetizing the debt are serious and potentially disastrous.[34] Finally, the government could cut benefits to Social Security recipients so that benefits equaled the level of revenues coming into the trust funds, but such an abrupt and substantial reduction in benefits would be politically difficult and unfair.

In short, if no action is taken, by approximately 2013 the federal government will have to raise taxes, increase the debt, reduce Social Security benefits immediately, or do some combination to fund the Social Security cash flow imbalance. The point is not that the government will default on the debt in the Social Security trust funds, but that paying that debt will have severe consequences for the U.S. economy.

In short, the so-called trust funds do not hold any real assets, but just future claims against federal revenues. In reality, the trust funds consist of nothing but internal government IOUs, effectively part of the national debt. If the Social Security trust funds do eventually total $2.9 trillion, that does not mean that the government has an additional $2.9 trillion with which to pay benefits. To the contrary, all it means is that the federal government has an additional $2.9 trillion in federal debt—an additional $2.9 trillion that will eventually have to be paid by taxpayers.

Another way to visualize the fraud behind the trust funds is to imagine what would happen if there never were any trust funds. In 2013, when Social Security begins running a deficit, the government would have to raise taxes, increase the debt, or cut promised benefits. But that is exactly what happens with the trust funds. In 2013, the government will have to redeem its bonds in order to pay promised benefits. In order to redeem the bonds it will have to raise taxes or increase the debt. Otherwise benefits will have to be cut. The trust funds become irrelevant.

Taxes upon Taxes

As Table 3.1 shows, payroll tax rates or earnings ceilings have been raised more than 30 times since the program began.[35] Even adjusted for inflation, Social Security taxes have increased more than 800 percent since 1935.[36] But these increases are nothing compared

Table 3.1
CONTRIBUTION AND BENEFIT BASE AND CONTRIBUTION RATES

Calendar Years	Contribution and Benefit Base ($)	Tax Rate (%)
1937–49	3,000	2.00
1950	3,000	3.00
1951–53	3,600	3.00
1954	3,600	4.00
1955–56	4,200	4.00
1957–58	4,200	4.50
1959	4,800	5.00
1960–61	4,800	6.00
1962	4,800	6.25
1963–65	4,800	7.25
1966	6,600	7.70
1967	6,600	7.80
1968	7,800	7.60
1969	7,800	8.40
1970	7,800	8.40
1971	7,800	9.20
1972	9,000	9.20
1973	10,800	9.70
1974	13,200	9.90
1975	14,100	9.90
1976	15,300	9.90
1977	16,500	9.90
1978	17,700	10.10
1979	22,900	10.16
1980	25,900	10.16
1981	29,700	10.70
1982	32,400	10.80
1983	35,700	10.80
1984*	37,800	11.40
1985*	39,600	11.40
1986*	42,000	11.40
1987*	43,800	11.40
1988*	45,000	12.12
1989*	48,000	12.12

(continued)

Table 3.1
CONTRIBUTION AND BENEFIT BASE AND CONTRIBUTION RATES,
continued

Calendar Years	Contribution and Benefit Base ($)	Tax Rate (%)
1990	51,300	12.40
1991	53,400	12.40
1992	55,500	12.40
1993	57,600	12.40
1994	60,600	12.40
1995	61,200	12.40
1996	62,700	12.40
1997	65,400	12.40
1998 and later	**	12.40

*In 1984 only, an immediate credit of 0.3 percent of taxable wages was allowed against the OASDI contributions paid by employees, which resulted in an effective contribution rate of 5.4 percent. The appropriations of contributions to the trust funds, however, were based on the combined employee-employer rate of 11.4 percent, as if the credit for employees did not apply. Similar credits of 2.7 percent, 2.3 percent, and 2.0 percent were allowed against the combined OASDI and Hospital Insurance (HI) contributions on net earnings from self-employment in 1984, 1985, and 1986–89, respectively. 1990, self-employed persons have been allowed a deduction, for purposes of computing their net earnings, equal to half of the combined OASDI and HI contributions that would be payable without regard to the contribution and benefit base. The OASDI contribution rate is then applied to net earnings after this deduction, but subject to the OASDI base.

**Subject to automatic adjustment based on increases in average wages.

with the tax hikes that today's young workers will face, unless the system is reformed.

According to the Social Security Administration's intermediate projections, under current law and policies, paying all promised benefits for a young worker entering the workforce today would require increasing the Social Security payroll tax from 12.4 percent today to approximately 18 percent, an increase of almost 50 percent![37]

The payroll tax increase is necessary to pay for Social Security benefits alone. It does not include tax increases necessary to provide benefits under Part A of the Medicare program, which is also funded out of the payroll tax.[38] Medicare Part A is already running an operating deficit and faces a future financial shortfall even larger than the projected Social Security shortfall.[39] In order to meet all the obligations of both Social Security *and* Medicare Part A, the payroll tax will have to be almost doubled from its current 15.3 percent to about 29 percent.[40]

Even these projections may underestimate the true size of the problem. All of the estimates discussed use the government's "intermediate" projections. Given the many variables involved in projecting over a 75-year period, the Social Security Trustees provide three different scenarios: optimistic, intermediate, and pessimistic projections based on such factors as mortality, disability, immigration and emigration, birth rates, wage and salary growth, inflation, unemployment, workforce participation, marriage rates, and changes in productivity and economic growth.[41] Because the intermediate projection lies between the "extremes" of the optimistic and pessimistic projections, this is the estimate used in most discussions of Social Security. It has also often been wrong.

In fact, the Trustees have been forced to adjust the system's projected solvency date forward 6 times in the past 10 years because intermediate assumptions proved too optimistic. Haeworth Robertson, former chief actuary for the Social Security Administration, points out that the Trustees' pessimistic projections have been right about as often as their intermediate projections in recent years.[42]

There are several reasons to believe that the intermediate assumptions contained in the *1998 Trustees Report* may be overly optimistic. For example, the Trustees assume an annual real wage growth of 0.9 percent.[43] However, as we have seen, real wage growth has actually been declining since 1973. Likewise, the intermediate projections assume relatively stable growth in life expectancy. As we saw, however, there is reason to believe that the growth in life expectancy is accelerating. The technical panel of the Social Security Advisory Council has suggested that the intermediate projections may underestimate the decline in mortality and has called for additional research.[44] As Richard Foster, chief actuary of the Medicare system, warns, "Much of the available evidence suggests that [the intermediate projections] may not be optimal."[45]

Therefore, we should examine the pessimistic projections. In doing so, it is important to understand that, although called pessimistic, these projections do not represent the most pessimistic view that it is possible, or even reasonable, to take.[46] For example, the pessimistic scenario assumes a real wage growth of 0.4 percent, about half that of the intermediate projection, but still higher than the actual growth over the past 20 years.[47] The pessimistic projections, therefore, merely represent a more cautious scenario than intermediate projections.

Under the pessimistic projections, paying all promised Social Security benefits to young workers entering the workforce today would require more than doubling the payroll tax from the current 12.4 percent to about 26 percent.[48] To pay all the benefits promised by both Social Security and Medicare Part A, the total payroll tax would have to increase from 15.3 percent to an astonishing 46 percent or more.[49] Young workers would be paying nearly half their paychecks in payroll taxes—even before paying income taxes. In fact, Laurence Kotlikoff of Boston University estimates that a young person entering the workforce today could eventually face total taxes, income and payroll, equal to nearly 71 percent of their incomes.[50]

Clearly tax burdens of that magnitude are unsustainable. Even at much lower levels, payroll taxes have very severe consequences for workers and the economy. Nearly 76 percent of Americans already pay more in payroll taxes than they do in federal income taxes.[51] Moreover, the payroll tax is particularly burdensome for low- and middle-income workers because it applies to the first dollar of income.[52]

The impact on the overall economy would be equally negative. According to the Congressional Budget Office, payroll tax increases between 1979 and 1982, for example, resulted in the permanent loss of 500,000 jobs.[53] A study of the 1988 and 1990 payroll tax hikes, by economists Gary and Aldona Robbins, estimated permanent job losses at approximately 510,000 and a reduction of the U.S. GNP of $30 billion per year by the year 2000.[54]

One alternative to an across-the-board payroll tax hike that has recently been discussed is removing the cap on income subject to the tax.[55] Raising taxes in this way would presumably not be as politically unpopular, since the tax increase would only fall on the "rich." But this would not solve Social Security's financial problems because benefits are based on taxable income. If the cap on taxable income is removed, benefits paid to upper-income people will soar as well, doing little to close the long-term financing gap, as well as creating the unappetizing spectacle of the federal government sending million-dollar checks to Bill Gates. If the cap is removed for tax purposes only, without its counting toward benefits, that would explicitly turn Social Security "contributions" into just another tax, ending the "social insurance" rationale for the program.

Some suggest that increasing the payroll tax now by just 2.2 percentage points would be sufficient to close the program's long-term financial gap. This suggestion is based on projections in the *1997 Trustees Report* showing that, under intermediate projections, Social Security's "actuarial deficit" is equal to 2.23 percent of taxable payroll over the next 75 years.[56] Supporters of the current system interpret this to mean a tax hike of 2.23 percent would be sufficient to pay all promised benefits over this 75-year period.

First, it should be pointed out that this is not a small tax increase. A 2.2 percent payroll tax hike would mean a $74 billion tax increase this year alone. Between fiscal years 1998 and 2002, the tax increase would total more than $407 billion.[57] Moreover, under pessimistic projections, the immediate tax increase under this logic would have to be 5.54 percentage points, a 36 percent increase in the current Social Security tax rates.

Of course, any tax increase will not solve the problems of the program, because higher taxes will make Social Security an even worse deal for today's workers. As discussed in more detail in the next chapter, Social Security is already an unacceptably bad deal for today's workers. Raising payroll taxes would also have severe negative consequences for the economy, as discussed in chapter 6.

Most importantly, however, a 2.2 percent tax increase will not work even on its own terms because it relies on a seriously misleading concept called "actuarial balance." Actuarial balance occurs when all of a program's assets match all of its liabilities.[58] But, this includes all "assets" of the program including the chimerical Social Security trust funds, which, as discussed above, do nothing to reduce the burden of financing future Social Security benefits.

If payroll taxes were raised by 2.23 percent today, any additional revenues would not be saved and invested to pay future Social Security benefits. Rather, like current Social Security surpluses, additional revenues would be lent to the federal government and would be immediately spent on other government programs. Social Security would simply accumulate more internal government IOUs in

Figure 3.2
Annual Social Security (OASDI) Operating Balance:
Intermediate Projection with and without 2.2% Solution

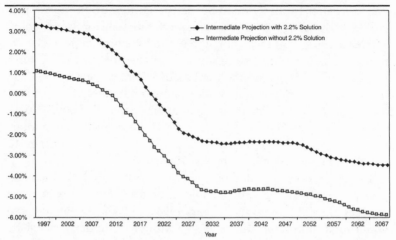

Source: Neil Howe and Richard Jackson, "The Myth of the 2.2% Solution," Cato Institute Social Security Paper no. 11, April 1998, p. 3, using data from the *1998 Trustees Report*.

the trust funds, which do nothing to make the future financing of Social Security any easier. When Social Security turns in those IOUs to pay promised benefits, the government will still have to find money with which to redeem the bonds. The government will still have to come up with the full amount of revenue needed—18 to 26 percent of taxable payroll—to pay promised benefits to the young workers entering the workforce today at their retirement.

As Figure 3.2 shows, a 2.2 percent tax hike would only increase the cash flow after 2013, buying a few extra years before Social Security runs a deficit, while doing nothing to help the program's long-term solvency. However, if the goal is only to increase the cash flow after 2013, there is no reason to raise taxes today. One can simply raise the tax in 2013 and achieve the same result.

So the suggestion that Social Security can be saved by raising the payroll tax by 2.2 percent is just a perpetuation of the trust fund fraud. Advocates of the tax increase simply assume that the trust fund accumulations will be available to finance benefits after the system starts running deficits in about 2013. But, as the previous discussion shows, the government will have to find the money to redeem trillions of dollars in trust fund IOUs. Paying off those government bonds will require revenues equal to another 3.7 percent of taxable payroll.

A few advocates of the 2.2 percent tax increase argue that it does not matter if the trust fund is not real because the revenue from the tax hike would reduce the federal deficit or create a budget surplus and increase national savings. Increased savings would lead to increased economic growth, creating new wealth that could be used to pay future Social Security benefits. But this argument betrays a naive view of budgetary politics in Washington. If payroll taxes were raised by $74 billion per year, the additional funds would be immediately gobbled up by the highly organized special interests in Washington. They certainly would not be used to run a federal budget surplus and increase savings. New money coming into Washington is never left in the bank for long.

The 2.2 percent payroll tax would only help pay future Social Security benefits if the trust fund fraud was abandoned and the additional funds were actually saved and invested in the private sector. This would increase national savings and would produce real new wealth that would flow back into Social Security, providing the revenues to help pay future benefits. But, as noted earlier, having the government invest directly would give the government enormous control over the U.S. economy and would have potentially disastrous consequences.

For the same reasons, simply adding revenue to the trust funds from other sources would also do nothing to solve Social Security's troubles. President Clinton has recommended that the expected federal budget surplus be used to shore up the Social Security system, and Deputy Treasury Secretary Lawrence Summers has said that if the surplus was transferred to the Social Security trust funds, it would extend the system's solvency from 2032 to 2039.[59] In reality, however, since federal budget surplus funds would still not be invested in real assets, adding new revenue to the trust funds would simply increase the amount of IOUs in the trust funds. Beginning in 2013, the government would still have no money put aside to redeem that debt. Social Security's problems would be unchanged.

Or Massive Benefit Cuts

The alternative to such massive tax increases is to reduce Social Security benefit amounts. If you cannot increase revenue to equal outflow, you can decrease outflow to equal revenue. However, such benefit cuts would have to be substantial and would have severe consequences for many elderly. Under the intermediate assumptions, Social Security will have sufficient revenue to finance only 77 percent of promised benefits beginning in 2032. That means, without higher taxes, benefits will have to be cut by nearly one-fourth.[60] Even worse, under pessimistic projections, Social Security will be able to fund only 66 percent of promised benefits, necessitating a one-third reduction in benefits.[61]

Benefit cuts may be packaged in many ways. For example, one of the most commonly discussed reductions is accomplished through recalculating the Consumer Price Index (CPI). The CPI is the government's general measure of inflation. As we saw in chapter 2, Social Security benefits, like those provided by many other government programs, are indexed to provide an automatic increase in benefits to offset inflation. These cost of living adjustments are based on the CPI.[62]

Although the CPI is often called the "cost of living index," it does not really measure the cost of living. Rather it measures prices for selected goods and services. Because this basket of goods and services is not revised regularly to reflect changes in consumer buying preferences or improvements in quality, the majority of economists believe that the CPI overstates the true effects of inflation. For example, when the price of apples rises faster than the price of oranges, people buy more oranges and fewer apples. But the CPI fails to take such substitutions into account. Likewise, the cost of improvements in a product is not accurately represented in the CPI. A telephone today may cost more than a telephone five years ago, but offers many new features not available on the old model.[63]

In 1996, the Senate Finance Committee appointed a special commission, chaired by Stanford University economist Michael Boskin, to study the accuracy of the CPI. The commission concluded that the CPI overstates the actual cost of living by 1.1 percent per year.[64] Other economists suggest different levels of overstatement. The Labor Department's Bureau of Labor Statistics estimates that the CPI overstates inflation by as much as 0.6 percent.[65] The Congressional Budget Office suggests that the amount of overstatement ranges from 0.2 and 0.8 percent.[66] The Federal Reserve Board puts the range of overstatement between 0.5 and 1.5 percent.[67]

Adjusting the CPI to more accurately reflect changes in the cost of living would reduce the expected growth in Social Security benefits. However, this approach has technical difficulties. First, given the wide range of estimates on the degree of overstatement, any change in the CPI mandated by Congress is likely to be arbitrary and reflect political compromise rather than an accurate measure of inflation. Moreover, once the door has been open to the political manipulation of the CPI, future Congresses are as likely to revise the measure upward as they are to reduce it. After all, what better way to seek favor with powerful voting blocs than to decree a high CPI and, hence, higher benefits?

In addition, some studies have indicated that a general measure of CPI, whatever it says for society at large, may actually understate the cost of living for the elderly, who are more sensitive to rising prices for some particular goods and services such as health care.[68] Regardless, any reduction in the CPI will amount to a real and significant reduction in future benefits for seniors, as much as $5,000 for an average retiree.[69] This could result in considerable hardship for low-income seniors who disproportionately depend on Social Security for their retirement income.[70]

Although often portrayed as a magic bullet for Social Security's troubles, changing the CPI would actually do relatively little to preserve the system's solvency. For example, reducing the CPI by 0.5 percent would move the date that Social Security begins running a deficit from 2013 to 2016. A full 1 percent reduction in CPI moves the deficit date to 2019. Therefore, whatever the merits of making the CPI more accurate, it should not be thought of as a fix for Social Security's problems.

A second much-discussed benefit reduction is an increase in the retirement age. The current retirement age of 65 is scheduled to increase very gradually to age 67 by 2027.[71] Table 3.2 shows the age at which individuals can expect to be eligible for benefits under current law.

There have been many proposals to speed up the scheduled increase and to raise the eligibility age for Social Security still further—perhaps to age 70. Raising the retirement age would reflect actuarial reality—people are living far longer than when the original age of 65 was chosen. If the retirement age was raised far enough and fast enough, it would significantly reduce future Social Security benefits.

Table 3.2
Age of Eligibility for Social Security Retirement Benefits,
by Year of Birth

Year of Birth	Normal Retirement Age
Before 1938	65 years
1938	65 and 2 months
1939	65 and 4 months
1940	65 and 6 months
1941	65 and 8 months
1942	65 and 10 months
1943–54	66
1955	66 and 2 months
1956	66 and 4 months
1957	66 and 6 months
1958	66 and 8 months
1959	66 and 10 months
1960 and after	67

NOTE: If you were born on January 1, refer to the year prior to the year of your birth. The Normal Retirement Ages shown are applicable for retired-worker and spouse's benefits. The Normal Retirement Ages for surviving spouse's benefits are slightly different (for instance, 65 years and 2 months for persons born in 1940 and 67 years for persons born in 1962 or later).
SOURCE: *Guide to Social Security and Medicare 1995.*

However, raising the retirement age would raise significant issues of equity. For example, the life expectancy at birth for African American men is just 65 years and 8 months.[72] Raising the retirement age means that a lot of African American men will pay Social Security taxes their entire lives, but receive few or no benefits. The poor, in general, would be similarly disadvantaged, since the poor generally have shorter life expectancies than do their wealthier counterparts.[73] (These issues of equity will be explored in more depth in chapter 5.)

Moreover, delaying retirement imposes only a modest burden on many white-collar and administrative workers, but can mean substantial hardship for many blue-collar workers and manual laborers. Surveys have consistently shown that white-collar workers are more likely to enjoy their work and are more willing to work beyond age 65.[74]

A third method of reducing benefits is means testing, meaning reducing or eliminating benefits for wealthier seniors. The rationale for such proposals is simple: if sacrifice is required (in the form of reduced benefits), the sacrifice should be greatest where federal largess is least deserved and where such sacrifice is least burdensome.[75] Clearly, cutting the benefits of, say, Ross Perot will have a different impact than cutting the benefits of someone with no other resources to support them.

There are three major drawbacks to means testing. The first is that it produces surprisingly little revenue unless it is imposed at such a low level of income that it would almost certainly be politically unacceptable. There are just not enough millionaires receiving Social Security benefits to make a difference. To yield substantial revenues, means testing would have to be aimed directly at the middle class. For example, phasing in means testing at incomes of only $40,000 per year (as suggested by the Concord Coalition) would still provide only 63.9 percent of the savings necessary to bring Social Security into actuarial balance, and only about a third of the savings necessary to pay all remaining benefits without redeeming the trust fund.[76]

Second, means testing (like eliminating the cap on payroll taxes) would explicitly break any link between contributions and benefits, transforming Social Security into a pure welfare program.[77] This would represent a fundamental change in the nature of the program and is unlikely to be accepted by seniors groups and other supporters of the program.

Finally, means testing would discourage private savings and earnings. In the same way that high marginal tax rates discourage work and investment, individuals will be less likely to accumulate assets on their own if the penalty for such accumulation would be the loss of their benefits.[78] For this reason nearly 100 economists from across the political spectrum signed an appendix to the Bipartisan Commission on Entitlement and Tax Reform opposing means testing, saying "Means testing would tax saving by cutting Social Security as income from private saving increases, conveying the message: Don't save or we will punish you for your frugality by denying you Social Security."[79] In addition to discouraging savings, there is evidence that means testing would reduce work effort as well.[80]

Moreover, any reduction in benefits should be looked at in light of the already poor rate of return that young workers will receive on their Social Security taxes. As discussed in the next chapter, individuals who retired years ago received more, often far more, in benefits than they paid into the system in taxes. Workers who retire today receive a barely positive return on their taxes. But young workers will receive a negative rate of return—less back in benefits than they pay in taxes. This does not even consider the opportunity cost of not being able to invest those taxes in private capital markets that provide far higher rates of return. Any reduction in benefits (or tax increase) will simply make the rate of return even worse.

That is not to say that any reduction in benefits is indefensible. Many of the above proposals may have to be part of any final Social Security reform. But, in the absence of fundamental structural reform of the system, they would merely make a bad deal worse.

Adding to the National Debt

In the absence of the type of tax increases or unprecedented benefit reductions that were described, the only way to finance Social Security's promised benefits will be through additional federal debt.[81]

As was demonstrated in the preceding chapter, surplus revenues from the Social Security payroll tax are currently being used to finance the government's general operating expenses, disguising the true size of the federal budget deficit. Thus, while the 1997 federal deficit is officially listed as $22 billion, in reality it is nearly $100 billion.[82] It appears smaller because the government borrowed $81.3 billion from Social Security. In 1999, when both the president and Congress are projecting a $9 billion budget surplus, the budget will actually be out of balance by nearly $77 billion, the balance being an illusion created by borrowing from the Social Security trust funds.[83]

In the short run, this has been bad for federal fiscal policy. Nobel Prize-winning economist James Buchanan and others have suggested that the existence of the Social Security surplus, and its use to disguise the true size of budget deficits, has enabled Congress to spend more than it would otherwise.[84] However, the real problem will start once that situation reverses in 2013. The government's general fund will have to provide the revenues necessary to redeem the trust funds, in effect repaying the Social Security system for the money it has been borrowing. Without tax increases or budget cuts, doing so will add to the federal budget deficit.

As Figure 3.3 shows, by 2020, Social Security will be adding more than $232 billion to the federal deficit, more than the entire deficit today. By 2040, that will grow to more than $1.3 trillion, nearly as

Figure 3.3

ANNUAL OPERATING BALANCE OF SOCIAL SECURITY (FEDERAL
OLD-AGE AND SURVIVORS INSURANCE AND DISABILITY
INSURANCE) TRUST FUNDS: OFFICIAL INTERMEDIATE PROJECTION

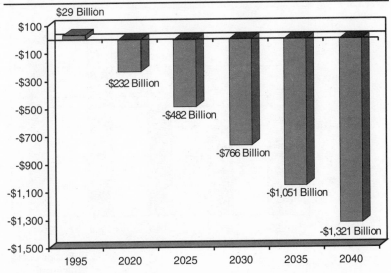

SOURCE: *1997 Trustees Report.*

much as the entire federal budget today.[85] The present value of Social Security's total unfunded liabilities over the next 75 years is more than $9 trillion.[86] By way of comparison, our current national debt is only $3.4 trillion.[87]

As Figure 3.4 shows, when Social Security's problems are combined with those of Medicare and other entitlement programs, the impact on the federal deficit becomes inescapable. By 2030, entitlement spending alone will consume all federal tax revenues, leaving not a single dime for any other operation of the federal government.[88] Since the federal government is not going to shut down, its operations will require either tax increases or deficit financing.

Clearly, there are significant problems with any of the ways of fixing Social Security's financial crisis that have been discussed.

Conclusion

Within just a few years Social Security will not be able to finance all the benefits it has promised. Only massive tax hikes or benefit

Figure 3.4
IMPACT OF FUTURE ENTITLEMENT SPENDING

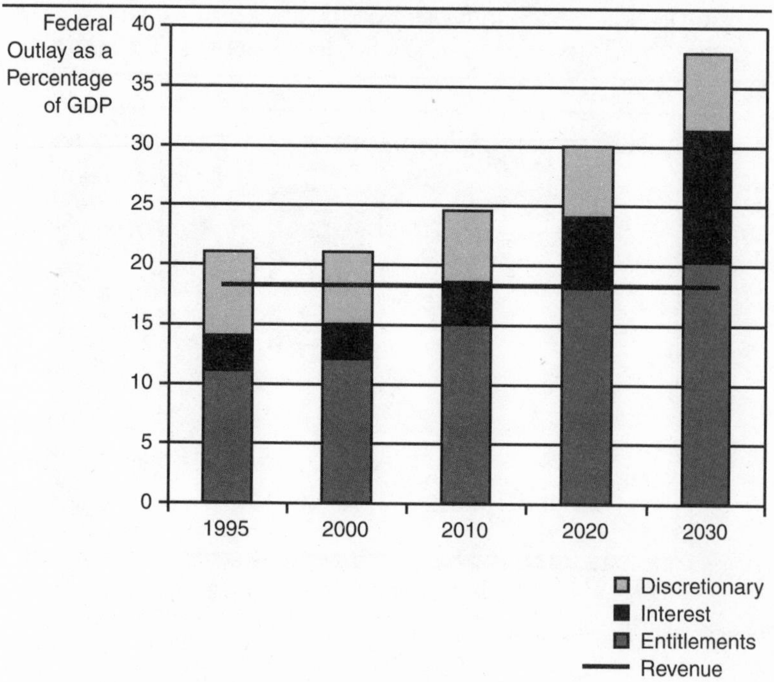

SOURCE: Bipartisan Commission on Entitlement and Tax Reform, *Interim Report to the President* (Washington: Government Printing Office, January 1995), p. 30.

cuts will keep the system afloat. But raising taxes or cutting benefits will have severe consequences for workers, recipients, and the economy. A new solution is needed.

Moreover, financing is not the only problem facing Social Security. The next chapters will examine an even bigger issue—how Social Security is robbing young Americans of the opportunity for a secure retirement.

4. A Bad Deal for Today's Workers

"We can't ask support for a plan not at least as good as any American could buy from a private insurance company. The very least a citizen should expect is to get his money back upon retirement."[1] So stated the report of the House Subcommittee for Finance in 1935, when Congress was considering passage of the Social Security Act.

Unfortunately, this promise is no longer true for today's young workers. For these workers, even if Social Security somehow pays its promised benefits, the program will pay a low, below-market return on the taxes paid into the program during their working years. Today's young workers could receive much higher returns and benefits investing in the private sector instead. In fact, this difference is now so great that Social Security is, on a relative basis, effectively impoverishing today's workers and future generations, by preventing the accumulation of real wealth that would otherwise be available through private investment alternatives.

Pay-As-You-Go vs. Fully Funded: Systemwide Returns

Social Security's bad deal for today's workers arises inherently because of the program's pay-as-you-go basis. As discussed in the previous chapter, the taxes paid into Social Security by today's workers are not saved to pay for their future benefits. Instead, tax revenues are in general immediately paid out to finance the benefits of current beneficiaries. The future benefits of today's workers will then be similarly paid out of the taxes of the next generation of workers.

In a private, fully funded system, by contrast, the money paid in is saved and invested in capital investments. The capital investments actually increase production, and the value of the new production is returned to investors in the form of a profit, rate of return, or interest payment on their investment. Over a lifetime, the return would accumulate to quite large amounts and could be used to finance retirement benefits. Because of the increased production, retirement benefits would be far higher than the amounts the workers had paid into the system over the years—and far higher than the benefits promised by Social Security.

But a pay-as-you-go system like Social Security, where, essentially, no funds are saved and invested, adds nothing to production. It simply transfers funds from one segment of the population to another. This means that individuals lose the amount of increased production and associated returns that they would have received if their money was invested in private income-producing assets. Since the pay-as-you-go system does nothing to increase production, each retiree can get no more out of the program in benefits than the simple amounts paid in taxes, unless the government increases the amount of taxes it collects from the next generation of workers.

Thus, the essential difference between the private, fully funded system and the public pay-as-you-go system is that the former relies on wealth creation while the latter relies on mere income redistribution. Because of this difference, a fully funded system will generally be able to pay much higher benefits than a mature pay-as-you-go system.

The Start-Up Phase

This is true even though those who retired in the early years of Social Security received above-market returns. Their experience was inevitable in a pay-as-you-go system, much as with initial participants in a Ponzi scheme. When a pay-as-you-go system is begun, the first generation of workers immediately begins to pay taxes into the system. Under a fully funded system, by contrast, the taxes of the first generation of workers would have to be saved and invested to finance their future benefits. But under the pay-as-you-go system no such savings are made, since the future benefits of this first working generation are supposed to be paid out of the taxes of the next working generation.

Consequently, instead of being saved, the taxes of the first working generation are immediately paid out in windfall benefits to workers in or near retirement at the time, even though these retirees paid little or nothing into the program during their working years—when the program did not exist. Benefits to initial retirees naturally represent very high returns on whatever relatively little amount of Social Security taxes the initial retirees may have paid.

One of the best illustrations of this point is the classic case of the very first Social Security recipient, Ida M. Fuller of Vermont. Ms. Fuller paid Social Security taxes for only three years before she retired in 1940. Because payroll tax rates were so low, she and her employer paid only a combined total of $44 in payroll taxes. Yet, she collected Social Security benefits for the next 35 years, until she died in 1975 at age 100. During that period she received a total of $20,933.52 in benefits, an enormous return on the taxes she paid into the system.[2]

Over the years, however, the returns paid by a pay-as-you-go system fall steadily. This is because, as each year goes by, retiring workers will have paid the program's taxes during more of their working years. The full benefits paid to later retirees out of the available revenue flow will naturally represent a lower rate of return on the larger amount of taxes they paid during their careers.

Ultimately, the system will reach a point at which retiring workers will have paid full Social Security taxes for their entire careers. At this point, the returns paid by the system reach a relatively steady state that would continue indefinitely in the absence of economic or demographic changes. The period before this point can be called the "start-up phase" of the pay-as-you-go system. The period after this point can be called the "mature phase."

The Mature Phase

The key issue in the mature phase is determining what return a pay-as-you-go system can pay, and how it compares to returns from a private, fully funded system. Since the pay-as-you-go system makes no investments, it produces and earns no investment return that can be used to pay retirees any return on what they paid into the system. As a result, with workers paying into a mere redistribution system, retirees might expect to get back only what they paid, with no real return or effective interest on the payments made into the system throughout their working years.

But there are two factors that naturally produce increased tax revenue over time in a pay-as-you-go system, enabling the system to pay some return to retirees.

The first is the rate of growth in real wages. As real wages increase over time, the total revenue collected through a fixed rate on wages increases by the rate of the wage growth. The higher revenue from these higher wages enables the system to pay retirees more than the taxes they paid on their lower wages during their working years, resulting in some effective rate of return on those tax payments.

The second factor is the rate of increase in the size of the working population relative to the size of the retired population. As the working population grows, the total tax collected by a fixed tax rate on the wages of this larger number of people grows by the rate of the population growth. However, this will not produce sufficient new revenue to pay a higher return to each retiree if the retired population is growing at the same rate as the working population. In this case, what workers pay into the system, apart from increased revenues due to wage growth, will be just enough to pay back retirees what they paid in during working years, with no return. There is only additional money to pay a rate of return on the funds paid in if the working population is growing faster than the retired population, again apart from the effects of wage growth.

In summary, because of these two factors, a pure pay-as-you-go system in the mature phase can pay a rate of return over time equal to the sum of the rate of growth of real wages plus the rate of growth of the working population relative to the retired population.

Long-established economic and demographic trends in the United States indicate the magnitude of this mature return for the U.S. Social Security system. As noted in the previous chapter, real wage growth from 1973 to 1993 was actually negative, declining 0.2 percent per year. The established long-term trend seems to be well under 1 percent.

Furthermore, because of long-standing fertility trends, the working population is likely to be stable in future years, with little or no growth. As discussed in chapter 3, the U.S. fertility rate has been below the level needed for a constant population for about 25 years. This low fertility reflects a long-term trend caused by powerful forces that have brought about similar or even more severe declines in other developed countries around the world.

At the same time, as discussed in chapter 3, life expectancy for the elderly continues to increase significantly, adding to the population of retired Social Security beneficiaries. This will cause a spread of available revenues from the pay-as-you-go system over more retirees, reducing the return available to each. Indeed, economic and technological trends will, if anything, cause life expectancy to accelerate even faster. As incomes rise over time, good nutrition, medical care, and improved general living conditions will be more widespread. Improvements will include increasingly high-tech medical care from biotechnology and other fields and may expand life expectancy much faster.

Consequently, the mature, pay-as-you-go, real return for Social Security will probably be less than 1 percent. Even under the best of circumstances it is unlikely to be more than 2 percent.

By contrast, a private, fully funded system produces and earns the full, before-tax, real rate of return to capital. This is the full amount of the benefits produced by the pool of savings and investments in such a system. Even if some of this return is taxed away, that just means that some of the benefits are being used to purchase government goods and services, rather than being channeled entirely into retirement income. But the new tax revenues are still to be counted as part of the full benefits produced by the fully funded system, as they represent new resources produced by the private retirement system. These new resources could be used for general tax cuts rather than for government spending. The before-tax, real rate of return to capital is consequently the appropriate return to compare to the mature, pay-as-you-go return discussed above, which represents the full amount of benefits resulting from the pure, pay-as-you-go system.

Martin Feldstein, professor of economics at Harvard and president of the National Bureau of Economic Research, estimates that the before-tax real rate of return to capital in the United States is about 9.3 percent.[3] This return is higher than the rate of return typically experienced by individual investors, primarily because of the heavy multiple taxation of capital caused by the current tax code. Even before the dividends, interest, and capital gains earned by individual investors, substantial federal, state, and local taxes on the capital returns have already been paid at the business level. Some investment vehicles, such as corporate bonds, also shift some of the return to others in exchange for reduced risk. Nevertheless, this full before-tax return is the appropriate return to consider for the analysis here, because it measures the full amount of the benefits produced and available through the private, invested system. The following section considers returns regularly received by individual investors in the market.

The full market return from a private, fully funded system is vastly superior to the 1 percent or less real return that can be expected from Social Security's pay-as-you-go system in the mature phase. Consequently, once the pay-as-you-go rate of return falls to its steady state in the mature phase, it will have fallen far below the full market returns earned in a fully funded system. A private, fully funded system, therefore, can naturally pay much higher benefits than a pay-as-you-go system in the mature phase.

Indeed, even comparing the 9.3 percent full, real, capital return to the 1 percent or less pay-as-you-go return is unfair to the private, fully funded system. That is because, again, the capital return results from increased production while the pay-as-you-go return results from redistribution. As a result, the capital return is earned without burdening others, while the entire pay-as-you-go return is taken from the output produced by others, making retirees better off only by making workers worse off. Under a pay-as-you-go system, workers and retirees together lose the full amount of the 9.3 percent before-tax real return to capital produced by a private, fully funded system, as the pay-as-you-go redistribution system again produces nothing. Therefore, the proper comparison is actually not 9.3 percent to 1 percent, but 9.3 percent to 0.

Some critics contend that those who tout the better returns of a private, invested system over Social Security are simply talking about switching from investment in bonds to investment in stocks, which would only provide a higher return in a tradeoff for higher risk. The analysis above shows how badly mistaken this criticism is. Pay-as-you-go Social Security does not invest in bonds. It does not invest in anything. It simply redistributes funds from workers to retirees. Payments into a private, fully funded system, by contrast, are saved and invested, creating new wealth that generates income equal to the before-tax, real rate of return to capital. Our analysis shows that the redistribution games of a pay-as-you-go system cannot hope to create even a phantom return anywhere near this return to capital. Investment in the private capital markets is inevitably going to produce much higher returns and benefits than a redistributionist scheme that does not invest in any real capital at all. The issue, therefore, is not investment in bonds versus investment in stocks; it is investment in private capital markets versus simple redistribution without any real investment.

The so-called Social Security trust funds are not a counter to this argument. Even today, with a supposed annual surplus, 86.5 percent of the tax revenues paid into Social Security are immediately paid out to current beneficiaries. Over the next 10 to 15 years, the percentage of the tax revenues immediately paid out will increase to 100. By 2012, under the intermediate assumptions, every dollar of Social Security tax revenues will be used to pay benefits—there will be no surplus.

If the annual surpluses remaining after benefits are paid were invested in private capital markets, a minor departure from a pure pay-as-you-go system would be involved and would garner a small fraction of the total investment returns of a fully funded system. In this case, because the vast majority of Social Security revenues would still be paid out immediately on a pay-as-you-go basis, the trust fund at its peak would never grow beyond 10 to 15 percent of the funds that would be necessary for a fully funded system.

But as discussed in chapter 3, the Social Security trust funds are not saved and invested. The money left in the trust funds each year after benefits are paid is lent to the federal government and immediately spent on other government programs, in return for IOUs from the federal government. So even with the trust funds, Social Security makes no real capital investment.

Social Security in the United States did not begin entering the mature phase until the early 1980s. Only then were workers retiring who had paid into Social Security for their entire working careers. At Social Security's mature phase, these retirees would have gotten higher returns and benefits by investing in a private, fully funded system than by paying taxes into Social Security system. But even these retirees avoided the sharp Social Security tax increases of the 1960s, 1970s, and early 1980s for much of their careers. The worst deal will be for those who pay these full taxes for their entire careers—today's young workers, in their 20s and 30s, as well as all future generations.

Individual Returns from Social Security

How will today's young worker fare under Social Security? What return will he or she receive on the taxes they pay?

One of the first comprehensive studies of this question was published in 1986 by the National Chamber Foundation, authored by

Peter Ferrara.[4] The study focused on a number of different hypothetical families composed of workers of different income levels. All workers were assumed to enter the workforce in 1985. Low-income workers were assumed to be 18 in that year and earning the minimum wage. Average income workers were assumed to be 22 in that year, with some earning the average income in Social Security covered employment each year, some earning the average income for full-time adult workers each year, and some earning the average income for heads of households each year. Higher income earners were assumed to be 24 in 1985 and earning the maximum Social Security taxable income each year.

The hypothetical families included examples of both married and single workers, and both two-earner and one-earner couples. Married couples were assumed to have one child when the oldest worker reached age 26, and another child when the oldest worker reached age 28. All workers were assumed to retire at age 67, which will be the normal Social Security retirement age when the young workers reach their senior years.

For each hypothetical family, the study calculated the amount that wage earners and their employers would have to pay in total payroll taxes (OASDI) throughout their careers, taking into account the probability that the worker would be alive in each year to pay the tax. The study next calculated the expected Social Security benefits to be provided to each family in return. This included retirement benefits, taking into account the probability of the worker continuing to live each year up until age 105. It included survivors benefits, taking into account the probability of death in each year. And it included disability benefits, taking into account the probabilities of disability incidence, recovery, or death in each year. The study assumed that Social Security would pay the full retirement, survivors, and disability benefits provided under current law, even though, as discussed in chapter 3, the government's own projections show the system will not have nearly enough funds to pay all these promised benefits to today's young workers. As such, with the projections showing Social Security revenues will cover only two-thirds or less of the benefits promised these workers, assuming full benefits will be paid is likely a substantial overestimate of the ultimate benefits these workers will receive.

Because the study counted the Hospital Insurance (HI) portion of the total payroll tax, it included Medicare's HI benefits as well. The study consequently counted all of the benefits currently financed by the payroll tax. But since the HI program is so much more badly underfunded than even Social Security, the calculation of HI benefits was adjusted to take those financial difficulties into account. The value of the benefits was assumed to be the average amount of HI revenue per beneficiary in each year. That represents the HI benefits that can be paid under current law, with current financing sources.

However, if the HI taxes and HI benefits so calculated were subtracted out of the calculation of Social Security returns discussed below, the returns presented would be little changed. The available HI revenues per beneficiary in retirement would just provide the same pay-as-you-go return on taxes paid as the rest of the Social Security system. So the returns calculated below can be taken as estimates of the returns provided by Social Security alone counting its retirement, survivors, and disability benefits.

The 1983 Social Security amendments mandated that Social Security benefits would be subject to federal income tax for the first time. But by law the income tax revenue resulting from the taxation of Social Security benefits does not go into the government's general revenues to help finance other government goods and services, like all other income tax revenues. The revenue from taxation of Social Security benefits is channeled exclusively back into Social Security to finance the program's taxed benefits themselves. Consequently, the benefits after such taxes represent the full benefits offered by Social Security. There are no additional benefits in the form of tax revenues produced by the system that finance other government goods and services, as with taxes assessed on the private, fully funded system. The taxation of Social Security benefits is actually a means of reducing the benefits on net rather than true taxation-raising revenue for the government. Therefore, the Social Security benefits in the study's calculations were reduced by the amount of income tax that would be paid on them, consistent with assumptions and projections of the Social Security Administration regarding the revenue that will result from such taxation.

Once the Social Security benefits and career payroll taxes were so calculated for each hypothetical family, the effective real rate of return for the family represented by the value of the benefits as compared to the value of the taxes was determined. It should be noted that the calculation does not require any assumption regarding the appropriate discount rate or market rate of return on private investments. It simply determines the rate of return paid by Social Security for different hypothetical families, and the return can then be compared to various market interest rates and returns.

All relevant economic and demographic assumptions necessary to calculate the Social Security returns were taken from the Social Security Administration's Intermediate Alternative IIB set of assumptions in the *1986 Trustees Report*.[5] This included comprehensive data regarding projected future changes in mortality, disability incidence, disability recovery, and similar factors. All calculations were performed by the international accounting firm of KMG Main Hurdman, which has since merged into the giant firm, Peat Marwick. Benefit calculations were checked for accuracy by the Social Security Administration.

Table 4.1 shows the calculated returns for family combinations in which the husband and wife both work. All the family combinations in the table involve families with two children. Families without children or only one child would have lower returns because some of the program's benefits depend on the number of children in the family. Families with more than two children generally would not have any significant increase in returns because of the program's maximum benefit limits.

Table 4.1 shows that almost all workers in two-earner couple families would receive real returns under Social Security of approximately 1 percent or less, with some actually receiving negative returns. The family combinations involving two average full-time income spouses includes a male worker earning the average income for full-time male workers throughout his career, and a female worker earning the average income for full-time female workers throughout her career. This is the best representative example of a family with two average income earners. The return for this family is significantly below 1 percent, at 0.78 percent. The family involving two Social Security average spouses includes two spouses earning the average income in Social Security-covered employment throughout their careers. This Social Security average is biased downward by the included earnings of teenagers, part-time workers, and other transient workers. Most full-time adult workers would have higher incomes over their careers than this Social Security average. The return for this family of two Social Security average earners, however, is still less than 1 percent.

Table 4.1
SOCIAL SECURITY RATES OF RETURN FOR TWO-EARNER COUPLES

Family Combinations	Real Rate of Return (%)
Two maximum taxable income spouses[a]	−0.45
One maximum taxable income spouse, one Social Security average spouse[b]	0.26
One maximum taxable income spouse, one low-income spouse[c]	0.64
Two average full-time spouses[d]	0.78
Two Social Security average spouses[e]	0.97
One average full-time spouse, one low-income spouse[f]	1.19
Two low-income spouses[g]	2.13

[a]Both spouses earn the maximum Social Security taxable income each year.
[b]One spouse earns the maximum Social Security taxable income each year, and the other earns the average income in Social Security covered employment each year.
[c]One spouse earns the maximum Social Security taxable income each year, and the other earns the relative equivalent of today's minimum wage each year.
[d]One spouse earns the average income for full-time male workers each year, and the other spouse earns the average income for full-time female workers each year.
[e]Both spouses earn the average income for Social Security covered employment each year.
[f]One spouse earns the average income for full-time male workers each year, and the other spouse earns the relative equivalent of today's minimum wage.
[g]Both spouses earn the relative equivalent of today's minimum wage each year.

The return reaches 2 percent only for a family with two low-income working spouses. These are workers who earn the relative equivalent of the minimum wage each year for their entire careers. This would be a rare earnings history indeed, as almost all minimum wage earners increase their incomes more rapidly after a few years of experience.

Table 4.2
Social Security Rates of Return for Single Workers

Family Combinations	Real Rate of Return (%)
Maximum taxable income worker[h]	−1.0
Average full-time worker[i]	0.31
Social Security average worker[j]	0.69
Low-income worker[k]	2.13

[h]Worker earns the maximum Social Security taxable income each year.
[i]Worker earns the average income for full-time workers each year.
[j]Worker earns the average income in Social Security covered employment each year.
[k]Worker earns the relative equivalent of today's minimum wage each year.

Table 4.2 shows the return to single workers. If anything, these returns are even lower than for two-earner couples. The great majority of these workers have real returns significantly below 1 percent, with many workers suffering negative returns. A single worker with the average income of all full-time adult workers throughout the economy would have a negligible return of 0.31 percent. A worker earning the average income in Social Security-covered employment throughout his career would have a return of 0.69 percent.

Given predominant social and cultural trends, most young workers entering the workforce today will be in two-earner couple or single-worker families, rather than in families with one wage earner.[6] Consequently, the returns in Tables 4.1 and 4.2 describe the experience facing most of today's young workers.

Table 4.3 shows the returns for married couples in cases in which only one spouse works outside the home. These returns are higher than for the other family combinations due to provisions favoring these families in the Social Security benefit formula, as discussed in chapter 2. Most important, a nonworking spouse receives 50 percent of the retirement benefit of the working spouse, even though the family paid no extra taxes for the extra benefits.[7] The nonworking spouse also receives extra survivors and disability benefits, if he or she continues not to work. Consequently, a family in which the worker receives the average income of male heads of households throughout his career—a good example for a typical, average income, one-earner family—would receive a return of 1.86 percent.

Table 4.3
SOCIAL SECURITY RATES OF RETURN FOR ONE-EARNER COUPLES

Family Combinations	Real Rate of Return (%)
Maximum taxable income worker, nonworking spouse[l]	1.31
Average head of household worker, nonworking spouse[m]	1.86
Average full-time worker, nonworking spouse[n]	2.02
Social Security average worker, nonworking spouse[o]	2.66
Low-income worker, nonworking spouse[p]	3.75

[l]Worker earns the maximum Social Security taxable income each year.
[m]Worker earns the average income of male head of household each year.
[n]Worker earns the average income of male full-time workers each year.
[o]Worker earns the average income in Social Security covered employment each year.
[p]Worker earns the relative equivalent of today's minimum wage each year.

Remembering again that most of today's young workers will be in two-earner couples or single-worker families, the returns in all three tables can be summarized as follows. For most young workers entering the workforce today, the real returns paid by Social Security will be 1 percent or less, with some workers even receiving negative returns.

However, this assumes that Social Security pays all promised benefits without increasing taxes. As we saw in chapter 3, this is impossible. Between one-quarter and one-third of Social Security's benefits are unfunded. Either taxes will have to be higher or benefits will have to be reduced. As a result, the rate of return for all the hypothetical workers in the study reviewed will be reduced still further, leading to negative returns for nearly all workers.

Several more recent studies provide similarly gloomy assessments of Social Security returns. The Tax Foundation estimates that most young workers will receive a negative rate of return, less money back in benefits than they pay in taxes,[8] while the Advisory Council on Social Security suggests positive rates of return of about 1 to 2 percent for most married couples, although some high-income workers and single workers would receive negative returns.[9] A new report from the Heritage Foundation also concludes that many young workers will receive a negative rate of return from their Social Security taxes, with particularly poor rates of return for African Americans and other ethnic minorities.[10]

The Historical Performance of Private Capital Markets

Receiving negative rates of return is bad enough for young workers. But there is an even worse problem—the missed opportunity of not being able to invest those taxes in private capital markets that could earn much better rates of return.

No one can predict how private investment instruments, such as stocks and bonds, will perform in the future. Still, it is possible to make reasonable estimates based on historical performance.

The most important thing to remember in evaluating the potential performance of private investments is that short-term trends do not matter. Capital markets fluctuate routinely. For any given day, month, or even year, stock and bond returns may go up, or they may go down. This volatility is extremely important to speculators, fund managers, and others trying to reap short-term profits. But, for the private investment of retirement funds, what counts is the long term. After all, individuals will be investing over a 45-year (or longer) working lifetime, and their funds will continue to be invested and support their benefits in retirement, covering a period of 60 to 70 years overall.

Over long periods of time, the trend of investment returns in U.S. capital markets has been inevitably upward. The longer the time frame, the easier this trend is to see. For example, Figure 4.1 shows the total nominal return index for U.S. stocks from 1802 until 1992. Periodic downturns, bear markets, and even the Crash of 1929, appear as little more than blips in the market's steady upward climb. In fact, $1 invested and reinvested in stocks since 1802 would be worth more than $260,000 in 1992.[11]

More important, even the far shorter periods relevant to a discussion of investing for retirement shows the consistently positive returns earned by private investment markets. Over the 70-year period from 1926 through 1996 the average annual nominal return on U.S. stocks was 10.89 percent. Adjusted for inflation, that is an

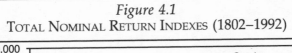

Figure 4.1
TOTAL NOMINAL RETURN INDEXES (1802–1992)

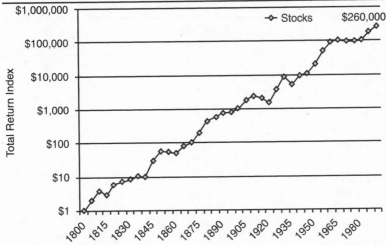

SOURCE: Jeremy J. Siegel, *Stocks for the Long Run* (Chicago: Irwin Professional Publishing, 1994), p. 13.

average annual return of 7.56 percent.[12] The returns cover an incredibly eventful period including the Great Depression, one world war, two comparatively minor wars, and the turbulent inflation/recession years of the 1970s.

In fact, as Table 4.4 shows, there is no 20-year period in U.S. history where stocks produced a negative rate of return.

Corporate bonds have also produced a consistently positive rate of return, although lower than the return on stocks. From 1919 to 1996, the average annual composite real rate of return paid on corporate bonds was 2.9 percent.[13] It is interesting to note, however, a distinct period from 1941 to 1951 with sharply lower returns than the rest of the 77-year period. During this time, a regime of government price and interest rate controls, not entirely removed until 1951, seems to have artificially reduced corporate bond rates. If we exclude this controlled period as not representative of market rates, then the average composite real rate of interest for corporate bonds is 4 percent.[14]

These returns over many decades, spanning a broad range of economic and political events, reflect basic, structural factors in our

Table 4.4
Annual Returns on Stocks & Bonds in the United States, 1802–1995

Years	% Stocks Total Return	% Bonds Total Return
1802–1809	4.77	6.60
1810–1819	2.68	6.41
1820–1829	5.31	5.92
1830–1839	4.53	6.25
1840–1849	6.73	4.89
1850–1859	0.45	5.35
1860–1869	15.73	6.65
1870–1879	7.58	7.96
1880–1889	6.72	5.53
1890–1899	5.45	3.92
1900–1909	9.62	1.63
1910–1919	4.69	0.30
1920–1929	13.86	8.16
1930–1939	−0.17	6.99
1940–1949	9.57	2.91
1950–1959	18.23	−3.75
1960–1969	8.17	−0.17
1970–1979	6.75	3.37
1980–1989	16.64	13.81
1990–1995	13.00	11.34
1802–1900	5.89	5.87
1900–1995	9.78	4.05
1802–1995	7.79	4.97
1950–1995	12.42	4.15

economy. In particular, they reflect the underlying productive power of capital.

Social Security Benefits vs. Market Returns

There have been several studies comparing promised Social Security benefits with the retirement benefits that could be earned if workers were allowed to invest their Social Security taxes in private markets.

One of the earliest of these was the National Chamber Foundation study by Peter Ferrara, discussed above.[15] For this book, the authors updated their study to report the results in constant 1998 dollars. We also modified the study to exclude the portion of the payroll tax for the HI program and the benefits paid by that program. So the results below cover only Social Security taxes (OASDI), and only Social Security benefits, including retirement, survivors, and disability benefits.

The study covers the same hypothetical families as discussed before and the real returns paid by Social Security were calculated. First, the amounts of OASDI taxes that would be paid by each worker (including the portion paid by the employer) over a career in the case of each of these families was calculated. It was then assumed that these amounts were invested in an IRA-type vehicle each year, further accumulating investment returns annually. The accumulated sums each year of the expected value of promised Social Security survivors and disability benefits were subtracted, assuming that workers would have to use some of their funds to purchase private life and disability insurance of equal value. The total accumulated sum each family would have at retirement was then calculated. Finally, the retirement benefits such a sum could pay were calculated. The updated and modified results are presented in the following, using three different assumed real rates of return–4, 5, and 6 percent. For comparison, we also present the Social Security benefits that would be paid to the workers under current law, even though we have seen that there are not sufficient funds in the system to pay those benefits.

The results are presented in Tables 4.5, 4.6, and 4.7. All figures are presented in 1998 dollars. The total of accumulated assets at retirement in the IRA vehicle for each family is shown in the first row of data in each table. The second row, labeled "Perpetual Annuity," shows the amount of benefits that could be paid out of the continuing returns on the assets alone, leaving the assets themselves intact to pass on to children or other heirs. The next two rows, labeled "Life Annuity," indicate the amount of benefits that could be paid if the accumulated assets were to be entirely consumed over the retirement period, leaving nothing for heirs. These annuity benefit values were adjusted, to pay more while both spouses were alive, to the same level that Social Security would pay for each family. The next two

Table 4.5

PRIVATE MARKET BENEFITS VS. SOCIAL SECURITY BENEFITS FOR DIFFERENT FAMILY COMBINATIONS. ASSUMED REAL RATE OF RETURN: 6%. (All Figures in Constant 1998 Dollars)

	Two Maximum Taxable Income Spouses	One Maximum Taxable Income Spouse, One Social Security Average Spouse	One Maximum Taxable Income Spouse, One Low-Income Spouse	Two Average Full-Time Spouses	One Average Full-Time Spouse, One Low-Income Spouse	Two Low-Income Spouses
Accumulated Assets at Retirement	2,846,460	1,995,932	1,643,642	1,628,297	1,259,826	693,395
Perpetual Annuity	170,788	119,756	98,617	97,699	75,590	41,603
Life Annuity						
Both spouses alive	419,121	273,325	217,682	229,348	167,129	100,418
One spouse alive	209,560	163,470	140,808	128,560	107,554	50,209
Social Security Pays						
Both spouses alive	45,380	37,635	34,036	33,394	28,481	18,404
One spouse alive	22,690	22,690	22,690	18,986	18,986	9,202

(continued)

	Maximum Taxable Income Single Worker	Average Full-Time Single Worker	Low-Income Single Worker	Maximum Taxable Income Worker, Nonworking Spouse	Average Head of Household Worker, Nonworking Spouse	Average Full-Time Worker, Nonworking Spouse	Low-Income Worker, Nonworking Spouse
Accumulated Assets at Retirement	1,413,562	855,583	333,885	1,397,370	1,059,505	982,591	338,031
Perpetual Annuity	84,813	51,335	20,034	83,843	63,570	58,955	20,281
Life Annuity							
Both spouses alive				184,269	139,954	129,735	44,395
One spouse alive	207,813	123,920	46,760	119,313	90,024	83,583	27,751
Social Security Pays							
Both spouses alive				34,036	29,301	28,481	13,802
One spouse alive	22,690	15,712	9,202	22,690	19,533	18,986	9,202

SOURCE: Authors' calculations.

Table 4.6
PRIVATE MARKET BENEFITS VS. SOCIAL SECURITY BENEFITS FOR DIFFERENT FAMILY COMBINATIONS.
ASSUMED REAL RATE OF RETURN: 5%.
(All Figures in Constant 1998 Dollars)

	Two Maximum Taxable Income Spouses	One Maximum Taxable Income Spouse, One Social Security Average Spouse	One Maximum Taxable Income Spouse, One Low-Income Spouse	Two Average Full-Time Spouses	One Average Full-Time Spouse, One Low-Income Spouse	Two Low-Income Spouses
Accumulated Assets at Retirement	2,191,490	1,536,028	1,263,987	1,223,602	953,604	506,920
Perpetual Annuity	109,574	76,802	63,199	61,675	47,681	25,346
Life Annuity						
Both spouses alive	293,952	190,905	151,674	157,458	114,649	66,968
One spouse alive	146,975	114,177	98,112	88,515	73,780	33,483
Social Security Pays						
Both spouses alive	45,380	37,635	34,036	33,394	24,481	18,404
One spouse alive	22,690	22,690	22,690	18,986	18,986	9,202

(continued)

	Maximum Taxable Income Single Worker	Average Full-Time Single Worker	Low-Income Single Worker	Maximum Taxable Income Worker, Nonworking Spouse	Average Head of Household Worker, Nonworking Spouse	Average Full-Time Worker, Nonworking Spouse	Low-Income Worker, Nonworking Spouse
Accumulated Assets at Retirement	1,083,349	645,555	243,355	1,074,586	802,015	743,716	246,591
Perpetual Annuity	54,167	32,278	12,167	53,729	40,100	37,185	12,329
Life Annuity							
Both spouses alive				128,394	96,003	88,990	29,421
One spouse alive	148,401	86,993	31,675	83,134	61,902	57,333	18,391
Social Security Pays							
Both spouses alive				34,036	29,301	28,481	13,802
One spouse alive	22,690	15,712	9,202	22,690	19,533	18,986	9,202

Table 4.7
PRIVATE MARKET BENEFITS vs. SOCIAL SECURITY BENEFITS FOR DIFFERENT FAMILY COMBINATIONS.
ASSUMED REAL RATE OF RETURN: 4%.
(All Figures in Constant 1998 Dollars)

	Two Maximum Taxable Income Spouses	One Maximum Taxable Income Spouse, One Social Security Average Spouse	One Maximum Taxable Income Spouse, One Low-Income Spouse	Two Average Full-Time Spouses	One Average Full-Time Spouse, One Low-Income Spouse	Two Low-Income Spouses
Accumulated Assets at Retirement	1,703,817	1,193,784	981,596	944,628	729,697	375,400
Perpetual Annuity	68,152	47,751	39,265	37,784	29,187	15,016
Life Annuity						
Both spouses alive	206,624	133,606	105,881	109,064	78,881	44,964
One spouse alive	103,313	79,907	68,490	61,136	50,763	22,458
Social Security Pays						
Both spouses alive	45,380	37,635	34,036	33,394	28,481	18,404
One spouse alive	22,690	22,690	34,852	18,986	18,986	9,202

(continued)

	Maximum Taxable Income Single Worker	Average Full-Time Single Worker	Low-Income Single Worker	Maximum Taxable Income Worker, Nonworking Spouse	Average Head of Household Worker, Nonworking Spouse	Average Full-Time Worker, Nonworking Spouse	Low-Income Worker, Nonworking Spouse
Accumulated Assets at Retirement	678,986	491,876	179,414	834,446	613,657	569,013	182,217
Perpetual Annuity	53,512	19,675	7,176	33,377	24,547	22,760	7,288
Life Annuity							
Both spouses alive				89,621	66,043	61,220	19,601
One spouse alive	106,431	61,372	21,513	58,029	42,584	39,441	12,253
Social Security Pays							
Both spouses alive				34,036	29,300	28,481	13,802
One spouse alive	22,690	15,712	9,202	22,690	19,533	18,986	9,202

rows in each table indicate the amount of Social Security benefits that would be paid to each family. These benefits are presented without any reduction for income taxes, as are the private benefits. It should be noted, however, that any taxation of the private benefits would produce revenues providing other government goods and services or reductions in other taxes, whereas by law the revenues from taxation of Social Security benefits merely go back into Social Security to fund the program's taxed benefits themselves, as discussed previously.

Given the historical trends discussed earlier, assuming a 6 percent real return would be a conservative estimate of the long-term return of a portfolio invested primarily in stocks. Even assuming this conservative return, the private, invested alternative would completely overwhelm Social Security.

For example, take a typical family consisting of two full-time workers. The husband earns the average income for full-time males throughout his career and the wife earns the average income for full-time females throughout her career. At a 6 percent real return, they would retire with a trust fund of about $1.6 million ($1,628,297) in 1998 dollars. This fund would pay them about three times as much as Social Security, while still allowing them to leave the $1.6 million to their children. Or they could use the fund to buy an annuity that would pay them about seven times what Social Security would pay.

Or take another example—a family where the husband works and earns the average income of a male head of household each year, and the wife works at home caring for the children. This family would retire with a trust fund of just over $1 million ($1,059,505) in 1998 dollars. That fund would pay them over twice what Social Security would out of the continuing returns alone, while still allowing them to leave the $1 million trust fund to their children. Or they could use the fund to buy an annuity that would pay them almost five times (4.77) what Social Security would pay.

Finally, take the case of two low-income spouses earning the equivalent of the minimum wage each year for their careers. These two low-income workers would retire with a trust fund of almost $700,000 in 1998 dollars. That fund would pay them more than twice what Social Security would pay out of the continuing returns alone, again allowing this low-income couple to leave almost $700,000 to their children. Or they could use the money to buy an annuity that would pay them about five-and-one-half times what Social Security would pay.

Even assuming a low 4 percent real return, the private, invested system still overwhelms Social Security. Two average full-time spouses would still retire with a trust fund of close to $1 million. That fund would still pay them more than Social Security out of the continuing returns alone, while allowing them to leave the almost $1 million to their children. Or the fund could be used to buy an annuity paying them over three times what Social Security would pay.

For our one-earner couple earning the average income of a male head of household, at a 4 percent real return they would retire with a trust fund of $613,657. The couple could use that fund to buy an annuity that would pay well over twice what Social Security would pay. Alternatively, that fund would pay them $24,547 each year for life out of the continuing returns alone, while allowing them to leave over $600,000 to their children. Social Security would pay $29,300 with both spouses alive, but only $19,533 after one died, with nothing left for the children. The couple could also match Social Security's benefits using only 45 percent of their funds, and still leave the remaining $341,000 to their children.

Finally, at a 4 percent real return the two low-income workers would retire with a fund of $375,400. The couple could use the fund to buy an annuity that would pay them about two-and-one-half times what Social Security would. Alternatively, that fund would pay them $15,016 each year for their entire lives out of the continuing returns alone, while still allowing them to leave almost $400,000 to their children. Social Security, by contrast, would pay $18,404 with both spouses alive, but only $9,202 after one died, with nothing left for the children.

This analysis shows that everyone would benefit greatly from shifting to the private, invested system. Our middle-income couple would gain three to seven times the benefits of Social Security under the examples shown. But our average one-earner couple would also gain from more than twice to almost five times Social Security's benefits. And even our low-income couple would earn two-and-one-half to five-and-one-half times Social Security benefits. The superiority of the private, invested system overwhelms even the special, redistributive subsidies for one-earner couples and low-income workers within Social Security.

Other comprehensive studies comparing Social Security and the private market have found similar results. In 1985, Peter Ferrara and economist John Lott, formerly of the Wharton School and now at the University of Chicago Law School, examined hypothetical families of different income levels entering the workforce in 1983.[16] The study looked at OASDI taxes and OASDI benefits, including retirement, survivors, and disability benefits. It excluded HI taxes and benefits. The study found that almost all workers of this age group could expect a real return from Social Security of 1 to 1.5 percent or less.

One example was two spouses earning the average income in Social Security-covered employment each year for their entire careers. Such workers would again be earning below average incomes for full-time adults, as the average Social Security-covered worker includes part-time workers, students, teenagers, and other secondary workers. Nevertheless, at a 6 percent real return, the study found that the couple would retire with a trust fund of $1.4 million updated to 1998 dollars. The fund would pay about two-and-three-quarter times what Social Security would pay out of the continuing returns alone, while still allowing the couple to leave the $1.4 million to their children. Or they could use the fund to buy an annuity paying over five times what Social Security would pay.

At a 4 percent real return, the couple would retire with a trust fund of $804,616 in 1998 dollars. This fund would still pay more than Social Security out of the continuing returns alone, while allowing the workers to leave the $800,000 fund to their children. Or they could use the fund to buy an annuity that would pay them about two-and-one-half times what Social Security would pay. The results for other family combinations were also similar to the results discussed for the study.

Finally, William G. Shipman, a principal with State Street Global Advisors, one of the largest pension investment management firms in the world, recently produced two studies comparing Social Security benefits to benefits available in the private sector.[17] In the first, Shipman examined hypothetical cases of workers born in 1930, 1950, and 1970, who would enter the workforce in 1951, 1971, and 1991, respectively. For each year of entry into the workforce, he examined two cases. One was a low-income worker earning 50 percent of the national average wage each year, which would be about $14,000 per year today. The second case was a worker earning each year the maximum taxable income under Social Security, about $67,000 this year.

For each case, Shipman examined two alternative investment scenarios. One is investment in a stock fund including a 75/25 percent mix of large and small capitalization companies. Based on historical experience, the fund was conservatively assumed to earn a real return over future years of about 6.5 percent. The second scenario is investment in a bond fund including a 50/50 percent mix of long-term corporate and government bonds. Based on historical experience, that fund was conservatively assumed to earn a real return over future years of about 3.5 percent.

For workers entering the workforce in 1991, investing in the stock fund, the high-wage worker would receive over six times the benefits of Social Security. Investing in the bond fund, the worker would still receive almost three times the benefits of Social Security. For the low-wage worker, the stock fund would produce over three times the benefits of Social Security. The highly conservative bond fund would still produce 41 percent more in benefits than Social Security.

In the later study, Shipman, along with Melissa Hieger, a vice-president at State Street Global Advisors, examined more closely the low-income worker cases.[18] In addition to a stock portfolio, with a 90/10 mix of large and small capitalization stocks, and a bond portfolio, with a 50/50 mix of corporate and government bonds, Hieger and Shipman added a mixed stock and bond fund. That fund was invested 60 percent in stocks and 40 percent in bonds, distributed among stocks and bonds as in the stock and bond funds above. In future years, the fund was assumed to earn a conservative real return of 4.3 percent, net of all costs.

With the mixed stock and bond fund, the low-wage worker would receive about 80 percent more than Social Security would pay. The stock fund would produce about three-and-one-half times the benefits of Social Security, while the bond fund would produce about 41 percent more.[19]

Other Advantages to a Private Alternative

The private, invested system offers additional important advantages over Social Security. Social Security retirement benefits are subject to an earnings test, which reduces benefits by $1 for every $3 earned above a certain amount. In the private, invested system, there would be no such restriction. People could continue to work and earn income in retirement to the extent they desired, without any reduction in their benefits.

A privately invested system would also provide better survivors benefits than the current system. Our discussion, comparing private retirement benefits to Social Security, included the survivors benefit to aged widows and widowers. When a worker dies under the privatized Social Security system, his family would inherit all the funds accumulated in the worker's individual account, providing benefits far in excess of those provided by Social Security. Since aged widows and widowers make up approximately 85 percent of all survivors, this would be true in the vast majority of cases.[20]

For workers who die before retirement, in a privatized system their families would inherit all the funds that had been accumulated until that time, including investment returns. Given even modest rates of return, it would take the average worker only about 20 years to accumulate enough funds in his account to provide benefits higher than Social Security survivors benefits.

Before enough funds have been accumulated for retirement, workers in the private system would use part of their annual contribution to purchase private life insurance, supplementing their accumulated funds to at least match the promised Social Security survivors benefits. Term life insurance can be purchased for individuals in their 20s for about $200 for $100,000 coverage.[21] This is inexpensive protection during the time one is just starting out. Coverage can be reduced as assets are accumulated.

Moreover *all* workers would enjoy this protection under a private system. Social Security, by contrast, provides no survivors benefits (prior to age 65) to couples without minor children or to childless single people.

In addition, under Social Security, survivors benefits are reduced if the surviving husband or wife remarries or places any children in the care of others. Moreover, preretirement survivors benefits are subject to an even stricter earnings test, reducing benefits by $2 for every $1 earned beyond a modest minimum ($13,500 for individuals between ages 65 and 69, $8,640 for individuals under age 65 in 1998).[22] However, if a family were covered by a private life insurance policy rather than by Social Security, there would be no reduction of benefits in any of those cases. The life insurance, as well as any inherited funds, would belong to the survivors to use as they please, regardless of remarriage, work, or child care arrangements.

The same situation holds true for disability benefits. If the wife of a disabled worker goes to work and earns over the same modest limit set for survivors benefits, then under the earnings test a portion of the family's benefits would be reduced by $2 for every $1 earned over the limit. The same applies to the work of a husband if a working wife is disabled. Benefits are also reduced if the children are placed in the care of others or if the spouses become divorced. But under a private insurance policy, the disabled worker would continue to receive full benefits to support his family regardless of the work and earnings of the nondisabled spouse, child care arrangements, or spouse's divorce.

Moreover, by the late 40s or early 50s for most workers, the individual retirement account for each worker in the private system would be enough to pay higher disability benefits than Social Security, as well as higher retirement benefits. Workers after that point would again not have to pay any more for this superior disability protection, which would be accruing automatically in their personal retirement accounts.

In addition, in the private system workers would be free to tailor their own packages of insurance and investment purchases to suit their individual needs and preferences. For example, through the private system single workers probably would choose appropriately to buy less life insurance than married workers, and married childless couples likely would choose less life insurance than married couples with children. Savings on unnecessary life insurance could then be devoted to retirement benefits. Social Security, by contrast, forces everyone to buy the same pattern of survivors and disability coverage, regardless of whether it is suited to them.

Workers in a private system would also have greater freedom of choice and control over their retirement age. Once they had accumulated enough to finance some minimum level of retirement benefits, they could be left free to choose whatever retirement age they desired. They could be allowed to contribute additional amounts in earlier working years to accelerate eligibility for retirement. They could also delay retirement as long as they wanted, without any penalty. Their retirement funds would continue to belong to them regardless of how long they worked. Indeed, they would continue to receive full market returns and increase future benefits even more rapidly the longer they worked.

In retirement, individuals would again have greater flexibility to pattern their retirement benefits to suit their personal needs and preferences. They could use part of their accounts to buy an annuity, guaranteeing a certain lifetime income, and retain personal control over remaining funds. They could use the funds to accelerate benefits when they needed or desired them. The funds would be on hand to pay for uncovered medical expenses, including superior care the retiree wanted. The funds would be there as well to buy a new home or car. The retiree would also have the funds to help out children or grandchildren with major needs, such as purchase of a home, health care, or education.

Finally, in addition to the higher benefits and other advantages noted, a privately invested system would also produce a large amount of new tax revenue. As discussed, these tax revenues result from taxation at the corporate level of the full, before-tax real rate of return to capital produced by the private system's investments. Therefore, as the privatized system generates new investment, it will yield new tax revenues that can be used to finance the transition to a private system (see chapter 8) or provide general tax relief.

Administrative Costs

A question often raised is how administrative costs would affect returns and benefits under a private, invested system. Of course, private investment fund managers would have to be paid some fee to cover the costs of administering the individual investment accounts of each worker and carrying out investment transactions. However, such costs would not have a significant impact on the returns earned under privatization.

Market experience shows that administrative costs of a private system should be quite modest. For example, Hieger and Shipman offer the example of the Vanguard Index 500 fund, which invests in a broad-based portfolio of U.S. stocks. That fund has an annual expense ratio of 0.2 percent of assets, or 20 basis points. They also offer the example of the Dodge and Cox Income Fund, which invests in a portfolio of U.S. bonds. That fund has an expense ratio of 0.54 percent of assets, or 54 basis points.[23]

Olivia Mitchell of the Wharton School of Economics reports average costs of broadly invested index mutual funds are 0.32 percent of assets, or 32 basis points.[24] The institutional market with large investment pools such as employer pension plans involves even lower administrative expenses. Mitchell reports examples of administrative costs in this market at less than 0.1 percent, or 10 basis points. For the Federal Thrift Plan, which offers individual account investment options to federal employees, Mitchell reports administrative costs of about 0.1 percent, or 10 basis points. Mitchell also reports that for the CREF national retirement system for teachers, which offers many more options in an individual account investment system, total administrative costs are 30 to 40 basis points.

Consequently, administrative costs for a national, private, fully funded system should be less than 0.5 percent of assets, or 50 basis points, per year for each account. Indeed, in the context of a national retirement system replacing Social Security, administrative costs are likely to be even lower than seen in the market today. Such a system would generate huge pools of investment funds, achieving economies of scale and driving down costs per participant. Fund collection costs would be minimized, with funds automatically distributed through payroll withholding. Standardized, low-cost investment options would become common. And the investment managers would be subject to close government scrutiny and regulation.

The private returns and benefits discussed leave far more than enough room for such administrative costs. With historical stock returns running at a real rate of 7.5 percent, an assumed 6 percent real return on a stock investment fund leaves over 1 percent, or 100 basis points, for any administrative costs. Indeed, a 7 percent real return net of administrative costs seems entirely plausible. Moreover, a 5 percent real return for a mixed stock and bond fund leaves about 50 basis points or more for administrative costs. And a 4 percent real return for such a fund leaves a huge cushion for administrative costs.

The Concern over Risk

Another concern about a privately invested system is market risk. After all, the market returns discussed are not guaranteed, and the stock market, in particular, is highly variable. In the market, some investments can go sour and losses can occur. How, then, will this market risk affect the returns and benefits of the private system?

Such investment risk can be minimized through a number of market mechanisms. Risk is sharply reduced by diversification through investing in broad-based pools of stocks. Some of the stocks in the pool may become worthless as some companies go bankrupt, and others will soar in value as successful new corporate giants emerge. The returns over the long run will reflect the above broad-based market returns. With a sufficiently broad-based investment pool, the investor would basically own a piece of the economy as a whole. No one is exempt from the risk of the performance of the general economy, not even the government. A very deep and prolonged general economic downturn would devastate Social Security and the government's ability to finance it as well.[25]

This diversification can be expanded across the globe by investing a portion of the funds in foreign stock markets. Then, when the U.S. economy is down, others may be soaring, and vice versa. Investing some of the funds in bonds would further minimize risk. Moreover, Hieger and Shipman point out that investment managers will commonly seek to diversify a portfolio's assets in investments that tend to be inversely correlated. In other words, some investments are likely to be up precisely when others are down, and vice versa.[26]

In a well-structured private system, these risk reduction strategies would be carried out by highly sophisticated investment managers, approved by the government and chosen by workers in a competitive market. Such managers would be investing huge pools of the funds of individual investment accounts. Such risk reduction mechanisms would enable workers to reliably receive the broad-based market returns and benefits discussed above.

Moreover, it is critical to remember that the privately invested retirement funds are long-term investments. As we have seen, the long-term trend of American capital markets is positive, regardless of short-term fluctuations. In the private system, workers are investing not only over their entire working careers, 45 years or so, but, since their funds will continue to be invested during retirement, over their entire adult lives, 60 or 70 years. While market investments may vary dramatically from year to year, over such a long period of time, returns are very likely to reflect the long-term returns discussed above.

Indeed, career investors planning for retirement have a great advantage over other investors, because they can commit funds for very long periods. They should consequently be able to get higher returns on their funds than most other investors, who may need to maintain the accessibility and liquidity of their investments over the next few years, if not sooner.[27] Most of the higher return on stocks is in fact not due to greater risk of failure (which can be minimized through diversification), but to the highly variable year-to-year returns on stocks, which are of much greater concern to most shorter-term-oriented investors. Since these short-term fluctuations are less important to career retirement investors planning for the long term, such investors are actually in a very good position to seek the higher returns offered by stocks.

Hieger and Shipman, in fact, point out that the worst 30-year period in the history of the U.S. stock market provided a 5.2 percent real return. The worst 63-year period in recorded stock market history, roughly the equivalent of investing over an adult lifetime (including retirement), yielded a 6.4 percent real return.[28]

Feldstein takes this analysis a step further. He calculates that with a contribution rate of just 2.74 percent of payroll, workers investing in private markets and earning full capital returns would be able to finance benefits at least equal to Social Security through age 100 with a 95 percent probability.[29] All of the remaining 9.66 percent payroll tax, minus a small portion for private life and disability insurance, would finance benefits in excess of those provided by Social Security. This provides more than enough cushion against risk.

Feldstein's analysis assumes that workers receive the full before-tax return to capital, but it also covers the risk of living too long in retirement. Covering just the risk of investment fluctuations would require less funds. Nor is there any reason why a private system could not be designed that allowed workers to keep the full before-tax return on at least a portion of their investments.

Moreover, workers could be protected from risk by having the government guarantee a minimum benefit level, as in Chile and other privatized social security systems. With a guaranteed minimum benefit equal to the average benefit provided by Social Security today, as discussed in chapter 8, the risk of the private system would be no greater than the risk of Social Security itself.

Given the risk-minimizing factors discussed above, our analysis of the returns and benefits of a private investment system left plenty of leeway for risk. With an average real stock market return over the last 70 years of approximately 7.5 percent, a real return of 5 to 6 percent would fully account for the worst long-term periods of stock performance in recorded history. A real return of 4 percent leaves room for an unprecedented poor performance, yet still provides three times more benefits than Social Security.

Of course, any real market investment return should be compared with the miserable 1 percent or so return offered by Social Security. The possibility of long-term market investment returns falling below the returns offered by Social Security is about as likely as that alien invasion anticipated by Generation X.

Depriving working people of the freedom to choose the higher returns and other benefits of the private investment market because of concerns about risk is not costless. It deprives working people of the full economic value of their earnings. In looking at the risk of investing in the market, we should also consider the risk of not investing, and losing the high level of benefits that would have resulted.

Finally, it is important that market risks be compared with the political risks of the current Social Security system. Contrary to common belief, Social Security is *not* backed by the full faith and credit of the U.S. government and is not a government-guaranteed investment. The U.S. Supreme Court has expressly held, in *Fleming v. Nestor*, that workers have no legally binding contractual rights to their Social Security benefits, and those benefits can be cut or even eliminated at any time. The Court said,

> To engraft upon the Social Security system a concept of "accrued property rights" would deprive it of the flexibility and boldness in adjustment to ever changing conditions which it demands.[30]

The Court also said,

> It is apparent that the noncontractual interest of an employee covered by the [Social Security] Act cannot be soundly analogized to that of the holder of an annuity, whose right to benefits is bottomed on his contractual premium payments.[31]

Moreover, as we have seen, even if Social Security can find a way to pay all its promised benefits, there is a virtual certainty of major losses compared to a private system. Virtually certain, as well, is that Social Security benefits will be cut, and/or taxes will be increased, further reducing the return of benefits on taxes paid. The bottom line is that a bad return from Social Security is more than a risk—it is a certainty.

5. The Poor, Minorities, Women, and Families

As we have seen, Social Security is a bad deal for nearly all Americans. However, bad deals are not all created equal. Some groups are particularly disadvantaged by the current system, including working women, the poor, and minorities. These groups are among those who would have the most to gain under a privatized system. The current system is such a bad deal that even groups that are subsidized by the system, such as traditional and extended families, would be better off with privatization.

The Poor: Social Security's Victims

Social Security currently accounts for approximately half of all retirement benefits. More than half of the elderly, however, receive no private pension, and more than one-third have no income from assets.[1] But that tells only part of the story. Low-income workers are far more likely to be dependent on Social Security when they retire than their high-income counterparts. As Figure 5.1 shows, the

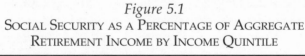

Figure 5.1
SOCIAL SECURITY AS A PERCENTAGE OF AGGREGATE
RETIREMENT INCOME BY INCOME QUINTILE

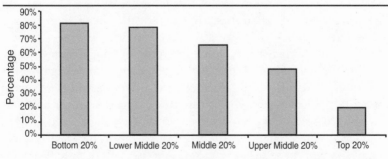

Quintile of Income Distribution

poorest 20 percent of the elderly depend on Social Security for 81 percent of their income, while Social Security provides only 20 percent of income for the wealthiest 20 percent of retirees.[2]

This trend has been slowly but steadily growing worse, with the poorest elderly depending more and more on Social Security. Projections indicate that the disparity between poor and wealthy seniors will grow wider in the future, with low-income elderly remaining extremely dependent on Social Security, while those with higher incomes will increasingly rely on private pensions and other income sources.

The question then becomes whether Social Security benefits are sufficient to provide an adequate retirement income for those elderly poor who have no other income. Perhaps the easiest way to look at this is to examine Social Security's "replacement value," that is, the proportion of a person's preretirement income that Social Security benefits equal.

Because of the progressive benefit formula described in chapter 2, Social Security replaces a higher proportion of income for a low-wage earner than for high-wage earners. The actual replacement rate fluctuates slightly from year to year based on a variety of factors. For an average-wage earner who retires this year, Social Security can be expected to replace approximately 42.4 percent of his preretirement income. A low-wage worker would receive benefits equal to 57.1 percent of preretirement income, while the replacement rate for a high-wage worker will be 25.6 percent.[3]

For a person who is 25 years old today, who will retire in 2037, projected replacement rates are 55.7 percent for low-wage earners, 41.5 percent for average-wage earners, and 27.5 percent for high-wage earners.[4] However, the relatively higher replacement rate for low-wage workers should be considered in light of their greater dependence on Social Security. As stated above, low-wage workers depend on Social Security for 81 percent of their income. Thus, total annual retirement income for the 25-year-old low-wage worker (from Social Security and other sources) will equal only 69 percent of preretirement income. In comparison, Social Security accounts for only 20 percent of postretirement income for high-wage earners. Therefore, when a high-wage worker retires, his income will actually equal 138 percent of his income before retirement despite the lower replacement rate.

Most financial planners suggest that if one's preretirement standard of living is to be maintained, retirement benefits of between 60 and 85 percent of preretirement income are probably necessary.[5] Clearly, then, Social Security fails to provide sufficient income to provide poor workers with a dignified and secure retirement.

Perhaps that is one reason why poverty rates remain higher for people over age 65 than for people ages 18 to 65. Although we have made extraordinary strides in reducing poverty among the elderly, in 1992, 12.9 percent of seniors were poor, compared with 11.7 percent of 18- to 65-year olds.[6]

Consider the advantages, therefore, that privatization of Social Security would bring to the elderly poor. As we saw in chapter 4, private investment of payroll taxes would provide retirement benefits several times higher than Social Security. For example, if private investment earns a 6 percent real return, a two-earner couple, with both workers earning the minimum wage their entire lives, would retire with more than $700,000 (in 1998 dollars) in their retirement accounts. They could use those funds to purchase an annuity that would pay them approximately five-and-a-half times as much as Social Security. Interest on the funds alone would pay them nearly twice as much as Social Security, and allow them to leave the $700,000 to their children—a substantial bequest, especially to a poor family.

Even with a 4 percent real return, the couple would retire with more than $375,000 in their accounts, enough to purchase an annuity paying approximately two-and-a-half times as much as Social Security. Alternatively, they could use about 45 percent of their funds to purchase an annuity paying the same benefits as Social Security, and still leave nearly $220,000 to their children.

Therefore, despite Social Security's progressive benefit formula, the superior returns and benefits under a privately invested system would provide the poor with a much better standard of living in their old age.

Of course, this comparison assumes that Social Security will be able to pay all the benefits promised. But as we saw in chapter 3, only a portion of those future benefits are fully funded. Thus, unless additional funding is found, benefits will have to be reduced and replacement rates will fall, perhaps by as much as one-third.[7] As a result, the poor would be even worse off, both in real terms and relative to a private system. The poor, of course, cannot afford the

97

Figure 5.2
MALES SURVIVING OF 100,000 REACHING AGE 20

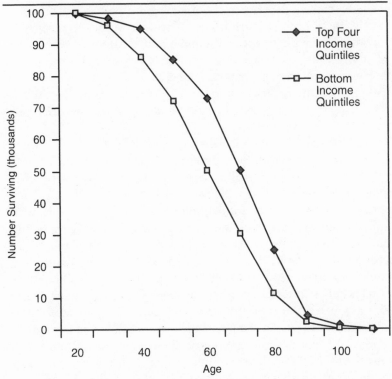

SOURCE: Daniel Garrett, "The Effects of Differential Mortality Rates on the Progressivity of Social Security," *Economic Inquiry* 33 (July 1995): 458.

reduced benefits or higher taxes necessary to bail out Social Security on our current course.

Moreover, this discussion assumes that the poor have the same life expectancy or mortality as other workers. But this is not the case.

For a variety of reasons, there is a well-established relationship in this country between wealth and longevity.[8] (Figure 5.2.) Put simply, wealthy people live longer than poor people. Therefore, wealthy retirees will likely receive Social Security for a longer period than will their poorer counterparts. This means that the returns and benefits under Social Security will be even worse for the poor than has been discussed.

Some studies have suggested that lower life expectancies for the poor completely offset the program's progressive benefit formula, leaving the poor with lower returns than high-income workers. One of the first economists to examine this issue was Henry Aaron of the Brookings Institution. In a 1979 study, when he was seeking an increase in benefits for low-income workers, Aaron concluded that the poor ultimately receive a lower return in retirement benefits on their past tax dollars than those with higher incomes.[9] However, after his work was cited by advocates of privatization, Aaron now warns against overreliance on it, saying that the calculations were incomplete, and the issue needs to be studied further.[10]

The next major study of the issue was by Eugene Steuerle and Jon Bakija of the Urban Institute. In their 1994 book, *Retooling Social Security for the 21st Century*, Steuerle and Bakija conclude that while differentials in mortality rates do weaken the progressivity of Social Security, they are not sufficient to completely offset the progressive benefit structure. Therefore, the system still includes a net internal redistribution toward the poor. The transfer is smallest for single men and largest for one-wage-earner couples.[11] A 1995 study for the Treasury Department reached a similar conclusion.[12]

However, Daniel Garrett of Stanford University, writing in *Economic Inquiry*, provides a different perspective.[13] While Steuerle and Bakija base their conclusions on the overall transfers over an entire income quintile, Garrett looks at the percentage of winners and losers within each quintile. According to Garrett, when mortality differentials are considered, slightly more than half (53.7 percent) of poor single-earner couples receive a negative return from Social Security. Because single-earner couples receive the highest return on their Social Security payments, the impact on other types of households is likely to be even greater. Garrett concludes that "differences in mortality eliminated the progressive spread in returns across income categories."[14] In other words, more poor workers lost money than received excess benefits.

The study by Steuerle and Bakija and the study by Garrett agree that the long-term progressivity of Social Security benefits is reduced, in addition, by the tendency of low-income workers to enter the labor force at a younger age.[15] The poor tend to start work right after high school, if not before, while the middle class and wealthy are more likely to delay full-time entry into the workforce until after they have completed college. Therefore, the poor will begin paying taxes several years earlier than the wealthy, but paying taxes for those additional years does not earn any additional benefits. [16]

A February 1996 study by the RAND Corporation also concluded that there was a positive correlation between total benefits and length of life based on lifetime earnings. As a result, they found that, while Social Security benefits retain some degree of progressivity, taking into account such factors as marital status and life expectancy shows that "the OASDI system is not as progressive" as generally believed.[17] Indeed, the study found that for unmarried men, the rate of return among high-wage earners was actually higher than among low-wage earners, making Social Security regressive for that category of recipients.[18]

These issues are particularly relevant because proposed reforms such as raising the retirement age would fall particularly hard on the poor and minorities already disadvantaged by their shorter life expectancies.

Some defenders of Social Security concede that shorter life spans mean that the poor receive less in retirement benefits from Social Security, but point out that the poor are more likely to receive survivors and disability benefits. They claim that if survivors' and disability benefits are included, Social Security retains its progressive structure.[19] While there is a certain logic to this theory, it has not been empirically validated. Indeed, the Social Security Administration actually refused a request by the Social Security Advisory Council to perform a study of this issue.[20]

In addition, as we saw in chapter 4, for a tiny fraction of what the person paid in OASDI taxes, he or she could have purchased a life insurance policy that would have paid at least as much as Social Security would have paid. Moreover, the vast majority of OASDI taxes go not to pay for survivors' benefits, but for the retirement benefits that he or she will never receive. Indeed, if the person is single or has no survivors, he or she receives nothing at all in exchange for years of payroll taxes. Overall, survivors' benefits accounted for only 5.3 percent of all OASDI payments in 1995. Therefore, a person who dies before age 65 receives the worst deal of all from Social Security, and that person is far more likely to be poor than rich.[21]

Privatization provides an answer to the problem of lifetime return in three ways. First, by transforming Social Security from a defined benefit to a defined contribution plan, privatization would disconnect total benefits from life expectancy. The benefits a worker would receive would depend on what was paid into the system plus the investment return on those payments, not on how many years the person lives. Annuities could be structured to take advantage of the lower life expectancy of disadvantaged groups, enabling them to receive higher benefits for their retirement funds. Second, under a privatized system, individuals would have a property right to their Social Security benefits. If a person were to die with money still in his or her retirement account, that money would become part of an estate, to be inherited by that person's heirs. Finally, individuals who begin work earlier, and therefore contribute more, would earn additional benefits as a result of their additional contributions.

Bad Deal for Black Americans

Perhaps no group in America is as ill served by Social Security as African Americans.

To begin with, 29.6 percent of African Americans over age 65 have incomes below the poverty level, a far higher poverty rate than their white counterparts.[22] As we saw, low-income workers are far more likely to be dependent on Social Security when they retire than are high-income workers.

In addition, since life expectancies for African Americans are shorter than life expectancies for whites, they receive far less in lifetime benefits from Social Security. The life expectancy for an African American man born today is just 65.8 years.[23] For African Americans who do reach age 65, life expectancies are still shorter than for their white counterparts. White men who reach age 65 can expect to live—and collect Social Security benefits—for an additional 15.7 years, white women for an additional 19.4 years. However, a 65-year-old African American man can expect to live only another 13.6 years. A 65-year-old African American woman can expect to live another 17.6 years.[24] Thus, whites will collect more in lifetime benefits than blacks who have paid identical amounts of payroll taxes.

The RAND study cited above concluded that the current benefit structure disadvantages African Americans, who have lower life expectancies and marriage rates. According to the study, whites consistently earn higher rates of return than blacks. In fact, on a lifetime basis, the income transfer from blacks to whites is as much as $10,000.[25] A 1998 study by the Heritage Foundation found that African Americans receive the lowest rate of return of any American ethnic group. Indeed, the study found that a single African American man pays $13,377 more in payroll taxes over his lifetime than he receives in benefits, a return of just 88 cents for every dollar paid in taxes.[26]

Of course, African Americans do receive both survivors and disability benefits at higher rates than whites. For example, African Americans are only 12 percent of the U.S. population, but receive 25 percent of survivors benefits for children of deceased workers and 14 percent of survivors benefits for widows and widowers. Blacks also receive 18 percent of all disability benefits.[27] However, as noted earlier, there are no empirical studies showing whether such benefits offset the loss of retirement benefits suffered by African Americans.

In contrast, a privatized Social Security system would provide important benefits to African Americans. First, the higher returns of a privately invested system would be particularly important to poor elderly blacks. Second, by breaking the connection between life expectancy and lifetime benefits, a private system would end the perverse redistribution of Social Security moneys from blacks to whites. Indeed, annuities could be structured so as to provide higher benefits to African Americans and other disadvantaged groups with shorter life expectancies. Moreover, since a private system would provide superior disability and survivors benefits, and blacks use those benefits more frequently, a private system would be of even more benefit to them.

A Penalty on Working Women

Under the current Social Security system, a woman is automatically entitled to benefits equal to 50 percent of her husband's benefits. A widow is automatically entitled to 100 percent of her deceased husband's benefits. A woman is entitled to those benefits whether or not she has ever worked or paid Social Security taxes.[28]

However, when a woman can claim Social Security benefits both as a retired worker in her own right and also as the wife or widow of her husband, the "dual entitlement rule" prevents her from receiving both benefits. Instead she receives only the larger of the two. Since many women work only part-time, take years off from work to raise children, or earn far lower wages than their husbands, 50 percent of the husband's benefits is frequently larger than the benefits she would be entitled to receive as a result of her own earnings.[29] She will, therefore, receive only the benefits based on her husband's earnings. She receives no credit or benefits based on the payroll taxes she has paid; a woman who never worked at all would receive exactly the same benefits.[30]

As a 1977 report on sex discrimination in government programs concluded, Social Security treats a woman "as an individual for the purpose of building an earnings record and as part of a family unit with dependents for the purpose of paying benefits." Women's benefits depend on whether the system paid them on the basis of their employment record or their status as "dependents" or "caregivers," resulting in serious inequities.[31]

As a result, approximately 71 percent of retired women are being penalized through the loss of at least some benefits based on their own earnings.[32] Even for women whose earnings generate benefits greater than 50 percent of their husband's, the dual entitlement rule reduces the marginal return on their payroll taxes. They receive some benefits for their taxes, but less than a dollar's value on each dollar paid.

To make matters worse, the marginal tax rate for married working women is already excessive. If a married woman chooses to work, her earnings are subject to taxation at her husband's highest marginal tax rate. The dual entitlement rule converts her Social Security "contributions" into still another tax on those earnings.[33]

Social Security was designed in an era when few women worked outside the home. However, those days have long since passed. Today, slightly more than 62 percent of married women work.[34] Add those women who work prior to marriage, and the vast majority of women have at some point in their lives worked the 40 quarters (a cumulative 10 years spread over time) necessary to qualify for benefits. This will be partially offset by rising incomes for women in the workforce and the likelihood that women will take less time off from work to raise families.[35] Therefore, it is projected that in the future, only about 53 percent of women will be subject to the full dual entitlement penalty. At the same time, the number of women subject to a marginal decrease in benefits will increase. The number of nonworking married women being completely subsidized through the Social Security system will decline from 36 percent today to just 15 percent in the next century.[36]

But, in a privatized system, there would be no dual entitlement penalty. An individual would receive credit for every dollar contributed to her individual account. A spouse's income would have no impact on this. Even if some form of earnings-sharing is required, redistribution would take place only within the family, not within the system at large.

Women would also benefit from the higher rates of return under a privatized system since they are less likely than men to have private pensions to rely on.[37] Only 22 percent of retired women currently receive a pension, either public or private, and their average pension is only 55 percent that of men.[38] For this reason, among others, women worry more about the adequacy of their retirement income.[39] Providing them with a source of high retirement benefits will help ease those worries.

Of course some worry that women generally invest more conservatively than men, meaning that their returns under a privatized Social Security system might be lower.[40] However, evidence suggests that women have a tendency toward conservative investment because they are relatively new to investing. Women who have been investing for a long time pursue investment strategies much closer to those of men.[41] Furthermore, the general level of investment knowledge among women is on the rise. According to a recent poll, 64 percent of women say that they are more interested in investment than they were five years ago. Seventy-one percent said they were more knowledgeable about investment than they were five years ago; 61 percent considered themselves knowledgeable investors.[42]

Moreover, even an extremely conservative investment strategy— for example, an all bond fund—will produce greater returns than Social Security.[43] In a well-structured private system, women as well as men could expect to rely on expert investment managers to help with investment decisions.

How the Traditional Family Loses

As discussed above, Social Security was designed in the 1930s with the assumption that the husband would be working, with the wife staying home to care for the children. Policymakers, therefore, structured the system to guarantee benefits for spouses who never worked. Nevertheless, Social Security has become a terrible deal for traditional families as well.

The current Social Security system does provide a substantial redistributive subsidy to such one-earner families, since it pays 50 percent of the husband's benefit to the nonworking wife, and 100 percent after the husband dies, even though neither she nor her husband ever paid any taxes in exchange for those benefits. However, as we saw in chapter 4, the superior returns and benefits of a privately invested system clearly outstrip any benefits resulting from such subsidies. Therefore, traditional one-earner families, as well as others, are made better off through the private system.

For example, in chapter 4, we discussed the case of such a traditional family: The husband works and earns the average income for a male head of household; the wife works at home caring for the children. Investing in the private sector, rather than Social Security, with a 6 percent real return on their investments, the family would retire with more than $1 million in their retirement fund (in 1998 dollars). That fund would pay more than twice the benefits of Social Security, while still allowing them to leave a $1 million inheritance to their children. Or they could use the fund to purchase an annuity that would pay nearly five times what Social Security would pay.

Even using a 4 percent return, just over half the average return earned in the stock market over the last 70 years, the private system would still provide this family with far better benefits than would Social Security. At that return, our hypothetical one-earner family would accumulate a fund of $613,657 by retirement, enough to purchase an annuity that would pay more than twice the benefits provided by Social Security. Alternatively, the couple could match Social Security's benefits by using just 45 percent of their accumulated funds to purchase an annuity and leave the remaining $341,000 to their children.

Traditional families, like all families, would undoubtedly prefer to receive the much higher returns and benefits of the private system, and to develop the substantial funds that they could leave to their children, rather than stay in the current Social Security system. Moreover, given Social Security's looming financial problems, traditional families, along with others, can soon expect to be hit with huge tax

105

increases. The family will also have to bear the burden of redeeming the trust fund bonds necessary to keep Social Security solvent after 2012. High federal taxes have already undermined the traditional family and forced many women into the workplace even if they would rather remain at home.[44] The coming tax increases needed to bail out Social Security will only place a further burden on traditional families.

In a privatized system, by contrast, returns will be so much higher that contributions can ultimately be significantly reduced from current payroll tax levels, making for a substantial tax cut. This would provide important relief to hard-pressed one-earner families.

In addition, a private system would keep retirement funds within the family and under its control. This would greatly enhance the power of family members to help one another, drawing the family closer together as an economic unit. For example, a retired couple might choose to use some of its accumulated funds to help pay for college for their grandchildren. Or, they could use the funds to make a down payment on a house for their children or grandchildren. Or the funds might help in a medical or other emergency.

With Social Security, by contrast, the money flows out of the family to the government. This helps pull the family apart as members look to the government for support and assistance rather than to each other. The family breakup that results is analogous to the family dissolution that occurs when welfare replaces the family as a source of support.[45] As Allan Carlson of the Rockford Institute puts it, "To begin with, socialized old-age pensions intentionally displace private economic bonds of families, and so contribute to the progressive destruction of society by the state."[46]

Social Security's damage to the family can be seen in living patterns. Without the need to rely on each other for support, retirees and their children increasingly live thousands of miles apart. Carlson reports that the proportion of elderly widows living with relatives declined from 60 percent in 1960 to 33 percent in 1980.[47] While many supporters of Social Security look on this as a good thing, it has led inevitably to a host of other government interventions in family affairs. For example, without grandparents available to help care for the children, the government has become increasingly involved in subsidizing and regulating child care.[48] Without children to care for elderly parents, the government progressively takes over long-term care. The result is both material and emotional impoverishment for American families.

For all these reasons, privatization of Social Security would be one of the most pro-family reforms that could be adopted.

Ownership in America

An important side benefit of Social Security privatization is that it would allow every American—including poor Americans—an opportunity to participate in the American economy by owning a part of that economy. In effect, privatizing Social Security will act as a nationwide employee stock option plan, allowing even the poorest workers to become capitalists. Through Social Security privatization, workers would become stockholders themselves. The artificial and destructive division between labor and capital would be broken down.

America has more economic and social mobility than almost any other nation, with people moving up and down the economic ladder. Most people who are poor today are unlikely to be poor 10 years from now.[49] However, there is reason to be concerned with the increasing disparity between rich and poor in the United States and the concentration of wealth in relatively few hands. For example, the bottom 50 percent of American income earners own just 2 percent of the nation's financial wealth. The top 1 percent own more than 56 percent of all net financial assets. The financial wealth of the top 10 percent is 4,653 times greater than the financial wealth of the bottom 20 percent.[50]

One of the biggest reasons for this is that many Americans are unable to participate in the surest route to wealth creation—savings and investment. Approximately one-third of all income in America comes not through wages, but through savings and investment.[51] As Louis Kelso, father of the Employee Stock Option, noted, "The bulk of wealth is produced, not by human labor as under preindustrial conditions, but by capital instruments. . . . Capital and not labor is the source of affluence in an industrial society."[52]

But most low- and middle-income workers do not have the financial resources to save and invest. Clearly, the imposition of the Social Security tax reduces private savings. (See chapter 6 for a more detailed discussion of this issue.) Workers are required by law to

107

pay Social Security taxes.[53] This precludes their investing those wages in private savings or investments.[54] For most low-income workers, the payroll tax is the largest tax they pay. Indeed, nearly 76 percent of Americans pay more in Social Security taxes than they do in federal income taxes.[55]

Consider this: a worker earning just $20,000 per year will pay $2,480 per year in Social Security taxes (including the employer share). That leaves very little money to invest privately. This can be seen through the low participation rates of low-income workers in company-sponsored 401(k) plans. Only 64 percent of low-wage workers contribute to 401(k) plans offered by their employers, compared with more than 90 percent of their higher wage colleagues.[56] Low-wage workers who do participate contribute an average of only 4.73 percent of their wages, compared with an average of 6.79 percent for high-wage workers.[57]

Low-income workers are also less likely to work for companies with private pension plans. For example, small businesses and service-sector employers are far less likely to offer pensions and other retirement benefits.[58]

Finally, it should be pointed out that Social Security may be contributing to this wealth gap even more by reducing the value of wages and increasing the value of capital. Because Social Security reduces savings and capital accumulation, it reduces the ratio of capital to workers, meaning that each worker will be less productive on average. As a result, wages are lower than they would be otherwise. At the same time, with less capital available, the return on capital may be higher than it otherwise would be.[59]

All this is particularly true for African Americans. According to a recent report from the White House Council of Economic Advisors, while the income gap between black and white families is declining, the total wealth gap is growing. The net worth of the typical black family is only about $4,500, a tenth of the figure for white families. The *New York Times* analyzed the government data and concluded that much of this gap is caused by investment patterns. White families have doubled the equity share of their savings since 1990, at a time of rising stock prices. But African Americans have been virtually shut out of this opportunity to gain real wealth. Nearly 95 percent of black families own no stock or pension funds.[60]

Privatizing Social Security would allow low-wage workers to participate in the wealth-creating mechanisms of saving and investment.

By being given the opportunity to save and invest 12.4 percent of his or her income, a low-wage worker would have the opportunity to accumulate a substantial nest egg. As we saw in chapter 4, a family with two workers earning the minimum wage for their entire life could accumulate nearly $700,000 by retirement.

It is this sort of worker empowerment and opportunity for the poor that has brought many liberal Democrats to support the privatization of Social Security. As Sen. Robert Kerrey (D-Neb.) has pointed out, privatizing Social Security is as much about "generating wealth" as it is about the system's financing. Kerrey says that "every American [should have] a chance to own part of his country."[61]

Sam Beard, a former aide to Sen. Robert Kennedy, calls this process the "democratization of capital," and points out that privatizing Social Security will give every American a real stake in our economic future. Beard also notes that the benefits are psychological as well as tangible, pointing out, "Personal participation will make savings and economic education part of everyone's day to day experience. . . . The benefits of this knowledge for individuals and families will include increased economic capability, a confident sense of the future, and more power to make fundamental choices that affect their lives."[62]

José Piñera, who was the architect of Chile's successful privatization of social security, explains that exactly those types of changes took place in his country:

> The new pension system gives Chileans a personal stake in the economy. A typical Chilean worker is not indifferent to the stock market or interest rates. When workers feel that they own a part of the country, not through party bosses or a Politburo, they are much more attached to the free market and a free society.[63]

The same worker empowerment is possible through privatization of Social Security in this country. As a result of the enormous accumulation of wealth by the working class through their retirement accounts, the socialist dream of workers owning the nation's business and industry would be effectively achieved.

Moreover, the distribution of wealth would then be far more equal than today. This would occur not through the counterproductive and illegitimate redistribution of existing wealth, but through the creation of new wealth in workers' retirement accounts. In fact,

Feldstein has estimated that if Social Security were privatized, the concentration of wealth in America would be reduced by half.[64]

Yet, as the division between labor and capital dissolved, with the nation's workers becoming capitalists, the social and political effect would be to sharply increase support for free market economic policies. Since workers would own part of the nation's businesses, they would demand an end to unnecessary tax burdens and regulatory interference in the market that harms business performance. Since workers would own much of the nation's capital, they would oppose harsh, multiple taxation of capital gains. General labor strife and antagonism between labor and management would be replaced with cooperation, since workers would benefit directly from the general prosperity of companies that they would effectively own. As Federal Reserve Chairman Alan Greenspan has explained, "[If workers] knew what they owned in their retirement programs as distinct from having a generic overall type of program, there [is] a considerable amount of pride in that, and it has a very important effect on people's citizenship in society."[65]

It is through these social and political effects that privatizing Social Security may ultimately have its biggest impact.

6. Social Security and the Economy

In addition to the huge losses for workers described in the previous two chapters, Social Security also harms workers and their families by damaging the U.S. economy. Privatizing Social Security would reverse these effects and lead to increased economic growth and a better standard of living for all Americans.

Few economists have done as much to study the impact of Social Security on the economy as Martin Feldstein. In fact, more than 20 years ago he noted,

> Because of the vast size of the Social Security program and its central role in the American system of financing retirement, it has major effects on all the significant dimensions of our economy. These effects are currently unintended, generally unperceived and frequently undesirable. . . . Social Security was the most important government innovation of the Great Depression. Forty years later nearly every major aspect of our economic life has changed dramatically. Yet, the basic structure of the Social Security program has not been reexamined and reshaped to fit the economic conditions of today. Instead the original program has simply continued to expand at an increasing rate.[1]

Today, the problems are more broadly recognized and understood. Based on the research discussed below, Social Security likely reduces U.S. GDP by 10 percent or more each year, a truly enormous amount. Indeed, Feldstein projects that fixing these economic problems by shifting to a private, fully funded system would produce a net gain to the nation of $10 to $20 trillion in present value terms.[2] For reasons discussed in this chapter, these figures may actually underestimate the economic benefits of privatizing Social Security.

Social Security and Saving

As we have discussed previously, Social Security operates on a pay-as-you-go basis. The money paid into the program is not saved

111

Figure 6.1
National Saving Rates

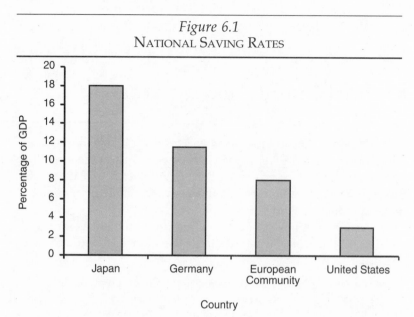

SOURCE: Bipartisan Commission on Entitlement and Tax Reform, *Interim Report to the President* (Washington: Government Printing Office, August 1994), p. 8.

and invested for current taxpayers as in a fully funded system. Rather, it is immediately paid out to current recipients. The future benefits of today's workers are then to be paid out of the future taxes of the next generation of workers. This pay-as-you-go system is what causes a massive decline in saving, which results in a decline in capital investment, and, in turn, a decline in national income and economic growth. Feldstein has long been a leading exponent of this view.

Virtually everyone agrees that countries that save and invest more grow faster and have more rapid improvements in their standard of living. Yet, as shown in Figure 6.1, the United States has the lowest national saving rate in the industrialized world.[3]

There are many reasons for this low national saving rate, including the deficits run by the federal government. However, personal saving has also declined substantially. This is particularly important because, with the government usually a negative saver, personal saving has become an increasingly important component of national

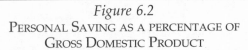

Figure 6.2
PERSONAL SAVING AS A PERCENTAGE OF
GROSS DOMESTIC PRODUCT

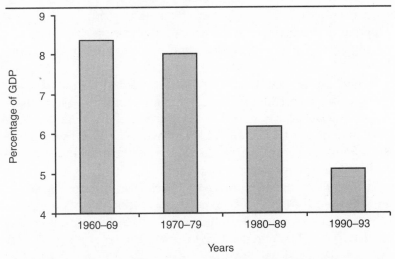

SOURCE: Bipartisan Commission on Entitlement and Tax Reform, *Interim Report to the President* (Government Printing Office, August 1994), p. 9.

saving. Indeed, because government saving has been negative, personal saving provided $1.24 of every net dollar of national saving in the 1980s, compared with 77 cents in the 1970s and 59 cents in the 1960s.[4] However, as Figure 6.2 shows, personal savings have declined to barely more than 5 percent of personal disposable income, from a high of more than 8 percent during the 1960s.[5]

The evidence seems overwhelming that Social Security is a major factor in decreasing personal saving, and therefore national saving. To understand why this is true, take the example of a typical worker. The worker is forced to provide for his retirement by paying into Social Security. These forced payments consequently take the place of private retirement saving. The worker, operating under the promise that his contributions to Social Security perform the function of personal retirement saving, reduces his own saving by an amount roughly equivalent to the taxes paid.[6]

If Social Security were run on a fully funded basis, each worker's payments into the program would be saved to finance his later benefits, and there would be no net reduction in total national saving.

Social Security saving would simply substitute for individual saving. However, since Social Security is run on a pay-as-you-go basis, the taxes are not saved but immediately paid out to current recipients. As a result, there is no offsetting increase in saving through the program to counterbalance the decline in private saving. Thus, the net impact on the economy is a decline in saving potentially as large as the full amount of Social Security taxes.

In 1997, Social Security taxes (OASDI) totaled $400.3 billion, compared with total private saving of $1.2 trillion.[7] On the basis of these figures, Social Security potentially reduced total saving for the year by about one-fourth. Even if taxpayers reduced saving by only half the amount of Social Security taxes, that reduction would reduce total saving for the year by one-eighth.

The reduction in saving caused by Social Security can be seen in another way. The individual taxpayer may focus on benefits instead of taxes and reason that with the promise of the benefits, he needs to save less for his retirement on his own. The taxpayer can in fact reduce retirement saving by the present value of the future benefits. Again, because Social Security operates on a pay-as-you-go basis, there would be no offsetting effect through the program to increase saving. The result is that total saved wealth will decrease by the full amount of the total present value of promised Social Security benefits.

Feldstein defines this total present value as Social Security wealth.[8] This "wealth" does not actually exist anywhere in the economy. It is not real wealth represented by any tangible assets. It is merely an implicit promise that the next generation will tax itself to pay currently promised benefits. In this sense, instead of Social Security "wealth," this concept may be more accurately labeled "the nation's Social Security liability," as Feldstein has recently suggested.[9] Indeed, Social Security "wealth" represents the amount of additional real wealth households may have in the absence of Social Security. In other words, Social Security "wealth" represents the amount of real wealth that may be lost because of the program.

Feldstein estimates the value of Social Security "wealth" as $9 trillion in 1996.[10] Total private wealth is about $15.7 trillion.[11] As a result, Social Security may have reduced total private saving or wealth by 40 percent.

These two arguments, focusing first on taxes and then on benefits, stem from the traditional life-cycle theory of individual consumption-saving behavior, which is a basic component of modern economic theory. According to the life-cycle theory, people attempt to even out their consumption over the course of their adult lives. Since the earnings capability of most individuals will increase as they grow older, individuals in their early working years will dissave by spending more than they earn and will borrow to make up the difference. Dissaving allows people to enjoy some of their future expected income earlier in life and thus partially even out their consumption over their working years. As people grow older and their incomes rise, they pay off their debts and begin to save for their retirement years, when their incomes from working will be much lower or nonexistent. This saving again allows individuals to partially even out their consumption over their lives by shifting some of their earnings from their prime earning years to their later retirement years.[12]

When a social security program is enacted that pays substantial retirement benefits, those attempting to even out their consumption in accordance with the life-cycle model need to save less during their high-earning years for their retirement years. In fact, if the theory holds, individuals will reduce their saving exactly by the full amount of the present value of the retirement benefits they expect to receive from the program because they will no longer need to save for the portion of their planned retirement incomes provided by the program. Indeed, after the program is enacted, people will be able to attain their planned relative levels of retirement and preretirement consumption if, and only if, they reduce their retirement saving by the present value of future social security benefits. Consequently, the widely accepted life-cycle theory fully supports the view that Social Security causes a substantial loss of private saving.

The Critics

One of the first serious criticisms of Feldstein's theory was advanced by Alicia H. Munnell, then of the Federal Reserve Bank of Boston and later a Treasury Department official in the Clinton administration. Munnell argued that Social Security induces a higher rate of earlier retirement among older persons, and this increased retirement will increase saving.[13] When a worker decides to retire earlier than he would have without Social Security, he will want to make sure that he has sufficient savings to attain his desired consumption level for those additional retirement years. Since Social Security is likely to provide less than an individual will desire in those years, he is likely to increase his saving so that he can supplement his Social Security benefits then.

Munnell called this effect the "retirement effect," juxtaposing it with Feldstein's theory, which she called the "asset substitution effect." Therefore, according to Munnell, the impact of Social Security on saving is indeterminate, depending on whether the early retirement effect or the asset substitution effect is stronger.

But, in fact, Munnell's argument that Social Security can have a major effect in causing increased saving through early retirement is extremely weak. Social Security may well induce early retirement. But examining this effect more closely makes clear that it is unlikely to cause a significant increase in saving.

Social Security may induce earlier retirement among shortsighted people who otherwise would not have saved for their retirement. By forcing them to provide for retirement, the program makes feasible retirement at age 65 or, with reduced early retirement benefits, at age 62, when otherwise it would not be. Yet, almost by definition, people who are too shortsighted to save for their retirement without Social Security are unlikely to save to supplement their Social Security during their early retirement years.

Moreover, as discussed in chapter 4, for the first generation of retirees, during the start-up phase of the program, Social Security paid a high, above-market rate of return. This increased wealth, focused in a lucrative retirement system, made early retirement easier and, therefore, more likely for members of this generation. But, as we also saw in chapter 4, Social Security no longer provides above-market returns. Therefore, it can no longer induce early retirement in this way.

Finally, the Social Security earnings test, which reduces benefits for earnings above a specified level, causes early retirement as well. People who might have retired at a later age will retire at age 65 to avoid losing the benefits they have paid for. Without the earnings test, a person who wanted to retire later could continue to work at age 65 and older and collect his Social Security payments at the same time, using these benefits for his later retirement.

Yet, the earnings test for retirees is being all but phased out at this time. It now applies to retirees only up to age 70. Moreover, the earnings limit at which the earnings test starts to apply is being increased over the next few years to $30,000 in wage income per year. In addition, Social Security provides a credit for those who choose later retirement, increasing their benefits for each month they delay retirement. This credit has been strengthened over the past 15 years so that it now seems to provide at least the same effective return as Social Security pays overall, if not better. As a result, even with the earnings test, people who wish to retire later can still do so, without suffering any significant loss of benefits. Therefore it seems unlikely that the earnings test will significantly increase saving under Munnell's theory.

Furthermore, any additional saving resulting from Munnell's early retirement effect would only be enough to supplement benefits for the few years of earlier retirement—the years that the retiree would have spent working without Social Security. Feldstein's asset-substitution effect, in contrast, applies to all years after the age at which the worker would have retired in the absence of Social Security, relying on a private retirement system instead, which is likely to be a longer period.

In addition, the saving induced by the retirement effect are only to cover the difference between the desired level of consumption in retirement and Social Security benefits during those few additional retirement years. Again, contrast this to the asset-substitution effect, which is equal to the full amount of Social Security benefits for the years in which the worker would have been retired without Social Security.

A second major critic was Robert Barro, professor of economics at Harvard University. Barro argued that any negative impact on saving due to Feldstein's asset-substitution effect would be largely offset by saving induced by Social Security through a full-bequest motive by parents.[14] Barro contended that in the absence of Social Security, parents would plan to save a certain amount over their lives so that, after their death, they could leave an estate or bequest to their children. With Social Security, parents would realize that the program was imposing a forced transfer of income from their children to them and that this was countering the parents' planned bequests to their children. Instead of receiving the full amount of their parents' planned bequests, the children would receive this amount minus the transfer imposed by Social Security.

Barro argued that parents would try to offset this reduction in their bequests by increasing their saving over their lives so that they could leave a larger estate or bequest to their children. Parents would in fact attempt to increase their final estate by the full amount of the transfer imposed by Social Security so that they would effectively leave to their children the equivalent of what they originally intended to leave. Since the amount of this transfer is equal to the amount of taxes collected from children over the years, parents would increase their saving by the amount of these taxes to increase their final estate by the necessary amount. Thus, even if children reduced their retirement saving by the full amount of such taxes because of the asset-substitution effect, this reduction in saving would be offset by increased saving by parents due to the bequest motive.

But any significant impact on saving from Barro's full-bequest theory is quite unlikely. His theory is, in fact, inconsistent with the very existence of the Social Security program. If people feel they have to increase their saving over their lives to offset the main intended effect of Social Security in transferring income from their children to them, then why do we have the program in the first place? It is brutally obvious that there is no widespread feeling among the public that people must increase their saving to make a bequest to their children because of Social Security.

Indeed, we may ask just when Barro's full-bequest saving supposedly occurred. When Social Security was first adopted, the program began to transfer income immediately from the first generation of workers to their parents, the first generation of retirees. If Barro's theory holds, then this first generation of retirees would have had to increase their saving sharply to offset this transfer. It is clear, however, that no such increase in saving occurred among the first generation of retirees in the start-up phase of the U.S. Social Security program. The members of this generation were considered relatively poor and in need of Social Security benefits to purchase basic necessities. The level of Social Security benefits they did receive was generally perceived as inadequate to provide for all their needs.[15] It should be beyond debate that the members of the first retired generation consumed their Social Security benefits. They did not save them to leave them to their children, as Barro's theory suggests.

118

Nor was there an increase in bequest saving among the first generation of workers paying Social Security taxes. The program imposed a transfer from this generation to their parents, the first retired generation. The individuals in the first working generation did not then feel compelled as well to save and leave a bequest to their children, the second working generation, in order to offset the transfer imposed by the program from this second working generation to them. In fact, their saving rate showed no increase over this period.[16] At no point, therefore, after the adoption of the Social Security program have we seen any increase in saving in accordance with Barro's full-bequest theory.

We should also note the irony that one of the popularly accepted rationales for Social Security is that people are too myopic to save for their own retirement. But Barro contends that, on the contrary, not only are individuals not too shortsighted to save for their retirement, they are so farsighted that they will save enough to provide a bequest to their children to offset Social Security. If Barro is correct, there is no need for a mandatory Social Security system at all.

Responding to Barro, Feldstein pointed out that children will tend to be wealthier than their parents were.[17] Parents are, therefore, likely to feel that it is worth more to them to spend their money on themselves now rather than to forgo that consumption and save for bequests to their relatively wealthier children.

This view is more consistent with actual saving and bequest behavior in the United States. Feldstein concludes,

> It is clear that, for the vast majority of the population, and therefore for most of the Social Security benefits, there are no significant bequests to children even in the presence of our current Social Security system. There is no evidence at all that the typical retired person wishes to offset Social Security's intergenerational transfer from the young to the old.[18]

Barro later appears to have abandoned the bequest theory and now offers a different—nearly opposite—reason why Social Security does not decrease national saving.[19] Barro now argues that in the absence of Social Security, retired people would be supported by direct payments from their children rather than by their own accumulated saving. Their children would then expect to be supported in retirement by direct payments from *their* children and would not save for retirement. But, if a Social Security system is adopted, individuals simply reduce their direct payments to their retired parents, paying into the Social Security system instead, so there is no effect on saving. Social Security would then simply be replacing a private pay-as-you-go system with a public pay-as-you-go system.

This is the most plausible theory advanced by Feldstein's critics, but it would probably be true today for only a small part of the population. Most workers would clearly prefer to rely on retirement saving, as this would give them more control over their retirement incomes and more independence, make their incomes more certain and secure, and remove a burden from their children. They could also maintain much higher retirement income in most instances through a well-funded retirement saving plan. If they did not have to pay Social Security taxes, workers could clearly afford such retirement plan contributions.

Moreover, widespread intrafamily retirement support is inconsistent with modern social developments. Bad as it is, family dissolution is a fact of life today. Adult children and parents rarely live together today, and often not even nearby. Divorce and remarriage are more frequent. Families are having fewer children and many married couples are choosing to remain childless. Most adults today do not think of their children as a major potential source of retirement support, and most grown-up children do not think of such support as a primary responsibility of theirs.

Thus, in practice, we see very little direct support from children to retired parents each year. As Feldstein writes,

> The survey evidence on gifts from children to retired parents shows that this second case is also of very limited importance. At no time have more than a small fraction of the retired received gifts from their children; moreover, the average gift received has been extremely small in comparison with concurrent income levels or to the corresponding rate of Social Security benefits to income today. It is beyond belief that the current working generation would, in the absence of Social Security, make gifts totaling $100 billion to retired parents in 1977.[20] [This was roughly the amount of Social Security benefits that year. In 1997, Social Security retirement benefits totaled over $300 billion.]

One possible criticism of Feldstein does not appear to have been well developed yet. In the absence of Social Security, some people will be shortsighted and fail to save or otherwise provide for their retirement. Others may rationally choose not to do so. They may plan to continue working beyond normal retirement age and anticipate needing less in savings. Such people would have little or no retirement savings to be reduced by Social Security.

However, economic science is based on the idea that the great majority of people are economically rational. This applies to retirement saving as well as everything else. Therefore, in the absence of Social Security, failing to save for retirement is likely to apply to relatively few people. Moreover, if Social Security is being compared to a mandatory private saving system (as described in chapter 8), there is no need to consider this issue in considering the relative impact on saving.

Empirical Analysis

Feldstein documented his theory with extensive econometric analysis showing a powerful effect of Social Security in reducing saving. In a 1974 study, Feldstein examined time-series data on saving. He concluded that Social Security reduced personal saving by 40 to 50 percent, and total saving, including corporate saving, by 32 to 42 percent.[21] In a subsequent study, examining cross-section saving behavior by individual households, Feldstein concluded that households reduced their private saving by almost one dollar for every dollar in the present value of expected future Social Security benefits.[22]

In yet another study, Feldstein examined international saving data and compared them with the social security programs in different countries. He concluded that countries with higher social security benefits and with more complete coverage of the population by a social security program have lower rates of private saving.[23]

Other studies also document Social Security's negative impact on saving. For example, Wharton School economists Bulent Gultekin and Dennis Logue suggest that Social Security contributions reduce national saving by roughly 80 cents per dollar of taxes.[24] Even a study cowritten by a researcher at the Social Security Administration concluded that "a dollar of Social Security wealth substitutes for about three-fifths of a dollar of fungible assets."[25]

The observed saving behavior of Americans is consistent with Feldstein's theories. Most American households do in fact save little for retirement on their own, accumulating few financial assets.[26] As MIT economist Peter Diamond has noted, this is entirely consistent with a rational decision to substitute Social Security benefits for private wealth accumulation.[27]

If Social Security reduces national saving, it will, in turn, reduce capital investment.[28] With less capital, less of the nation's resources are devoted to production and to the materials necessary to increase that production. The result is less production and lower levels of national income and economic growth. For example, Paul Samuelson and William Nordhaus estimate that a 1 percent reduction in the saving rate decreases GDP by 0.8 percent.[29]

Of course there are competing econometric studies showing a wide range of different relationships between Social Security and saving.[30] As a group, these studies show that with enough computer manipulation it is possible to reach almost any conclusion from the same data. However, Feldstein recently said that he interpreted cross-sectional studies as showing that each extra dollar of Social Security wealth reduces private saving by approximately 50 cents. This would reduce national saving by 20 to 25 percent. If this is true, Feldstein estimates that the annual loss of national income would exceed 5 percent of GDP.[31]

But, if the impact of Social Security is much larger, reducing national saving by 40 to 60 percent, as Feldstein's econometric studies show, then our GDP would be reduced by much more, on the order of 10 percent or more. Such reductions are truly enormous. GDP in 1997 was about $8 trillion. If Social Security had reduced GDP by 10 percent to that level, it would mean a loss in that year alone of almost $900 billion. If Social Security had reduced GDP by just 5 percent, it would mean a loss for the year of $421 billion.

Wages and Employment

Social Security has three separate effects that tend to distort the labor supply, discourage employment, and create economic inefficiencies.

The Wedge Effect

The first effect is caused by the payroll tax, which creates an economically destructive wedge between what an employer pays and what an employee receives. This wedge is equal to the full amount of the tax, including both the employer and employee shares.

At 12.4 percent, the payroll tax creates a rather large wedge, equal to about one-eighth of total wages.

The full amount of this wedge or tax is borne by the employee.[32] That is because the employer will never pay more in total labor costs for a worker than the marginal product of labor.[33] If labor costs rise above the marginal product of labor, the employer would simply be losing by continuing to employ the worker, and would lay him off. As a result, any labor costs such as a payroll tax would be fully offset by the employer by reducing the employee's wage commensurately, so that the tax plus the wage would not be greater than the marginal productivity of labor.[34]

As a result of this wedge, the employee will never receive the full value for his work and the full amount paid by his employer, but only this amount minus the wedge or tax. For example, with a 12.4 percent payroll tax, if an employee is offered $100 a week in wages, it actually costs the firm, which ostensibly pays the tax, $106.20 a week to hire him. This is what the employee's work is really worth to the employer and what the employer is willing to pay to hire him. But the worker only takes home $93.80 after paying his share of the tax, even though his work is worth $106.20.

This wedge or tax thus reduces the compensation of workers, and consequently discourages them from working. The result is a reduced labor supply and reduced employment. The payroll tax is essentially a tax on employment, and as always, the result of taxing something is that there is less of it.

Indeed, the result of this wedge effect is that there will be less employment than both workers and employees desire. The wedge prevents an employer from hiring as many employees, or as much of their labor, as he might like because it prevents him from paying employees what they are really worth and attracting as many workers, or as much of their labor, as he is able and willing to hire at that wage. It prevents employees from working as much as they would like at the full wage the employer is willing to pay because they can only receive the after-tax wage, for which they are not willing to work as much.

This in turn means misallocation of resources and economic inefficiency. Because labor does not receive its full worth, the labor supply is below the optimal amount. Workers who can produce $10.62 per hour but receive only $9.38 will not put forth the same labor supply that they would if they were paid their full value. Workers who could be producing and taking home $10.62 an hour will instead be consuming leisure time, which is only worth $9.39 to $10.61 to them. In the meantime, employers have to make up for the decreased labor supply with increased capital. The mix of capital and labor that results is a more expensive and less efficient way of producing the output than the mix of capital and labor that would exist without the tax.

Workers who are likely to be able to vary their labor supply easily in response to the wage rate are especially affected by the payroll tax. Part-time workers and secondary workers who are not always in the labor market by necessity are likely to be very discouraged by reduced compensation. A college or high school student who is working during the summer might take an extra few weeks off if his wages are reduced and he no longer feels it is worth his time to work and miss a vacation. A housewife who works 25 hours a week may feel that at a reduced compensation rate she will work only 15 hours and give the extra attention to her children.

Full-time family breadwinners are less likely to vary their work in response to the wage rate. Yet, even here, many might stay in school longer, take more vacations, forgo overtime, and so forth, because of the reduced compensation. They might choose less demanding jobs, or fail to move to a new location for a better job, or just put out less effort, because the reduced compensation is not worth the sacrifice. Workers may also seek to avoid the tax by shifting cash wages into untaxable fringe benefits, or nicer working conditions such as fancier offices.

These effects mean not only less labor supply, but also lower labor productivity, more misallocation of resources, and greater economic inefficiency. And all of these effects mean, in turn, lower income and less economic growth.

These labor and employment effects would not occur if the worker perceived the tax payments as directly buying him a service or benefit, like retirement benefits, or insurance protection. If the worker believed he would get back his tax payments plus full interest in retirement, then these payments would effectively be part of his compensation for working. The worker would be buying deferred compensation, with the full interest compensating for the deferral. The payments would be like putting money in the bank, which would eventually be withdrawn by the worker. The payments would then not be a tax, but part of the inducement to work, about as much as his cash wages.

But Feldstein has shown that, given full-market returns, a small fraction of the total payroll tax, about 2 percent, would be sufficient to finance all promised Social Security benefits.[35] As a result, the remaining 10 percent or so of the payroll tax is a pure tax not buying any benefit for the worker. Therefore, at least 10 percent of the payroll tax has all the negative consequences described.

Moreover, even the remaining 2 percent of the tax, supposedly buying retirement benefits, may be perceived as a pure tax as well. This is because benefits are not directly related to taxes paid. They depend on whether there are other family members, whether the recipient is working or divorced, and other factors. The benefit formula is also redistributive, shifting benefits to lower-income recipients. Consequently, the worker may not see a direct link between taxes and benefits and, therefore, may view Social Security payments as just another tax rather than as payments for later direct compensation.

Feldstein estimates that even apart from this last effect, the prior impact of the Social Security tax discussed above would produce a total economic loss of about 1 percent of GDP.[36] This would be about $80 billion per year today.

Capital Effect

As discussed above, Social Security reduces saving, which in turn reduces capital investment. This loss of capital investment has several negative effects on the labor market.

Capital investment increases the demand for labor and thereby drives up wages. Because of investment in new and expanding businesses, employers seek employees to staff the expansion, which translates into increased labor demand and, as a result, increased wages. This same effect can be seen by recognizing that capital investment results in improved worker productivity. Workers with steam shovels are more productive than workers with manual ones; workers with copy machines are more productive than workers with carbon paper. Higher worker productivity results in higher wages. A reduction in capital investment like that caused by Social Security leads to lower worker productivity and a loss of these higher wages.

These higher wages might also have induced a greater labor supply, so a loss of capital investment means less employment and less national income.

Capital investment also tends to upgrade jobs and thereby provide more of what are considered good jobs. It does this not only by increasing wages, but by improving the status of some jobs. For example, capital investment can make a steam shovel operator out of a ditch digger. And, in an economy with persistent involuntary unemployment, capital investment will decrease unemployment. As new businesses are created and old ones expanded, the increased demand for workers will reduce unemployment. Reduced capital investment again results in the loss of all these advantages.

The loss in capital investment caused by Social Security, therefore, results in lower wages, lower worker productivity, less employment, lower GDP, fewer good jobs, and more unemployment.

The Earnings Test

Social Security's earnings test causes additional disruptions in the labor market. The earnings test reduces benefits for retirees and other beneficiaries who earn wages above certain modest limits. This test reduces employment by reducing the compensation for that employment. If benefits are reduced by $1 for every $2 earned above a certain limit, as they are for preretirement spousal survivors and disability benefits, then the worker is in effect receiving only $1 for every $2 worth of work above that limit. The earnings test alone consequently places a high marginal tax rate of 50 percent on such income. If benefits are reduced by $1 for every $3 earned above a certain limit, as they are for retirees below age 70, then the worker is effectively suffering a high marginal tax rate of 33 percent on such income from the earnings test alone.

Those who choose to continue working after eligibility for Social Security benefits must also continue to pay Social Security payroll taxes. This has a particularly harsh effect on elderly workers, as they face very high marginal tax rates. In fact, economists Peter Diamond and Jonathan Gruber have found that a 69-year-old worker with average earnings faces an effective Social Security tax rate of more than 45 percent.[37]

In response, workers receiving Social Security benefits will reduce their labor supply and employment will decrease. The elderly in particular may choose to retire earlier, leaving the labor force entirely.

Discouraging employment through the earnings test results in the same negative impacts as discussed for the payroll tax. It results in less employment than both workers and employers desire, making both worse off. It results in economic inefficiency and a misallocation of resources because it induces a suboptimal labor supply and suboptimal mix of capital and labor. Finally, it results in less GDP by causing less employment and producing economic inefficiency and misallocation of resources.

Indeed, the economic impact of encouraging seniors to leave the labor force is particularly harsh. As Nobel laureate Gary Becker has pointed out, Social Security encourages workers to withdraw from the labor force at a time when they are highly productive and making important contributions to the economy.[38]

As discussed previously, the earnings test for retirees is being sharply cut back, with the applicable earnings limit being increased to $30,000 by 2002. This will sharply reduce the negative effects we described.

The Economic Impact

As discussed, the reduction in saving caused by Social Security is likely to lead to at least a 5 percent reduction in GDP. If Feldstein's econometric studies, which we find most plausible, are correct, the much larger reduction in saving would produce a much larger reduction in GDP—perhaps 10 percent or more.

In addition, Feldstein estimates the economic loss due to the effects of the payroll tax on labor and employment to be 1 percent of GDP. And this does not fully account for all the negative labor effects that were described.

Overall, therefore, Social Security may be reducing GDP by as little as 6 percent to as much as 11 percent or more. This means an annual loss to the economy of from a low of $500 billion to a quite plausible $1 trillion or more.

Feldstein offers an estimate of $10 trillion to $20 trillion as the present value of the economic benefits of correcting those problems through privatizing Social Security.[39] That would translate into at least a million new jobs and an increase in annual income of $5,000 for an average family of four.[40]

This, of course, is more than enough to warrant privatization. But as a matter of valid analysis, the authors believe Feldstein has accepted so many qualifications and overly conservative assumptions in reaching this estimate that it now seriously underestimates the ultimate likely positive effects of such reform.

Whatever the precise effect, a consensus is emerging among economists that privatizing Social Security would have a significant impact on improving economic growth. For example, Michael Darby, former assistant secretary of the Treasury, and now Warren C. Cordner, professor of money and financial markets at UCLA, estimates that Social Security has already reduced U.S. capital stock by 5 to 20 percent and real income from 2 to 7 percent.[41] As Laurence Kotlikoff of Boston University says, "The net impact [of privatizing Social Security] will be a rise in national saving, investment, and, at least in the short term, real wage growth."[42] A survey of economists by *Business Week* concludes that privatizing Social Security would increase investment in U.S. plants and equipment by 25 percent by 2020.[43]

This improved economic performance will provide important benefits to workers beyond the much higher returns and benefits described in chapter 4. Privatizing Social Security will mean higher wages, more jobs, reduced unemployment, and expanded economic opportunity for the entire nation.

7. Social Security Privatization around the World

America's Social Security problems are far from unique. Around the world, pay-as-you-go social security systems are running up against the hard-edged reality of demographics. Indeed, many social security systems are in far worse condition than our own. However, out of this crisis new and innovative alternatives are developing as other countries experiment with different forms of privatization. The experience of these countries provides valuable lessons for the United States.

A Worldwide Demographic Nightmare

Demographic changes are a worldwide issue. By 2030, the proportion of the world's population over age 65 will have more than doubled, from approximately 8 percent to more than 16 percent. This trend is most apparent in the industrialized countries of Europe, the United States, and Japan, where the percentage of elderly will grow from about 18 percent to more than 32 percent. But, developing countries are experiencing similar strains. In Latin America, the percentage of seniors will explode from 7 percent to more than 17 percent; in China it will grow from roughly 9 percent to more than 23 percent.[1]

Moreover, as Figure 7.1 shows, the trend toward longer life spans is accelerating dramatically. It took 140 years for the elderly population of France to double from 9 to 18 percent; China will accomplish this in just 22 years.[2]

At the same time, as a result of increased economic growth and efforts at population control and family planning, worldwide fertility rates are declining. Worldwide, the fertility rate has declined from 3.3 as recently as 1990 to just 2.96 today. By 2020, the rate is projected to decline to under 2.5. In fact, in every Western European nation except Ireland, fertility rates are now below the 2.1 necessary

Figure 7.1
Number of Years Required or Expected for Percentage of Population Aged 65 and Over to Rise from 7% to 14%

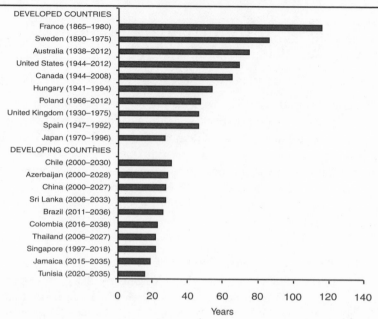

Source: Japan Ministry of Health and Welfare, UNDESIPA, U.S. Bureau of the Census, Int'l Programs Center, Int'l Database, Country Sources.

to replace the current population.[3] That means that the population in those countries will actually begin to shrink.

As a result, fewer and fewer workers are supporting more and more retirees. In some countries of Europe, such as Austria and Belgium, the ratio is already below 2:1. By 2025, nearly all the countries of Europe will have fewer than two workers supporting each retiree. Many countries, including Germany, will have more retirees than workers, a ratio of less than 1:1. The same is true of Japan.[4] While most developing countries are not in quite such bad shape, their worker-to-retiree ratios are also declining. (See Figure 7.2.)

These demographic changes will put enormous strains on the flawed pay-as-you-go retirement systems of Western Europe and Japan. How bad is the problem? Consider this:

Figure 7.2
RATIO OF RETIREMENT-AGE TO WORKING-AGE POPULATION

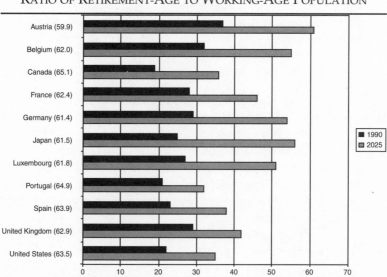

NOTE: Ratios represent the number of persons at or above average retirement age per 100 persons between the ages of 20 and average retirement age in 1984. Each national average retirement age is in parentheses after the country name.

- Payroll taxes for pensions already exceed 25 percent in Brazil, Spain, Italy, and much of Eastern Europe. In Germany, the combined payroll tax (for pensions, health care, and other forms of social insurance) already exceeds 40 percent. To pay all promised benefits, it will have to exceed 50 percent by 2030, with the pension portion alone exceeding 25 percent.[5]
- Italy's public retirement system already consumes 14 percent of the nation's GDP and represents 37 percent of government expenditures.[6] Unless changes are made in their pension programs, Germany will have to increase its total government spending by 5.5 percent of GNP in the next 20 years. Japan will have to increase government spending by 9.5 percent of GNP.[7] The OECD projects that government retirement benefits alone will exceed 16 percent of GDP annually in Germany, France, and Italy by 2030.[8]

131

- According to the OECD, the current unfunded liabilities of the public pension systems in Germany and Japan are well over 100 percent of their respective GDPs. In France and Italy, unfunded liabilities exceed 200 percent of GDP. In most industrialized countries, the implicit debt of unfunded pensions is two or three times greater than their explicit national debts.[9]

Although developing countries do not face the immediate crisis of the industrialized world, they too face significant problems in caring for an aging population. In Latin America and Eastern Europe, pay-as-you-go systems face high payroll taxes and benefits that have been severely eroded by inflation.[10] In Africa and Asia, countries that have been hard pressed to meet basic needs are struggling with the need to develop a retirement system that can handle a burgeoning aged population.[11]

Perhaps the problem was best summed up by the World Bank in its 1994 report *Averting the Old-Age Crisis*:

> [Pay-as-you-go] pensions have proved unsustainable and very difficult to reform. In some developing countries, these systems are nearing collapse. In others, governments preparing to establish formal systems risk repeating expensive mistakes. The result is a looming old age crisis that threatens not only the old, but also their children and grandchildren, who must shoulder, either directly or indirectly, much of the increasingly heavy burden of providing for the aged.[12]

Chile: Individual Accounts

The remarkable political turnaround for Social Security began with the South American nation of Chile, which adopted a private option for its social security system in 1980. Interestingly, Chile was the first country in the Western Hemisphere to adopt a social security system, doing so in 1925, 10 years before the United States. But by 1980, their system had many of the same problems the U.S. Social Security system faces today. Payroll taxes were greater than 26 percent, yet the system still ran deficits that drained the federal budget. Long-range projections showed the program's financial gaps growing ever larger. Yet benefits were inadequate and far below what workers could have earned by saving and investing in the private sector.[13]

Chile's private-sector reforms were developed by a group of economists (many with graduate degrees from the best American universities), led by Labor and Social Security Secretary José Piñera. Rather than postpone problems with Chile's social security system through tax increases or benefit cuts, they developed a completely new system based on individually owned, privately invested retirement accounts called Pension Savings Accounts (PSAs). The new plan took effect on May 1, 1981.[14]

Under Chile's PSA system, neither workers nor employers pay a social security tax to the state. Nor does the worker collect a government-funded pension. Instead, during working years, 10 percent of each worker's wages are automatically deposited by the employer each month into the worker's own, individual PSA. A worker may, if he chooses, contribute an additional 10 percent of his wages each month (over and above the minimum required 10 percent), on a tax-deferred basis (like an American IRA). Generally, a worker will contribute more than 10 percent of his salary if he wants to retire early or obtain a higher pension.

A worker chooses one from about 12 private, expert, investment companies (known as AFPs for Adminstradoras de Fondos de Pensiones) approved by the government to manage his PSA.[15] These companies choose the stocks, bonds, and other investments for the worker's account, subject to government regulation prohibiting high-risk investments. As a result, workers do not have to be experienced stock and bond investors to participate in the private system. Each AFP is required to pay at least a minimum investment return, set as a proportion of the average return earned by all companies.

Because workers are free to change from one AFP to another, there is strong competition among the companies to provide a greater return on investment, better customer service, and lower administrative fees. Each worker is given a PSA passbook and every three months receives a statement that reports how much money has accumulated in the retirement account and how well the investment fund has performed. The account bears the worker's name, and the money in the account is the worker's property.

At retirement, workers can use the accumulated funds in their individual pension accounts to buy an annuity from any private insurance company. The annuity pays a specified monthly income for the life of the worker, indexed to inflation. The annuity also pays survivors benefits for the retiree's spouse or other dependents after the worker dies.

Alternatively, instead of buying an annuity, a retiree may leave the funds in the PSA and make regular withdrawals, subject to limits based on the life expectancy of the retiree and dependents. When the worker dies and there are funds remaining in the account, the account can be left to the spouse, children, or other heirs.

The Chilean government also guarantees a minimum retirement benefit to all workers. If a retiree's private benefits fall below the minimum benefit level for any reason, the government will pay additional benefits to the retiree to bring total benefits up to the minimum. The minimum benefit is equal now to 40 percent of average wages, which is about what the U.S. Social Security system pays to average-income workers, and is funded out of general government revenues—not through a payroll tax.

The retirement age under the new system is 65 for men and 60 for women, but workers can retire earlier if they have accumulated sufficient funds to pay a minimum level of benefits. Workers can speed up their accumulation of funds, and retire even earlier, by making extra, voluntary contributions during working years or earning higher than expected returns. Workers can continue to work after retirement to any extent they choose, but are no longer required to contribute to their retirement accounts.

Workers in the private system also contribute an additional 2.6 percent of wages for private life and disability insurance, as well as for the overall administration of their accounts. The insurance replaces the survivors and disability benefits paid by the old system for disability or death occurring during the preretirement years of the worker. The entire private system is indexed for inflation.

Workers who were already in the workforce at the time of the reform had, of course, paid taxes into the old system for several years. For those who switched to the new private system, the government issued special bonds, called recognition bonds, to compensate them for their accrued rights under the old system. The bonds are held by individual workers in their PSAs. The amount of the bond is set for each worker so that by retirement it will be sufficient to pay the accrued proportion of the old system's benefits.[16]

Workers were given the choice of moving to the new private system or remaining in the existing government-run social security

Figure 7.3
REAL RATE OF RETURN TO CHILEAN AFP ACCOUNTS 1981–1996

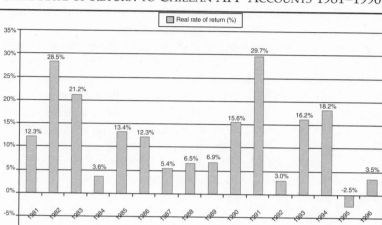

system. Within 18 months, more than 90 percent of workers chose the new private system.

After 17 years of operation, Chile's experiment has proven itself. As Figure 7.3 shows, since the system began to operate on May 1, 1981, the average real return on investment has been 12 percent per year (more than three times higher than the anticipated yield of 4 percent).[17] Of course, the annual yield has shown the oscillations that are intrinsic to the free market—ranging from minus 3 percent to plus 30 percent in real terms—but the important yield is the average one over the long term.[18]

Pensions under the new system have been significantly higher than under the old, state-administered system, which required a total payroll tax of around 25 percent. The typical retiree is receiving a benefit equal to nearly 80 percent of his average annual income over the last 10 years of his working life, almost double the U.S. replacement value.[19] Survivors and disability benefits are also substantially higher.[20]

The resources administered by the private pension funds amount to $30 billion, or around 43 percent of GDP as of 1997.[21] By improving the functioning of both the capital and the labor markets, pension privatization has been one of the key reforms that has pushed the growth rate of Chile's economy up from the historical rate of 3

135

percent a year to 7 percent on average during the last 10 years. The Chilean savings rate has increased to 27 percent of GDP, and the unemployment rate has decreased to 5 percent since the reform was undertaken.[22]

Moreover, due to the earning and investments rapidly accumulating in the private retirement accounts, in less than 10 years the average Chilean worker will have more retirement savings than the average American worker, even though the average American worker earns seven times the annual income of the average Chilean worker. Chilean labor union leader Eduardo Aguilera says, "The bottom line is that the private pension system has been an enormous advancement for the Chilean workers." Like many labor union leaders in Chile, Aguilera was initially opposed to the reform, but is now an enthusiastic supporter.[23]

Critics of the Chilean System

Despite its success, the Chilean system has not been without critics. They claim that Chile's privatized system is too costly, fails to provide full coverage, and cannot be sustained in the future. But, while the Chilean system is certainly not perfect, most of the criticisms aimed at it are far off the mark.

For example, one area that has received the most criticism is the relatively high administrative fees and commissions charged by the Chilean AFPs. Critics often claim that such costs run as high as 18 percent of an average worker's contributions to his account.[24] As Figure 7.4 shows, in the earliest years of the program, administrative fees did indeed reach such levels but they have been declining in recent years; fees now amount to just 10 percent of contributions.[25] This is not surprising, as economies of scale and advances in computerization have made data collection far more efficient. Competition between AFPs has also contributed to declining administrative costs.[26] Unlike the United States, Chile had no experience with private pensions or large numbers of individual investors. It had to invent capital markets and investment products virtually from scratch. This led to high initial costs, which are now declining as the system matures.

However, looking at fees as a percentage of contributions is a misleading way to look at the issue. Most of the funds in the workers' accounts do not come from the contributions themselves, but from

Figure 7.4
MANAGEMENT FEES FOR CHILEAN AFPS

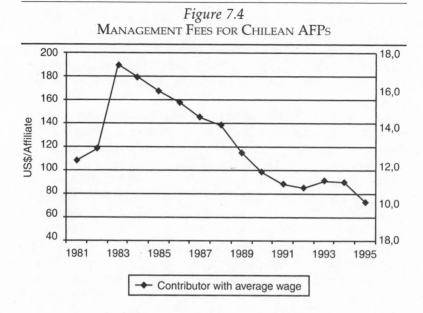

Contributor with average wage

the return on investment that the accounts have earned. A more accurate measure of administrative expenses, therefore, is to compare fees to the total amount of assets managed by the accounts. That is the basis on which American mutual funds compare costs, for example.[27] Using this measure, estimates of the cost of administrative fees is only about 1.2 percent of assets managed.[28] This is slightly higher than the approximately 1 percent charged by American mutual funds, but hardly outrageous.[29]

That is not to say that there is no room for fees to decline further. Administrative costs remain somewhat higher than they might otherwise be because of high marketing costs. Promotional expenses may amount to as much as 30 percent of operating costs for the average AFP.[30]

Moreover, the commission structure of the Chilean system was changed in 1987, for populist political reasons, creating some difficulties. The government mandated that commissions be paid at a flat rate in order to create a cross-subsidy from high-income to low-income workers. However, the flat rate policy means that AFPs are not allowed to offer incentives to salesmen who develop customer loyalty, nor may they offer discounts to workers who commit to remain with an AFP for long periods of time. Since all commissions are based on "new sales," salesmen focus on convincing workers to switch from one AFP to another. Approximately 25 percent of all Chileans transfer their accounts each year.[31] This has resulted in a great deal of "churning," or instability in the system, which has raised costs.

However, in 1997, the Chilean government approved some basic rules making it slightly more difficult to transfer accounts. This has resulted in a dramatic decline in the frequency of transfers, proving that this problem can be addressed with rather minor changes.

More important, as Monica Queisser of the World Bank has noted, the bottom line is that "since the real returns have been very good, the costs have not affected members' retirement incomes negatively."[32]

Critics of the Chilean system also claim that many Chilean workers have been left out of the new system and are in danger of having no retirement benefits in their old age. They often claim that approximately 40 percent of Chilean workers are not participating in the private system.[33] However, that claim is seriously misleading.

More than 95 percent of Chilean workers are participating in the system in the sense that they have an AFP account.[34] However, only about 61.5 percent of the labor force is actively making payments to their accounts at any given time.[35] There are many reasons for this. Approximately 26.4 percent of the Chilean workforce is self-employed and therefore not required to participate.[36] Only about 10 percent of self-employed workers regularly contribute to their accounts, a percentage that has remained stable since the system's inception.[37] Workers who are temporarily unemployed or disabled are also not making payments to their accounts, as are women who have temporarily dropped out of the workforce to care for children.[38] However, unlike the old system where workers without enough time in the labor force to qualify for a pension received nothing, workers who move in and out of the labor force keep their accounts while they are not working. Those accounts continue to earn investment returns and the workers can renew their payments when they go back to work.

In addition, a Chilean worker who chooses the "programmed withdrawal" option for receiving benefits retains an active AFP account, but for obvious reasons is no longer required to make contributions.

The most important reason for less than full participation may simply be that tax evasion is a time-honored tradition throughout Latin America, where the underground economy has often been more important than the official, state-regulated and taxed sector.[39] In fact, under Chile's old social security system, from 1976 to 1980, an average of only 49 percent of the labor force participated sufficiently to earn pension coverage, and participation was declining.[40] Therefore coverage today is actually more extensive than under the old system.

Some critics also claim that the new system fails to do enough to help the poor. They allege that the old social security system contained a significant element of redistribution. For example, workers with the lowest 40 percent of incomes paid approximately 10 percent of all social security taxes, but received 15 percent of all benefits.[41] The privatized system, with its strict link between contributions, does not redistribute wealth between workers. As a result, they blame the privatized system for a growing gap between the rich and poor.[42]

But, while it is true that the rich have gotten richer in Chile, so have the poor. Nearly half of all Chileans lived in poverty in the early 1980s. Today, the poverty rate has been cut in half. Fewer than 25 percent of Chileans have incomes below the poverty level.[43]

Moreover, as mentioned above, Chile maintains a safety net in the form of a minimum benefit. That minimum is equal to approximately 80 percent of the minimum wage. Few workers are likely to need this minimum benefit. Current projections indicate that more than 80 percent of Chilean workers will accumulate enough funds in their accounts to provide benefits in excess of the minimum.[44]

Finally, some critics admit that Chile's social security system has been successful so far, but warn that that success cannot continue in the future. In particular, they warn that the phenomenal 12 percent real rate of return cannot be sustained, the most pessimistic among them suggesting that in the long term real rates of return are more likely to be in the range of 3 to 5 percent.[45]

It may be true that the rate of return will decline in the future. The current high rate of return is largely due to the phenomenal growth of the Chilean economy. That growth will cool in the future. Moreover, most pension funds remain heavily invested in bonds.[46] While this provides a high degree of safety and stability for investors, bonds are not likely to outperform equities over the long term.

But declining rates of return do not mean that the Chilean system will fail. According to a 1992 study, even if rates of return fell to as low as 5 percent, the replacement rate for men would still be between 81 and 86 percent of preretirement income. Women's replacement rates would be lower, because of lower wages and longer periods outside the workforce, but would still be between 52 and 57 percent.[47] Under the old social security system, the replacement rate for manual laborers was officially targeted at 70 percent of the unindexed average of wages for the laborers' last five working years.[48] Because the wage base was not indexed, during periods of high inflation, such as the 1970s, the effective replacement rate was far less.[49] In fact, 93 percent of manual laborers received only the minimum rate of 85 percent of the minimum wage.[50]

It is not likely that rates of return will fall as far as the critics portend. Labor economist Raúl Bustos Castillo, for example, believes that long-term rates of return will be between 5.5 and 6.5 percent.[51] Regardless, when the plan was designed it was modeled on the assumption that a 4 percent real rate of return would yield replacement rates better than those under the old system.[52] Thus, even if returns decline dramatically, workers will still be better off under the new system than they were under the old. (Of course, all this assumes that the old system was viable, which it was not.)

These same critics warn that the Chilean government has accepted substantial obligations in making the transition to the new system, particularly the debt represented by the recognition bonds. While this does not actually represent new debt—merely a recognition of unfunded liabilities under the old system—making the debt explicit limits the government's option to repeal promises already made in the event of an economic downturn or renewed inflation.[53] However, Chile has already passed the worst of its exposure and wisely used its extraordinary economic growth to buy down its debt. Obligations under the new Social Security system have declined from a peak of 7.8 percent of GNP in 1984 to under 4 percent today.[54]

Of course, declining rates of return or a severe economic downturn could increase the number of Chileans receiving the minimum benefit. That would result in additional pressure on the Chilean budget. However, it is difficult to see how the budget impact of economic slowdowns could have been avoided under the previous system either. Indeed, the new system makes economic slowdowns less likely.

Where problems do exist with the Chilean system, they are likely to be a result of too much regulation rather than too little. For example, AFPs are penalized if their portfolios perform below a maximum deviation from the average performance of all AFPs. This is designed to discourage speculation and protect workers. However, the result has been that most AFPs offer very similar portfolios, reducing worker choice. Also, restrictions on the amount of foreign investment may reduce future returns and makes portfolios more sensitive to local economic conditions.

Still, given the program's remarkable success over the past 16 years, most of the criticisms directed at Chile's program seem little more than quibbles.

Variations on the Chilean Theme

In the wake of Chile's success, six other Latin American countries have privatized their social security systems along the lines of the Chilean model. The first was Peru in 1993, followed the next year by Argentina and Colombia. Mexico, Bolivia, and El Salvador privatized their social security systems in 1997. All of those countries followed the basic Chilean outline—a defined contribution system with individually owned, privately invested accounts. However, the political and economic conditions in each country resulted in variations on the Chilean theme.

Argentina

Like Chile, Argentina had one of this hemisphere's oldest social security systems. By the beginning of the 1990s, the pay-as-you-go system had accumulated enormous unfunded liabilities despite payroll taxes of 27.5 percent. The government attempted to respond by slashing benefits only to find most cuts blocked by lawsuits from beneficiaries. With unemployment high, further payroll tax hikes were impossible. A drastic change was required.[55]

In 1994, Argentina established an alternative social security system. The old pay-as-you-go system was not eliminated, but workers were given the option of paying a portion of their payroll tax into individually owned, privately invested accounts. Essentially, Argentina has a two-tiered system. All workers pay 16 percent (the employer's portion of the payroll tax) into the government-run social security system to fund a universal basic pension payable to every worker with at least 30 years of contributions. The basic pension is low, equal to approximately 27.5 percent of the average covered wage.[56]

Argentine workers then have the option of paying the 11 percent employee portion of the payroll tax into the government-run system to receive additional benefits, or workers can divert that portion of the payroll tax into individual accounts. The individual accounts are privately managed as in Chile and invested in private capital markets. There are no recognition bonds. Individuals who select the private option receive an increase in their basic pension to partially compensate them for past taxes paid to the system. (The formula used caps the recognition benefit at 52.5 percent of previous income.)[57]

Although it is far too early to determine the program's long-term success, initial results have been positive. Approximately 65 percent of Argentine workers have chosen the private alternative.[58] The annual real rate of return has been near 20 percent.[59] Although no one expects such returns to continue, Argentines can realistically expect higher retirement incomes than under the former government-only system.[60]

There are some reasons for caution, however, most importantly Argentina's ability to finance the transition. The government was counting on the new program to provide incentives that reduced evasion, using the additional contributions to help pay for the transition. But improved participation has been marginal, meaning that continued reliance on a payroll tax may not have been the best method of meeting transition costs.[61]

Colombia

Colombia's social security system was much newer than most in Latin America, only about 20 years old, and therefore was not yet showing the demographic strains of more mature pay-as-you-go systems like those in Chile or Argentina. However, the system was beset with other problems, particularly widespread evasion that meant that barely 25 percent of the population was covered.[62] Projections for the future suggested that problems were coming. The number of retirees was increasing at 7 percent per year, while the number of workers was increasing by only 3 percent. Promised replacement rates were extremely high, leaving unfunded liabilities equal to 80 percent of GDP.[63]

As in Argentina, Colombia was not able to completely abandon the system. Instead, political compromises forced the adoption of a dual system—a system of privately invested individual accounts operating side-by-side and in competition with a pay-as-you-go system run by the government.[64] Workers may choose to pay into either the government-run pay-as-you-go system or a system of individually owned, privately invested accounts. They may switch between systems every three years. The government collects all payroll taxes regardless of whether the worker is enrolled in the public or private system. For workers in the private system, the government is supposed to transfer the money to the management company of the worker's choice. In practice, there have been frequent delays in making this transfer.[65]

Individuals who switch to the private system receive recognition bonds to compensate for past taxes paid to the public system. Because individuals can switch back and forth between the public and private systems, the bonds must be constantly recalculated, adding greatly to the administrative costs of the system. In addition, because of the extreme decentralization of the Colombian fiscal system, the cost of redeeming the bonds will fall heavily on local and provincial authorities. This has resulted in a lack of confidence in the safety of the bonds.[66]

It is far too early to judge the success of Colombia's system. Only about 15 percent of workers have switched to the private system.[67] There are three general reasons for the low participation rate: a history of evading the country's social security taxes; exemptions for the self-employed, petrochemical workers, teachers, and others; and incentives for workers over age 40 to remain in the government-run system.[68] However, the program is increasingly popular among younger workers. About 65 percent of all those enrolled in the private system are under age 35.[69]

Real rates of return in the private system have been modest, just 4.5 percent.[70] One reason for this low rate of return is that Colombian pension funds are very heavily invested in bonds and other fixed-income securities rather than in equities, choosing lower rates of return in exchange for greater stability.[71] However, it is important to note that the Colombian economy is performing sluggishly in general. Chile and Argentina accompanied the privatization of social security with other reforms, which helped boost economic growth

143

and the return on investments. Colombia's economy remains mired in central planning and government control.[72]

Peru

Like Colombia, Peru had a relatively young social security system that was beset with inefficiency, corruption, and noncompliance. Only about 20 percent of Peru's population was making sufficient payments to qualify for coverage.[73] Future demographic trends were threatening. In 1993, therefore, President Alberto Fujimori established a Chilean-style alternative to the government-run system.

As in Colombia, Peru's privatized system operates side-by-side with the government's pay-as-you-go system. Workers can choose to remain in the government system or switch to the private one. Unlike Colombia, the choice is irrevocable. Individual accounts are invested by private management firms, with workers able to switch between companies. Workers who switch to the private system receive recognition bonds to compensate for past payroll taxes. Alone among countries with a Chilean-style system, Peru offers no minimum benefit or guaranteed rate of return.[74]

There have been several problems with the implementation of Peru's privatized system, most due to the often chaotic and corrupt nature of Peru's government. Some employers have failed to make required payments, and the government has been slow in issuing recognition bonds.[75] In the program's early years, individuals switching to the private system had to pay a *higher* payroll tax than individuals who remained in the government system, which depressed participation, particularly among low-income workers. The tax differential was corrected in 1995.

Despite these problems, initial results have been encouraging. About 60 percent of Peruvian workers have chosen the privatized system.[76] The average real rate of return annually since the program's inception has been 7.1 percent, solid but modest compared with returns in Argentina and Chile.[77]

Mexico

In July 1997, Mexican workers were given the option of diverting their payroll taxes to privately invested, individual accounts, known as AFORES, or remaining in the current government-run pay-as-you-go system. New entrants to the labor force will be required to enter the new system. Therefore, the government-run system will eventually be phased out. [78]

The AFORES system covers retirement benefits only. Disability and survivors benefits will continue to be provided through the government system, financed by a separate payroll tax. Unlike Chile, the government did not issue recognition bonds for past contributions. However, there is an indirect recognition of past payments because, at retirement, workers who chose the AFORES system can choose to receive their benefits from either that system or the government system, whichever is higher. Any shortfall in revenues to the government system will be made up out of general revenues.[79]

Although the program is just beginning, there are several elements of its design that are cause for concern. For example, allowing workers at retirement to choose which system they wish to collect retirement benefits from will both encourage speculation in the private accounts and make it difficult for the Mexican government to budget its future obligations. Also troubling is the "social contribution," equal to 5.5 percent of the minimum wage, paid into the pension accounts by the government. By weakening the link between the worker's contribution and benefits, the payment opens the door to fiscal mischief. Maintaining the link between contributions and benefits is particularly important in a country like Mexico where corruption and expropriation are rife. A third mistake is allowing the government social security system to regulate and audit the AFORES system. This presents a serious conflict of interest. Finally, the government has adopted an overly restrictive policy on the types of investments allowed by AFORES. At least initially, AFORES will be required to invest most of their funds in government debt. This will lead to lower rates of return and could turn into a backdoor way of financing government spending.[80]

Yet, even with these caveats, the Mexican pension reform represents a significant accomplishment in a country hardly noted for free market policies.

El Salvador

Of all the countries in Latin America with privatized social security systems, El Salvador has come closest to adopting a pure Chilean model. Under the reform, adopted in 1996, employers pay 6.5 percent of payroll into an individual account for each worker. The worker pays another 3.5 percent into the account, as well as up to 3 percent for life insurance, disability insurance, and administrative fees. Workers choose from a range of private investment management firms approved by the government to handle their accounts. These firms then pick the individual investments for the workers. At retirement, the accumulated funds finance an annuity that pays monthly benefits to the retiree for life. The system also guarantees workers a minimum retirement benefit. If the private benefits that can be financed by the accumulated account funds fall below the minimum for some reason, the government will pay supplemental benefits to bring total benefits up to the minimum. As a percentage of preretirement income, this minimum is close to the average benefit under the U.S. system. Those already in the workforce who switch to the new system receive recognition bonds to compensate them for their past taxes paid into the old system.[81]

Other Countries

Bolivia and Uruguay have also adopted privatized pension systems very similar to Chile's.[82] Several other Latin American countries are on the verge of privatizing their social security systems, including Guatemala, Honduras, and Venezuela.

Eastern Europe

If Latin America has led the way in privatizing social security, the former communist nations of Eastern Europe have not been far behind. Eastern Europe is fertile ground for social security reform in part because the public pension systems inherited from the old communist regimes had been largely discredited. Despite payroll taxes of between 30 and 50 percent, many Eastern European countries were already having trouble paying promised pension benefits. No one believed that they would be able to meet obligations in the future.[83]

Hungary was the first country in the region to privatize its social security system. Under the new Hungarian system, which took effect January 1, 1998, Hungarian workers divert approximately half their payroll taxes to individually owned, privately invested accounts. The remainder of the payroll tax is used to provide a low-floor benefit as well as to finance transition costs.[84] The former Soviet republic of Kazakhstan adopted a similar partially privatized system this year.[85]

146

Several other Eastern European countries are close to enacting similar reforms. The Polish legislature is putting the finishing touches on legislation that will allow workers in that country to privately invest a portion of their social security taxes. Final approval is expected sometime in 1998.[86] Perhaps even more significantly, Russia has passed legislation allowing new entrants to the workforce to invest privately for their pensions. After visiting Chile in 1997, Russian Deputy Prime Minister Boris Nemtsov told reporters, "Until now Russians only know Chilean wines and juices. Soon they may get a taste of their pension system."[87]

Albania, Bulgaria, Croatia, the Czech Republic, Macedonia, Romania, and Yugoslavia are all reportedly developing privatization proposals.[88]

Singapore: Provident Funds

Like pay-as-you-go social security, provident funds have their origin in the 19th century, but are generated from private rather than from government sources. Throughout Europe, employers established occupational provident funds to protect their workers in old age. Early in the 20th century, British colonial administrators picked up on the device as a way to attract and retain expatriate employees. Gradually, other workers were absorbed into the system. When decolonization arrived after World War II, many former British colonies saw provident funds as a foundation for their emerging social security systems.[89]

Beginning in 1955, Singapore introduced a compulsory savings program that now covers about three of four Singaporean workers.[90] Both employers and employees contribute to the government-run Central Provident Fund (CPF), which maintains accounts for each worker. Employees have a property right to the funds that accumulate in their accounts and are able to withdraw funds to purchase a home and to buy life insurance or home mortgage insurance, and may borrow money from their accounts to pay for the college education of a family member. Funds may be withdrawn at retirement, in the event of permanent disability, or if the individual emigrates from Singapore.[91]

Unlike Chile, there is a single fund *and its investment policy is controlled by the government.* Until 1986, the government directed all the fund's investment. However, recently the government has allowed individuals to control more and more of their own investment decisions. Currently, individuals are allowed to direct the investment of a portion of their accumulated balance (approximately 80 percent of funds in excess of S$35,400) in certain government-approved stocks, government bonds, and annuities.[92]

The funds not directed by individuals must be invested in Singapore government bonds. However, because the Singaporean government is running a budget surplus, the funds used to purchase those bonds are not used to finance government expenditures (as is the case in the United States, for example), but are invested through the Singapore Government Investment Corporation. No information on the investment portfolio is made public (it is, in fact, a state secret), but it is believed that most funds are invested abroad. The Singaporean government provides a return on the bonds based on the rates provided by the nation's major banks, with a guaranteed minimum of 2.5 percent.[93]

Similar systems have been implemented in many countries of Southeast Asia and the Pacific (Sri Lanka, Fiji, and Nepal, among others), Africa (Kenya, Gambia, and Tanzania), and the Caribbean (Dominica, Grenada, and St. Lucia). The success of these systems has been mixed. Because provident funds are compulsory monopolies, with government control of investment, the system's success has depended on the success of the government's investment policy.[94] Some countries, such as Malaysia and Singapore, have pursued conservative investment strategies, heavily focused on their own government debt, which have produced stable—but low—rates of return. In some other countries, however, governments have been tempted to politicize their investment policy, using invested funds to shore up unprofitable state enterprises or make other unproductive investments. Figure 7.5 shows the return on investment in selected provident funds.[95]

Even in Singapore, the government's investment strategy has brought returns that are unlikely to yield retirement income equal to the benchmark target of two-thirds of preretirement income. The problem is compounded by withdrawals from the system for purposes other than retirement, such as housing, and the lack of any "safety net" or minimum pension guarantee.[96] As a result, the system may not provide an adequate level of retirement income for a substantial portion of the population.[97]

Figure 7.5
AVERAGE ANNUAL INVESTMENT RETURNS FOR SELECT PROVIDENT
FUNDS

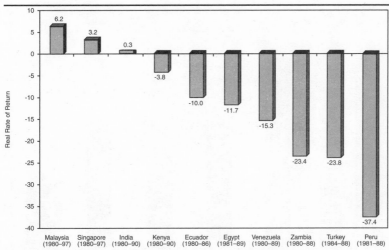

As Figure 7.6 shows, returns from privately managed investment funds have been substantially higher. It would appear, therefore, that the biggest drawback of the Singaporean system has been its centralization and insistence on government control. (This should be a warning to U.S. politicians who want the government to invest the Social Security trust funds.)

Britain: Model for a Two-Tier System

While most examples of social security privatization have taken place in countries that may be unfamiliar to many Americans, a very successful program of public pension privatization has quietly taken place in one of America's closest allies—Great Britain.

Since 1986 Britain has had a partially privatized two-tier system of Social Security benefits.[98] All British workers pay a progressive-rate payroll tax to a National Insurance Fund. Out of this fund, all retired workers receive a Basic State Pension (also known as the Old Age Pension), a flat-rate benefit equal to £62.45 ($99.92) per week for single retirees and £99.80 ($159.68) per week for couples. Workers also pay a payroll tax, also on a progressive-rate schedule, to the State Earnings Related Pension Scheme (SERPS), which provides

Figure 7.6
AVERAGE ANNUAL INVESTMENT RETURNS FOR PRIVATELY
INVESTED FUNDS

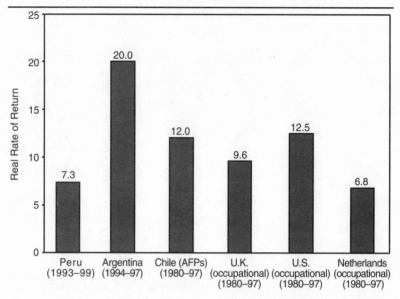

retirement benefits equal to approximately 25 percent of preretirement wages. Both the SERPS and the National Insurance Fund operate on a pay-as-you-go basis.

Workers may choose to opt out of SERPS, either by having an approved employer-provided pension plan, or through enrollment in a personal pension plan. An eligible employer-provided plan may be either a defined-benefit or defined-contribution plan, but must provide a guaranteed benefit at least equal to the benefit provided by SERPS. If a worker chooses to enroll in an employer-provided plan rather than in SERPS, he receives a tax rebate of 1.6 percent of earnings. His employer receives a rebate of 3 percent of earnings. Workers may also choose to invest in an Appropriate Personal Pension (APP) plan, similar to American mutual funds or IRAs. If a worker chooses this option, the government will rebate 4.6 percentage points of his payroll tax directly into this account. (A worker cannot receive a rebate for both an employer-provided plan and an APP, but may make additional contributions to either option on a tax-preferred basis.)

The private alternative has been both popular and successful. Approximately 73 percent of British workers have chosen one of the private options.[99] The reason for this popularity is simple—much higher rates of return. Studies show that younger workers in the private system can expect a pension at least twice as high as that provided by SERPS.[100]

The political debate in Britain is now over how fast and how far to extend privatization. In the last parliamentary elections, the Tories proposed a significant extension of privatization.[101] The victorious Labour Party was more cautious, but strongly endorsed the privately invested portion of the current system and declared itself willing to consider further privatization. [102] Frank Field, Labour's Minister of State for Social Security and Welfare Reform, is known to be a fan of the Chilean system.[103]

Australia

Recently the Labour government in Australia adopted reforms designed to gradually move the country to a privatized social security system. Previously, Australia's old-age pension system provided everyone over age 65 with a flat benefit unrelated to individual earnings. The benefit was financed not out of payroll taxes but through general tax revenues.[104] The payment was relatively low, equal to approximately 25 percent of the average wage.[105]

Beginning in 1996, Australia began requiring workers to contribute to private savings plans called "superannuation funds." Workers may choose from several different types of funds: small, self-managed pension funds resembling American IRAs; trustee-managed funds, run by employers and unions, either individually or through industry-sector groups; and retail funds, managed by banks, insurers, and security firms, similar to American mutual funds. In addition, public employees must contribute to public-sector funds managed by the government, similar to American federal and state employee pension programs. The required contribution rate is 6 percent of income today, but is scheduled to rise to 9 percent by 2002. Workers may voluntarily contribute additional amounts and receive preferred tax benefits.[106]

At the same time, benefits under the government-run system were frozen and a stiff means test was imposed. As a result, the vast majority of workers will eventually be covered through the private system.

While the system is relatively new, initial results have been positive. The superannuation funds have averaged a real rate of return of 5.5 percent.[107] It has been estimated that even if returns decline to just 4 percent, retirees will receive nearly double the total retirement income they would have received before privatization.[108] At the same time, the new system has led to a substantial increase in national savings and economic growth.[109]

China: Changes in the World's Most Populous Nation

Any discussion of social security reform around the world should include recent changes in the world's most populous nation. China has one of the world's fastest aging populations. Yet, for much of China's rural population, government-provided retirement benefits have been rudimentary, often little more than emergency relief for "five guarantee" families. Meanwhile, until recently, urban workers relied on pensions from state-owned enterprises, financed by government budget grants. But employment at state-owned companies is no longer the centerpiece of the Chinese economy. At the same time, declining tax revenue and the increasing cost of an aging population have made it difficult for the government to continue financing its pension obligations.[110] As a result, China will soon be facing important decisions over the future of its retirement system.

China has correctly rejected a pay-as-you-go system as the sole basis of retirement security.[111] Despite China's robust rate of economic growth, demographic realities will eventually make a pay-as-you-go system unsustainable. Indeed, given the declining ratio of workers to retirees, maintaining a pay-as-you-go system could eventually require payroll taxes as high as 44 percent.[112]

The Third Plenary Session of the 14th Central Committee of the Communist Party of China called for a system "integrating social pooling with personal accounts" for urban workers.[113] Urban workers, in both state enterprises and private companies, including the self-employed, contribute a portion of their wages to a personal pension account. Their employer also contributes to the individual account as well as to a pooled social insurance system.[114] The individual accounts are invested in a single government-managed fund, similar to the system in Singapore, and are paid a uniform rate of interest determined by the People's Bank of China.[115]

Although rudimentary, this system provides China with a solid basis for future reforms. Several reforms are under consideration, including allowing a wider range of investment options, phasing out the portion of the payroll tax devoted to social pooling, and extending the pension plan to rural areas.[116] Thus, even this communist giant may soon have a privatized social security system.

Private Alternatives in the United States

Finally, even in the United States there are examples of alternatives to Social Security. Prior to 1983, county, municipal, and state governments could opt out of the traditional Social Security system and provide public employees with an alternative system. Today, more than one million state and local employees are participating in private alternatives to Social Security.[117]

For example, in 1981, employees of Galveston, Brazoria, and Matagorda counties in Texas voted overwhelmingly to leave the Social Security system. Today, county employees pay 9.73 percent of their income (split equally between the employee and the county) into a retirement fund and pay an additional 4.05 percent to purchase private life and disability insurance. Each county chooses a company to manage the retirement portion of the plan, with funds invested in annuities. The managing company, chosen by bid, must provide a guaranteed rate of return. [118] This guarantee may not be ideal; it protects workers in the event of a market downturn, but also limits the gains during a bull market.[119]

Although the total contribution rate is slightly higher than the Social Security payroll tax (13.78 percent vs. 12.4 percent), the benefits are far higher than those provided under Social Security. The rate of return on the retirement portion of the system has averaged 6.5 percent above inflation since the program began.[120] As a result, retired workers are receiving benefits three to six times higher than they would have under Social Security. A worker earning $20,000 per year can expect to receive about $775 per month in Social Security benefits at retirement, whereas a county employee in Galveston earning $20,000 per year can expect retirement benefits of $2,740 per month. A Galveston county employee earning $50,000 per year can expect retirement benefits of $6,843 per month, compared with just

$1,302 per month at retirement if that worker had remained in Social Security.[121] Survivors and disability benefits also significantly exceed the benefits offered by Social Security. The life insurance benefit is three times the worker's salary (with a minimum benefit of $50,000), and disability benefits equal 60 percent of the worker's salary.[122]

Other public employees participating in private alternatives to Social Security include state employees in Colorado, Maine, Nevada, and Ohio; teachers in California and Ohio; and city workers in Los Angeles.[123] While the details of the plans vary, all provide significantly higher rates of return than Social Security.[124]

Conclusion

All around the world, social security is changing. Demographics and the flawed structure of pay-as-you-go social security programs are forcing countries to reexamine how they provide for an aging society. Every country must adapt its pension policy to its own specific circumstances, but clearly the trend is away from pay-as-you-go systems toward systems based on individual accounts and private investments.

Chile has provided the model for such a program. Sixteen years after its inauguration, the Chilean system can be judged a clear success, providing higher retirement benefits while generating economic gains to the society at large. As a result, the Chilean model is being increasingly copied by other countries—from Latin America to Eastern Europe. The experience of Britain, Singapore, Australia, and even of some public employees in the United States provides overwhelming evidence that privatizing Social Security is both desirable and possible.

Unless the United States acts soon, we will be left behind.

8. Social Security Freedom for America

The case for private Social Security has now matured into a viable, mainstream political issue. The future financing problems of the system are just one small part of the broader case. The far bigger problem is that American workers are losing a fortune *today* by being deprived of the freedom to choose the far higher returns and benefits of a private, invested system. All workers, including the working poor, minorities, women, two-earner families, one-earner families, and others would receive much more from a private invested option. All workers would benefit as well from the improved economy that would result.

Moreover, as indicated in chapter 1, the American people know this, by overwhelming margins. The American people know that Social Security is headed for deep bankruptcy. They know they could now do far better through the private sector. Ultimately, what workers want today is the freedom to control their own money and to make their own decisions about these questions. On these grounds, there is now a huge reservoir of public opinion to support such reform, particularly among people under age 40.

Finally, these concepts no longer constitute high theory, as private social security is sweeping the globe, with both great economic and political success. American workers will not long tolerate being left out of the resulting freedom and prosperity that workers in other countries around the world are now enjoying.

But how would such a private social security option work in the United States? What specifically would it involve? What would be its main features?

Basic Issues of Reform

In developing a plan for privatization of Social Security, each of the issues discussed in this chapter must be considered and addressed.

Benefits for Current Retirees

Any privatization proposal should begin by assuring current retirees that they will not be affected by the reforms. The proposal should irrevocably commit and emphasize that *currently promised benefits for current retirees would not be reduced or changed.* The government has led current retirees to rely on its promises, and at this late stage in their lives, and after all the money they have paid into the system, it is too late for them to make alternative arrangements.

Relief from Payroll Taxes

Those who opt for the private system should expect that they would no longer pay taxes into Social Security, so that they can use the funds to pay into the private system instead. But two competing views are developing on this issue.

One view follows the Chilean reforms. Chilean workers who opted out of the government-run Social Security system were no longer required to pay anything into the old system. They were allowed to keep all their money and invest it in the private system instead.

The other view essentially follows the British model of reform. In that country, workers choosing the private, individual account option are relieved from paying only part of the payroll taxes to invest in the private system. They are still required to pay a substantial part of the taxes into the old system to help finance the continuing benefits of that system. Based on this approach, some suggest that we should relieve workers of just enough of the taxes to get them to choose the private option, with the rest of the taxes continuing to be paid into Social Security. This is advocated as a major way to finance the transition to the new system.

The Chilean approach is vastly preferable. That approach allows workers to receive the full benefits of the private system. As a result, it will maximize the proportion of workers who choose that system. Requiring those who opt for the private system to continue to pay substantial amounts into the old system is essentially a bias against the private option, or effectively a tax on it, which undermines the appeal of that option.

Moreover, the Chilean approach ensures that workers will benefit greatly from the private option, which ensures, in turn, that the reform will be a stable, lasting success. Workers will rightly feel cheated if privatization reform is promoted by telling workers they will receive far higher benefits through the private investments, if then the actual privatization plan allows them to receive only a fraction of those benefit gains.

Finally, there are better ways to finance the transition, which will be discussed below. We should not finance the transition costs through means that directly undermine the appeal of the private option itself.

However, as a compromise between the two views, it would not create a serious problem to require those who opt out to continue paying only a small amount into the old system for a temporary period. That would provide some funding for the continued benefit payments under the old system during the transition, without undermining the appeal of the private option in any significant way.

Required Payments for the Private System

A privatized retirement system would not require payments as large as the current Social Security system. That is because the investment returns of the private system provide so much more in benefits over the long run. As we saw in chapter 4, studies indicate that for today's young workers, the private system can provide several times the benefits promised by Social Security for the same amount of payments. Therefore, the private system can require substantially less in payments than Social Security, while still paying far more in benefits.

This would effectively provide a substantial tax cut for those who choose the private option. A reasonable approach might be to require the worker and employer to each pay 5 percent of salary, for a total of 10 percent, into the private system, instead of the Social Security payroll tax of 6.2 percent each on worker and employer, for a total of 12.4 percent. Workers would then pay 20 percent less into the private system, and could still expect over twice as much in benefits, and quite possibly much more.

However, to help provide funds for the transition to the new system, the effective tax cut from choosing the private option could be delayed for a few years, with the funds going into Social Security to help finance its outstanding benefit obligations. For example, workers and employers could each pay 5 percent into the private option as suggested, and continue paying 1.2 percent each into the old system for 10 years or so, keeping the total at the current 6.2 percent each in those years. As indicated, this represents a compromise between the views described in the previous section. Such a compromise involves a well-defined limit on how much will be paid into the old system—the amount of the eventual effective tax cut from choosing the private option. Committing these funds to an eventual effective tax cut also limits those continued payments to some temporary period.

Refund of Past Taxes Paid into the System

For those who have already been in the workforce for many years when the private option is adopted, a question arises as to what will happen to the taxes they and their employers have already paid into Social Security if they opt out. Will they get some sort of refund for these past taxes?

Social Security is now such a bad deal for younger workers that up until about age 40 or 45 they will probably still be better off in the private sector even without the refund of any past taxes, as long as they no longer have to pay into Social Security in the future and can use all those funds for their private investment accounts instead. The private individual account option in Great Britain in fact provides no refund for past taxes paid. The big advantage of this approach is that it substantially reduces costs during the transition. For example, if all workers under age 40 opt out of Social Security without any refund for past tax payments, once those workers reach retirement age and the older workers are paid off, there will be no further payments for benefit obligations under the old system.

On the other hand, this approach has no effect in reducing costs until those workers opting out do reach retirement. For example, if only workers under age 40 opt out, there will be no effect of reducing Social Security obligations until 25 to 30 years later when those workers reach retirement. Reducing costs so far in the future would significantly reduce long-term obligations, but would provide little help in managing the short-term transition to the new system. The big transition issue is really in the first 10 to 15 years. The projections in the next chapter in fact show that 25 to 30 years after the reform, the transition deficits have long been offset, and the new system is producing huge surpluses.

Moreover, this approach again creates an effective bias against the private option. Past Social Security taxes are counted for the worker who stays in Social Security, but not for the one who chooses the private option. One result of this bias is that the benefits from the privatization option will vary greatly based on age. The youngest workers will benefit the most, and those benefits will decline sharply by age, until reaching zero for those at age 40 to 45 and above. Many may see this sharp variance by age as unfair; one practical result is that no workers above age 40 to 45 will opt out, thus effectively eliminating any privatization option for them. In addition, even apart from any age difference, many may view the government paying nothing for past taxes as simply unfair.

The opposite approach would be to pay all workers who opt out a full refund for their past taxes. Ideally, this would involve calculating the proportion of lifetime taxes the workers and their employers already paid. The refund would then equal this same proportion of expected lifetime benefits, in present value terms. Workers could be given this refund in government bonds for private retirement accounts. The bonds would accrue interest over the years, reaching at retirement the present value of the proportion of retirement benefits the workers should receive based on the past taxes paid. These bonds could then be partially cashed in each year to help finance the workers' retirement benefits. The government would not have to make any actual expenditures for the past tax refunds until this point, cashing out some of the bonds each year in retirement. Workers would then receive each year a proportion of promised Social Security benefits equal to the proportion of lifetime Social Security taxes paid. This is basically how the Chilean reform worked.

This Chilean approach again seems superior. Workers under this approach receive the full benefits of the private system. Moreover, all workers have an equal incentive to opt out of the old system for their remaining working years regardless of age. Workers at every age would each receive the full net advantage of the private system over the public system for their remaining working years. Consequently, the great majority of workers of all ages would likely opt out, resulting in immediate maximum privatization, as in Chile. Workers are also likely to see this approach as the most fair. Since it will benefit workers of all ages, it will draw support from workers of all ages.

It should be noted that instead of a refund for past taxes, the same effect can be achieved simply by paying workers a proportion of benefits based on past taxes paid. The bonds paid into their personal accounts can then be dispensed with altogether. However, having actual bonds in their own accounts would probably appeal more to workers, as it would be a firm and concrete legal obligation, whereas the courts have ruled that there is no right to Social Security.

Finally, there is no need to put any maximum age limit on those who could opt out, which will only make some who might want to opt out feel excluded.

Government Regulation and Guarantee of Investments

Another key question is government regulation of the private retirement investments. Some would favor strictly limiting the investment options to those deemed safe, so that workers would not risk losing their retirement funds. But such regulation would also sharply limit the returns to the private investments and consequently sharply reduce the retirement benefits they could pay.

Ideally, the restrictions on the private retirement investments should be minimal, to maximize the reasonable returns and retirement income workers could expect to receive. The current regulations that apply to individual retirement accounts are a good model, prohibiting only the most high-risk investment alternatives. Workers must have broad freedom to invest in corporate stocks in the United States and abroad, as well as in corporate bonds and government securities. This would provide very high returns and benefits compared with Social Security, while maintaining reasonable risk that does not seriously threaten long-term retirement security.

A related question is whether the government should guarantee the private retirement investments. Such government guarantees are in fact counterproductive and unnecessary. By ensuring against losses, such a guarantee encourages investors and investment firms to take greater risks to get greater returns, knowing that the government will make up any losses. This will induce more losses than would occur otherwise, with taxpayers bearing the cost.

Moreover, investors are always free to choose government-guaranteed investments that already exist in the market, if that is what they want. These include U.S. government bonds, treasury bills, and certificates of deposit, among others. This provides a government guarantee without the drawbacks cited.

However, workers would have all the investment security they need simply investing in broad-based mutual funds that own shares in a wide range of companies. This avoids significant risk from the losses of any one company and yields investment returns that track the performance of the economy as a whole. No one, not even the government, is immune from general economic performance. With a calamitous and persistent economic downturn, for example, the government would not be able to get the tax funds to pay all Social Security benefits either. Market investment risk is discussed in more detail in chapter 4, pp. 89–93, and chapter 10, pp. 216–19.

Finally, all needed assurance could be provided in any event by a simple government safety net for the private system, without government guarantees of investments or overly strict regulation of investment options. That safety net would involve a guaranteed minimum benefit level. If the benefits payable by the private investments fell below that minimum level for some reason, the government would make up the difference. Such a minimum benefit is included in the Chilean system.

This minimum benefit would guarantee that no one's retirement income would fall below a basic level. Yet, with the likely performance of the private system described above, government expenditures for this minimum benefit are likely to be quite small. Indeed, the reform overall would probably reduce current government income assistance spending by far more than is spent on the minimum benefit, because workers would retire with far higher benefits through the private system and would need less government assistance than today. The public can consequently be assured that no one would be left destitute, while still allowing workers to enjoy the freedom and prosperity offered by the private system.

Chile also adopted a good system for avoiding fraud and abuse of unsophisticated investors. Workers there were required to choose an investment company to manage and invest their pension funds. Only companies that had applied for and received government approval could handle such investments. There are about 14 such companies in Chile, and workers can switch among them.

Such a system also avoids the problem of unsophisticated workers not knowing what private-sector investments to choose. As in Chile, workers would choose among the approved investment managers, and these experts would then choose the particular private investments. This system has worked quite well in Chile, even for the most unsophisticated workers. In Australia, by contrast, workers are able to manage their own, individual investment portfolios.

In the United States there would be hundreds and perhaps thousands of such approved companies. Workers might be allowed to choose self-direction of investments for any funds they contribute to their retirement accounts above the mandatory amounts. Over time, provisions could be adopted to allow more individual self-direction of the investments under appropriate circumstances. For example, workers could be allowed self-direction of accumulated funds in excess of the amount needed to pay benefits equal to the guaranteed minimum discussed.

Taxation of the Private Option

The private retirement accounts should receive the same tax treatment as IRAs. That removes the harsh, multiple taxation of savings and capital in the current tax code. Therefore, if the contributions to the private accounts are tax deductible, then the retirement income they pay should be included in taxable income. If the contributions to the private accounts are not deductible, then the retirement income they pay should not be taxed. Under this overall approach, the private accounts are taxed once, at the beginning or the end, which is fair and minimizes the negative impact of taxation on the private system.[1]

Today, the employer's share of the Social Security payroll tax is deductible. But the worker's share of the tax is not deductible. Making the worker's share deductible would produce a major revenue loss, which is probably intractable at the same time the government is financing the transition to a new private system. The employer's share, however, probably should remain deductible because it is a business expense, like wages. A revenue-neutral private option would, therefore, allow the employer's contributions to the private accounts to be tax deductible but not the worker's. This means, however, that half the retirement income paid by the accounts should be subject to tax and half not. At some point, however, this should be rationalized and simplified, providing for either deductibility of all contributions and taxation of the retirement benefits, or nondeductibility of the contributions and tax exemption for the retirement benefits.

Under this approach, while the returns paid directly to the accounts would not be taxed, substantial taxes would still be paid on the investments at the business level. Business enterprises would use the capital investments to generate on average the typical before-tax rate of return to capital. They would then pay their full taxes on that return and other tax assessments before paying the after-tax interest, dividends, and other returns to the investment accounts. This would still leave the investors with sufficient returns to receive the high benefits discussed earlier. At the same time, substantial new tax revenues would be generated for the government to help finance remaining Social Security benefits during the transition to the new system and, ultimately, to reduce and possibly eliminate the entire long-term federal debt.

Another question is whether workers should be allowed to voluntarily contribute more than the required amounts to their private accounts. In Chile, workers are required to include 10 percent of wages, but can voluntarily contribute an additional 10 percent, for a maximum of 20 percent. This encourages savings and allows workers to better control their retirement finances. They can contribute more, for example, if they want to retire earlier. Consequently, this would be a desirable component of reform.

A Social Security Option

Another issue is whether workers should remain free to stay in Social Security if they prefer. This would be valuable in the early stages of reform because it would assure skeptics that they will not be forced into the private system if they do not want it. Advocates of the private option would then be free to focus on the irresistibly appealing principle of allowing each worker the freedom to make his or her own choice. Over time, as the superiority of the private system is demonstrated, the public Social Security option will make little difference, as few if any workers will choose it.

Some economists have suggested that allowing workers a choice of opting out of Social Security creates a risk of adverse selection. The wealthy, it is suggested, being more sophisticated and experienced with private investment, would opt out of Social Security, leaving only the poor behind in the government-run system. With upper-income workers fleeing the system, Social Security's redistributive formula would be undermined and the system would not be able to pay promised benefits to low-wage workers.

However, this argument fails to recognize that low-income workers would also do far better under the privatized system than they do under Social Security. As a result, there simply is no basis for such an adverse selection problem. Simply because people are poor does not mean that they are unintelligent or unable to determine their own best interest. Given the higher returns and benefits even for low-wage workers discussed in chapters 4 and 5, we can expect workers at all income levels to choose the private option.[2]

Future Social Security Benefits

A continued Social Security option raises the question of what future Social Security benefits will be promised to those who might choose to remain in the current government system. On the one hand, workers should not be offered the current benefits that are well in excess of what Social Security will be able to pay in the future. If workers are going to have the option to stay in Social Security, they should be offered only the future benefits that the system can finance in a steady state. The World Bank, in its study advocating privatization, in fact recommended bringing future Social Security benefits in line with revenues as the first step of reform.[3] These future Social Security spending reductions would also help to finance the transition to the private system, as discussed further in the next chapter.

The future spending reductions raised by the national Entitlement Commission and proposed in legislation by Sen. Robert Kerrey (D-Neb.) would bring future benefits in balance with steady-state revenues.[4] These involve primarily delaying the retirement age to 70 and reducing the growth in benefits by indexing them to prices rather than to wages during working years. These changes would again have no effect on anyone already in retirement.

On the other hand, such adjustments to future Social Security benefits may not be worth the political difficulties. If, as seems likely, almost all workers would ultimately choose the private system, which is far superior even to currently promised Social Security benefits, then reducing such benefits will not make much difference over the long run.

Should Retirement Savings Be Mandatory?

If workers are allowed to participate in a private option to Social Security, they would still be required to contribute to one or the other system. However, there is good reason to question whether the United States should have *any* mandatory retirement program.

Essentially, the argument for mandating retirement savings is that people are simply too shortsighted to save on their own. Because people are myopic, choosing current consumption over preparing for the future, they will reach retirement without enough savings to take care of themselves in their old age. The rationale for mandatory savings is therefore a paternalistic one—people must be forced to participate in either Social Security or an alternative, private plan for their own good.

However, mandating savings is not cost free. First, any such program, by its very nature, seriously restricts the freedom of individuals to control their own lives. It forces people to live by the government's standards of what is best rather than their own. It prevents people from pursuing their own goals and objectives merely because other people believe those goals are mistaken. But, as Nobel laureate Milton Friedman notes,

> Those of us who believe in freedom must believe also in the freedom of individuals to make their own mistakes. If a man knowingly prefers to live for today, to use his resources for current enjoyment, deliberately choosing a penurious old age, by what right do we prevent him from doing so? We may argue with him, seek to persuade him that he is wrong, but are we entitled to use coercion to prevent him from doing what he chooses to do? Is there not always the possibility that he is right and we are wrong? Humility is the distinguishing characteristic of the believer in freedom, arrogance of the paternalist.[5]

The government paternalism inherent in any forced savings plan violates the foundational principle that your life belongs to you. Paternalism implies that your life belongs to the government, and therefore it has the right to make sure that you care for it properly, according to the government's standards. But, if your life truly belongs to you, then you have the right to live it any way you choose, according to your own desires and tastes. No one has the right to compel you to live your life according to their desires.

If the government has the right to force us to save, what other things can it force us to do for our own good? Might not the government justify on equally paternalistic grounds a law requiring everyone to take vitamins, eat yogurt, jog, read Shakespeare, and go to the opera? The point is, once paternalism is accepted as a valid function of government, there is no limit to the actions that it may take in controlling our lives and restricting liberty. The ultimate result, as Friedman writes is "dictatorship, benevolent and maybe majoritarian, but dictatorship nonetheless."[6]

Some suggest that forcing individuals to save for retirement is justified on the basis of "moral hazard." That is, because America is a compassionate nation that will not allow the improvident to starve or live in misery, we will feel compelled to provide those who do not save with costly welfare benefits. Therefore, if a person chooses not to save, it does not solely affect their own life, but potentially imposes costs and harm on others who will be forced to provide support later in such a person's life. Furthermore, the improvident may tend to rely on the prospect of welfare payments and become even more likely to fail to provide for themselves. Therefore, it is argued, the public has a right to force people to provide for their old age to prevent some people from imposing unwanted costs on the public.

There is some weight to the moral hazard argument, but not enough to justify mandated savings. First, it suggests the inevitability of government tax-funded welfare programs. However, welfare is far more properly handled by the civil society through private charity.[7] If tax funding, and therefore government coercion, is removed from the welfare equation, the moral hazard issue becomes far less compelling. In this case, the moral hazard argument would be claiming that, because some individuals, out of compassion, offer benefits to those in need, these individuals have the right to use force to compel potential recipients of their charity to behave in ways that will reduce their costs.

Moreover, some individuals might rationally choose to invest in a business or in their children's education, believing that this type of investment is a better route to a comfortable retirement. Who is to say that person is wrong? Certainly not the government. As John Stuart Mill put it, "Speaking generally, there is no one so fit to conduct any business, or to determine how or by whom it should be conducted, as those who are personally interested in it."[8]

Beyond philosophical grounds for opposing a mandatory Social Security system, there is no evidence that such a program is necessary. There are no empirical studies showing that, in the absence of Social Security, people really would fail to save for their own retirement. It is true that Americans do not save as much as we might hope they would. But, as we saw in chapter 6, Social Security itself is a cause of that. Americans fail to save because they believe that Social Security is saving for them. In the absence of evidence that Social Security is necessary, there can be little justification for such a massive intrusion into the personal decisions of Americans.

The American public seems to recognize this. In a 1994 Gallup Poll, 54 percent of Americans supported making Social Security voluntary.[9]

However, despite the preceding arguments, we recognize political reality. Any privatization proposal likely to pass Congress will replace Social Security with a mandatory savings program. Therefore, we have based our proposal that follows, and all the calculations we have made, on an assumption that the system will be mandatory. However, that does not mean that the plan we support will not increase liberty.

As Friedman noted, the current Social Security system restricts freedom in three ways: (1) by requiring that individuals make some provision for their old age and other contingencies; (2) by requiring that this provision be made by buying one single type of insurance—Social Security; and (3) by requiring that this one type of insurance be purchased from one monopoly "seller"—the federal government.[10]

A system of mandatory individually owned, privately invested accounts, as outlined hereafter, would not do anything about element 1, but would eliminate elements 2 and 3. Thus, the total amount of individual liberty would be increased.

A Proposal for Reform

Based on the preceding discussion, a specific and concrete proposal for privatization of Social Security is offered. Our proposal is not meant to be the last word on how to privatize Social Security. There are numerous variations of possible privatization plans that will work well. But the proposal outlined here is carefully designed to produce a highly appealing and successful private option, maximizing the freedom and prosperity of working people.

Move Social Security Completely Off Budget

The first step in any reform plan is to move Social Security completely off budget, including the program's taxes and expenditures, surpluses and deficits. This would save the current surpluses in Social Security to be used to help finance continuing benefits during the transition to the new system. It also means any net deficits within

167

Social Security created during the transition to the new system will be completely off budget. The transition will consequently not interfere with the effort to balance the rest of the budget.

As a result of this change, current Social Security surpluses would no longer be lent to the rest of the government and spent. The amount of the surpluses lost to the rest of the budget would be around $25 billion to $30 billion per year in 1998 dollars for the next 10 to 15 years, as only the surplus of Social Security tax revenues over expenditures would be lost. The interest on Social Security trust fund bonds, which is not an immediate expense in any event, should continue to cancel out in federal budgeting practice as both income to and an expenditure of the government.

If there is a general federal deficit, the government would have to make up for this lost revenue, preferably by cutting overall government spending. If there is a general federal surplus, then that surplus would be reduced by the amount of revenue left in the Social Security trust funds.

This change could be packaged as a highly popular initial proposal in itself. The public bitterly opposes using the trust funds surplus to fund the rest of the government. Ending that would draw strong bipartisan support among the general public. Moreover, the change would immediately force consideration of fundamental reform, and ultimately privatization, as something must be done with the surpluses if they are no longer spent on the rest of the budget.

The Private Option

The next reform step would be to allow workers the freedom to choose to provide for their retirement, survivors, and disability benefits through a private investment account, like an IRA, rather than through Social Security. For those who choose this option, the worker and employer would each pay 5 percentage points of the current 6.2 percent Social Security tax on each into the private account, up to the maximum taxable limit, calculated as is done today. Workers and their employers would have the freedom to contribute more if they choose on a tax-preferred basis, up to an overall limit, equal to 20 percent of wages. This option would apply to all workers without any age limit.

The remaining 1.2 percent of the current tax on each employer and employee (a total of 2.4 percent) would continue to be paid for

10 years after the worker opted out. These funds would be used to help finance continuing benefits to today's retirees during the reform's transition phase. After that, the worker and employer would each no longer have to pay this portion of the tax, meaning workers would receive a tax cut. As discussed previously, workers do not need to be required to pay as much into the private system as Social Security, because the benefits payable through the private system are so much higher than Social Security.

Some form of protection would be built into the system to protect spouses, particularly nonworking spouses, in the event of divorce. One option is to require earnings sharing between spouses. Half of a worker's contributions would be credited to the worker's account and half to the worker's spouse's account. Where both husband and wife work, funds from both workers are credited to each other's accounts. A second option would be to treat a worker's retirement account as community property in divorce cases.

Some questions have been raised about how contributions would be collected and dispersed. If individual workers are free to select any private management fund they wish, employers could be forced to send checks to dozens of different funds. This could be costly to administer, particularly for small employers. We believe that modern computer technology has minimized this problem. However, if, in practice, the burden proves too heavy, we believe it could be eased in one of two ways. Employers could be allowed to "nest" their payments, choosing a single investment fund for all their workers. Workers would be free to move their funds to a different manager, but at their own initiative. As a less attractive alternative, the government could establish a central clearinghouse to collect all payments and then electronically disperse the funds to the manager of the worker's choice. In any event, we do not believe that this technical detail should be a major impediment to privatizing Social Security.

Life and Disability Insurance

Part of the funds in the investment account would have to be used to purchase private life and disability insurance covering at least the same survivors (preretirement) and disability benefits as Social Security. Workers consequently would be covered for these contingencies through the private system as they would through Social Security. Since Social Security only pays preretirement survivors benefits to workers with children, workers without children would be free to forgo the life insurance and devote the funds to their retirement benefits. Similarly, workers would not have to buy disability insurance providing any greater benefits than Social Security would. In order to avoid any problems with adverse selection, all investors in a particular retirement fund would be treated as a common pool for underwriting purposes, with the insurance purchased by the investment management company, purchasing a group policy, rather than by individual workers.

Investment Regulations

The same rules, regulations, and restrictions would apply to the private retirement accounts as apply to IRAs today, except no withdrawals would be allowed until an individual has accumulated sufficient funds to purchase an annuity providing benefits equal to at least the minimum guaranteed benefit discussed below. Once a worker has accumulated that amount of money, funds in excess of that amount could be withdrawn, even preretirement. As a result, individuals would be free to choose their own retirement age.

As in Chile, workers would also be required to choose from among approved private investment companies to manage their account investments, with the freedom to change companies. Companies would apply to the federal government to obtain such approval, upon demonstrating their financial soundness, stability, and reliability. As discussed, this would make the system simple for inexperienced investors and avoid concern over fraud and abuse.

Workers could choose self-direction of their investments for any funds contributed above the 10 percent minimum. Eventually, the program could be revised to allow workers to self-direct all investments in the accounts above the amount necessary to purchase an annuity equal to the guaranteed minimum benefit. Self-direction would work just as it does for IRAs today. Workers would tell the investment company exactly what investments they want to purchase with those funds, again subject to the usual IRA regulations. (Of course, workers could just let the investment manager decide where to invest these funds, as well as the rest of the retirement account funds.)

Taxation of the Retirement Accounts

Employee contributions to the private accounts would not be tax deductible, just as employee Social Security taxes are not deductible.

Employer contributions would be deductible as a business expense like wages, just as employer Social Security taxes are deductible today. Investment returns to the accounts over the years would be tax exempt until withdrawal, just like the IRAs. In retirement, half the benefits would be included in taxable income and half not, unless the worker made voluntary, nondeductible, supplemental contributions. Then a formula would have to determine what proportion is taxable and what is not.

At a later time, this taxation policy would be reformed to provide for either deductibility of all contributions and taxation of the retirement benefits, or nondeductibility of the contributions and tax exemption for the retirement benefits.

Retirement Benefits

This would be a "defined contribution" plan. Benefits at retirement would equal what the individual has paid in over his working lifetime plus the return on investment that those funds have earned. The worker could use the accumulated funds to purchase an annuity, paying promised benefits for the rest of the worker's life. Annuities could also be structured to provide benefits not just over the worker's life, but also over the spouse's life. Or the worker could make regular, periodic withdrawals. Regulations would limit such withdrawals so the retiree could not use up all the funds early and then be left without retirement support. If the worker chooses this option and dies before all the funds in the account are used up, any remaining money would become part of the estate and would be inherited by the heirs. The worker could also combine the two options, buying an annuity with some of the funds and making limited periodic withdrawals with the rest.

Some have argued that adverse selection makes it difficult to purchase actuarially fair annuities. There is some evidence that this may be true in the current annuity market and might cause difficulties if only a small number of individuals chose the annuity option upon retirement. This has led some supporters of privatization to advocate mandatory annuitization. However, evidence from Chile and common sense suggest that the vast majority of workers will, in fact, choose an annuity rather than risk outliving their benefits. Therefore the actuarial characteristics of annuity purchasers will be substantially the same as the population as a whole, meaning that annuity prices will begin to more closely approach actuarial fairness.[11]

Moreover, there may even be benefits to allowing annuities to reflect differences in life expectancies. For example, as discussed in chapter 5, annuities could be structured in such a way as to allow disadvantaged groups such as African Americans to receive higher benefits to compensate for their lower life expectancies.

Finally, it is important to understand that any cost associated with difficulties in pricing annuities is likely to be extremely small compared with the benefits offered by privatization.

Workers in the private system could retire at any age after 59-and-a-half. They could even retire earlier if their accumulated retirement funds were sufficient to satisfy a specified standard of benefits. This is one reason why workers may want to make additional, voluntary contributions during their working years. Workers could also continue to work after they begin to collect their benefits without any penalty or earnings test.

Recognition Bonds

For workers who choose the private option, the government would pay into their accounts recognition bonds to compensate them for past taxes paid into the Social Security system. The bonds would be credited with interest over the years. The amount of the bonds would be set so that with interest they would pay a proportion of future benefits equal to the proportion of lifetime Social Security taxes paid. However, those benefits would be calculated against the benefits Social Security could pay under a financially sound system and thus would likely be lower than currently promised benefits. At retirement, workers could turn in the bonds to the government over time for cash to finance their benefits, along with the benefits payable from the private savings and investment accounts accumulated after the worker shifted to the private system. This system would give all workers a proportionally equal incentive to opt out for their remaining working years.

Minimum Benefits

The government would guarantee all workers a minimum benefit as in Chile. Given the strong likelihood that the private benefits would be so much higher than Social Security benefits, this minimum benefit could be set at a generous level, such as the average benefit paid by Social Security. This would create great confidence in the reform for lower-income workers, who would be guaranteed higher benefits than promised by Social Security today.

This minimum benefit would be financed out of general revenues, supplementing private benefits to the extent necessary to reach the minimum benefit level. As discussed above, this would ensure that no one would fall below a basic benefit level, with probably no significant cost to the government.

Right to Stay in Social Security

Workers would have the complete freedom to choose to stay in the public Social Security system if they prefer.[12]

Social Security Benefits

There would be no benefit reductions for anyone currently receiving Social Security. Current law already provides that starting in the year 2000 the retirement age will be delayed two months per year until the retirement age reaches 66 in 2005. The reform proposed here would continue to delay the retirement age two months per year after that until it reaches age 70. Early retirement would still be available at age 62, with a full actuarial reduction in benefits. In addition, the indexing of future Social Security benefits during working years would be changed from wage-indexing to price-indexing. As discussed above, these benefit changes are justified to bring the system's expenditures into line with steady-state, long-run revenues.

Conclusion

We believe that the system we described is a practical and workable plan to ensure that today's young workers will have a secure and dignified retirement. It is a system that will enhance individual liberty, provide higher retirement benefits, increase economic growth, and lead to greater social equity.

The only remaining question is how do we get there from here? That is, how do we make the transition to this new system? The next chapter will discuss this important issue in depth.

9. Financing the Transition

One crucial question remains. If we adopt the reform plan in the last chapter, or any privatization reform plan, how do we finance the transition to the new system?

The problem arises from Social Security's pay-as-you-go method of operation. Almost all of the payroll tax revenues from today's workers are immediately paid out to finance the benefits to today's retirees. If we allow workers to save and invest those payroll tax funds in the private sector, where will we get the money to finance the program's continuing benefits to today's retirees? In a way, it is analogous to trying to stop a chain letter without anyone at the top of the chain being hurt.

Critics of privatization rely heavily on this transitional financing question. They suggest that addressing this question will deeply undermine many of the most important benefits of the reform we have advanced. In particular, critics argue that financing the transition will eliminate any higher returns and benefits from the private system for the first generation of workers. Critics further suggest that financing the transition may well eliminate any net saving increase from privatization and most of the resulting general economic benefits.

These concerns are greatly exaggerated. Governments around the world are successfully addressing this question and greatly benefiting their workers and their economies in the process.

In this chapter, we will explain exactly how the transition can be financed without significantly detracting from the overall benefits of the reform. The central reason why this transition is workable is this—most of the necessary transition financing can be paid out of the benefits resulting from the reform.

Paying for Two Retirements?

A rallying cry for those opposed to privatization has been that any such reform would effectively require the first working generation at the time of transition to pay for two retirements. They would have to save and invest in the private system to finance their own retirement. Yet they would still have to pay for the retirement of the elderly generation, by continuing to pay for their outstanding benefits through Social Security.

Yet "paying for two retirements" is a simplistic mischaracterization of what is going on in a privatization reform plan. Indeed, we will show in this chapter that under the reform plan we have proposed, the first working generation will not in fact pay for two retirements.

Privatization of Social Security involves a shift from the current pay-as-you-go system, where funds are immediately paid out in current benefits rather than saved for the future, to a fully funded system, where today's payments are saved to finance the future benefits of today's workers. The cost of transition is simply the cost of making the increased saving for the fully funded system. The cost of increased saving is the same as the cost of any saving increase—forgone current consumption equal to the amount of the saving increase. That cost is worthwhile because of the investment returns earned by the saving increase, adding to income and economic growth.

In other words, paying the benefits owed to current retirees will occur under both the current system and privatization. So those payments are not a net cost of privatization. All that privatization adds is increasing saving to fully fund the system, which is worthwhile because of the returns on that saving.

This analysis can be demonstrated by a simple example. Assume a Social Security system in the year of reform with $100 billion in revenues and $100 billion in benefit expenditures. Suppose the workers invested the $100 billion in a private system instead.

Now suppose for illustrative purposes that the government financed the continuing $100 billion per year in benefits by issuing $100 billion in new government bonds each year (a course that we do not favor). Then, all else being equal, saving would increase each year by $100 billion due to the investment in the private retirement accounts, but issuing the new government bonds would decrease saving by $100 billion each year, by taking saving out of the private sector to pay Social Security benefits. Assume also that the returns on the private accounts each year were taxed sufficiently to pay the interest on the new government bonds. No increased saving would result under such reform. And workers would not be paying for two retirements. They would not be paying anything more than under the current system.

Now suppose that instead of issuing $100 billion in new bonds each year to pay the continuing Social Security benefits, the government cut spending on other programs by $100 billion and used those funds for Social Security benefits. All else being equal, the result would be $100 billion in increased saving each year, through the private retirement system, with no offsetting reduction by the government. The $100 billion in reduced government spending involves forgone present consumption equal to the $100 billion saving increase.

As a result, what workers are paying for in the transition to the new system is simply the cost of the increased saving involved in fully funding the system. That is the same as the cost of any other saving increase—forgone present consumption equal to the amount of the saving increase.

Therefore, it is wrong to speak of "transition costs" involved in the privatization of Social Security. For such reform does not involve "cost" in the true sense of that word, meaning a sacrifice or consumption of resources. The funds paid into the private system are not lost; they are saved for the future and are put to productive use in the meantime, earning a return that further helps to pay for future benefits. Therefore, what is involved in privatization of Social Security is an issue of transition financing, not transition "costs." It is a question of how to finance the saving for the fully funded system, not paying a cost that involves a permanent loss.

Another way to illustrate this argument is to look at a balance sheet. Social Security has unfunded liabilities of more than $9 trillion.[1] Privatization of Social Security does not increase those liabilities, adding new costs. Rather, it reduces and ultimately eliminates those liabilities. It does so by generating new assets through the saving and investment of the private system that offset and eventually pay off the liabilities. Indeed, those assets and the returns they generate are a less costly way to pay off those liabilities. Consequently, privatization does not increase costs, it reduces them.[2]

Sources of Transition Financing

There are numerous possible sources of transition financing to pay off outstanding benefit obligations under the current Social

Security system, while workers switch to the new private system. Each of these is discussed in the following.

Replaced Social Security Benefits

As workers opt for the private system, they will receive fewer benefits from the old Social Security system in the future as a result, with those benefits more than replaced by the new private system. This effect alone would eliminate the transition financing gap in the long run. But it will start off relatively slowly. In the first few years, new retirees who opt out for their last few working years will receive a little less in benefits from the old public system as a result. This benefit saving will grow over time until about 65 years down the road, at the death of the last worker who opted for the private system and was entitled to some Social Security benefits for his past tax payments into that system. All outstanding Social Security benefit obligations for today's retirees and today's workers already in the system who opt for the private system will then have been paid off, ending the transition financing.[3]

Another effect will reduce benefit costs much more in the early years. Starting in the very first year, the disability and preretirement survivors benefits for everyone who opts out and becomes eligible the first year would be paid through the private disability and life insurance rather than Social Security. This adds up to significant saving right away.

Continuing Payroll Taxes

Under the reform proposal discussed in the last chapter, workers and employees will each pay 5 percent of wages into the retirement accounts, instead of the current 6.2 percent payroll tax paid by each. But workers and employers will continue to pay an additional 1.2 percent each in payroll taxes for a temporary 10-year period to help finance the transition. This will generate significant revenue during that time to close the transition financing gap.

Social Security Surpluses

For the next 10 years or so, Social Security is projected under intermediate assumptions to produce a surplus of taxes over expenditures of $25 billion to $30 billion per year in 1998 dollars, declining to 0 by 2012. (The surpluses do not include interest on trust fund bonds, which is not revenue to the government because it is paid by the government itself.) The surpluses create a cushion that will partially offset the shortfall of revenue to pay Social Security benefits due to the private option. The net shortfall of revenue to pay the benefits each year will be reduced by the amount of the Social Security surplus for the year, which can be used to pay the benefits.

If there is a total unified budget surplus for the year at least equal to the Social Security surplus, then using the Social Security surplus to help finance the privatization transition will just reduce the total budget surplus by the amount of the Social Security surplus. If there is a total deficit or lower surplus than the Social Security surplus, using the Social Security surplus for the transition means the government will not be able to use that surplus to help finance its other spending, as it has in the past. The government would then have to cut its other spending to make up for the unavailability of Social Security funds, or find some other way to finance that spending.

However, these spending cuts or other means of general government financing are not a cost of the privatization plan. Using the surpluses to pay for continuing Social Security benefits during the transition is simply a matter of using these funds to pay such benefits now rather than later, after lending them to the government for current spending and then claiming them back with interest after Social Security goes into deficit. This only involves the elimination of cover for higher government spending on other programs, which is not a cost of Social Security privatization. Preferably, legislation to eliminate the use of Social Security surpluses for other government spending would be adopted concomitantly with any Social Security privatization plan, along with any reduction of other government spending that may be necessary as a result.

Unified Budget Surpluses

If during the years after the privatization reform is adopted there are unified budget surpluses beyond the level of Social Security surpluses, those general surpluses would be available to help pay continuing Social Security benefits as well.

However, suppose the federal government would otherwise maintain those general surpluses and use them to pay down the national debt. A general budget surplus reducing the national debt would increase saving, as federal debt is retired and the funds are freed for private-sector investment. Using the surplus instead to pay Social

179

Security benefits during a privatization transition would eliminate this increased saving, and consequently reduce national saving from the level that would otherwise prevail. This would offset to that degree any saving increase resulting from the privatization reform.

Suppose, however, that absent the privatization reform the federal government would not maintain the total federal surpluses, but use it for increased spending or tax cuts. Using the surplus for Social Security benefits instead would then have no effect on national saving. Consequently, there would be no reduction in any saving increase resulting from privatization. Given federal budget history and the political pressures in Washington, this latter alternative seems far more likely. So using total federal budget surpluses to help finance the transition is unlikely to have any negative, offsetting effect on saving.

Revenue Feedback

Perhaps the most powerful source of transition financing would be the generation of substantial new tax revenue for the government as a result of the new saving and investment in the private system. This new saving will generate the full, before-tax rate of return to capital. As discussed in chapter 4, businesses will pay substantial taxes on these returns before they pay the interest, dividends, or other returns to the tax-exempt private retirement accounts.

Feldstein estimates that the full, real, before-tax return to capital is 9.3 percent.[4] Of that, he estimates that 3.9 percent would go to the government in taxes paid at the business level before remaining returns are paid to the retirement investment accounts. With the private retirement account saving growing to huge amounts relatively rapidly, this would result in the generation of huge amounts of new tax revenue to help with transition financing.

It should be noted that the private system can and should be structured in any event so that this portion of the full, before-tax return to capital, or some other reasonable portion, is taxed away to help finance the transition. Those full, before-tax returns are so high that even after this taxation, the private benefits would still be significantly higher than those paid by Social Security. Indeed, we assumed in chapter 4 that the private retirement investments would only earn real returns of 4 to 6 percent. This effectively assumes substantial taxation at the business level of the full, real, before-tax return of 9.3 percent, of the magnitude estimated by Feldstein. So even with such taxation of the full, before-tax returns, workers will still be able to get the benefits through the private system discussed in chapter 4.

Moreover, the full, before-tax return to capital does not go completely untaxed in any other saving vehicle. Consequently, this seems to be the least painful way to help finance the transition. It simply follows a basic principle of successful privatization strategies in general—using some of the benefits of the reform to offset any costs.

Sale of New Government Bonds

Another source of funding for the transition would be to give the Social Security Administration authority to sell new government bonds to the public to raise the money. This is in fact how Nobel prize-winners Milton Friedman and James Buchanan have advocated financing the transition.[5] They have correctly argued that these bonds would not involve new government debt, but only explicit recognition of the implicit debt the government already owes through the unfunded liabilities of Social Security. Financing a large proportion of benefit obligations each year through such bonds would be feasible because of the huge amounts of saving that would be generated through the private retirement accounts. The World Bank supported financing the transition mostly through this method as well in its 1994 report on the subject.[6] Chile also financed about half its transition in this way. Bonds effectively allow the transition to be financed over several generations, as the bonds are paid off over a more extended period instead of being imposed all on the first generation.

Since Social Security would be off budget under the reform plan, these bonds would be off budget as well. That is sound because the bonds are again not a new debt but in fact explicit recognition of a debt already incurred. As a result, they are not a part of each year's budget on a current basis. The transition is a temporary, one-time event, not a permanent, recurring program.

To the extent the transition is financed by issuing new bonds, however, the saving generated by the reform would be reduced, until the bonds are ultimately paid off. The saving increase resulting from contributions to the private retirement accounts each year would be offset by the government borrowing private saving

181

through the bonds. As a result, the increased income generated by the reform, and the revenue feedback helping to finance the transition, would not be as great. For these reasons, it would be wise to limit such bond financing as much as possible.

The projections that follow in fact show that it is possible to finance the transition under the proposed reform plan by issuing new bonds for only the first 12 years or so of the reform, totaling only about $500 billion in today's dollars. This would offset only a small fraction of the saving produced by the reform. Moreover, after another 10 years the reform would produce sufficient surpluses to pay off and retire these newly issued bonds, thus restoring the saving lost by issuing the bonds in the first place.

Sale of Social Security Trust Fund Bonds

At the end of 1998, the Social Security trust funds will hold about $700 billion in government bonds. Instead of eventually turning these bonds in to the government to raise money from the taxpayers to pay continuing benefits, the law can be changed to allow these bonds to be sold directly to the public, over time, to help finance the transition shortfall under a privatization plan.[7] The proceeds of these sales would be used to pay continuing Social Security benefits during the transition phase. The trust fund bonds were intended to be eventually redeemed precisely to fund Social Security benefits in any event.

These Social Security bonds could be sold to the public instead of issuing new government bonds. The trust funds currently hold enough in bonds to cover the portion of the transition deficits under the projections we give that would otherwise be covered by issuing new government bonds. Consequently, the transition could be financed without issuing any new government bonds at all, by relying instead on the sale of existing trust fund bonds.

Selling the Social Security trust fund bonds would have the same economic effect as described for selling new government bonds. But it may be easier for people to see that selling the trust fund bonds does not involve creation of a new debt, but just recognition of a debt that already exists and will inevitably become due. Selling the trust fund bonds may also be easier under Congress's budget rules.[8]

Nevertheless, opponents of any privatization reform might caricature the sale of Social Security trust fund bonds as raiding the program's trust funds to finance the privatization reform, leaving Social

Security without any trust funds. These opponents could be countered by noting that the bonds would be sold only to finance Social Security benefits as they were intended, and the bonds are soon going to be liquidated for this purpose anyway. Moreover, the Social Security trust funds are not real trust funds but just debt that does not help finance future benefits. In addition, with most workers opting for the private system, Social Security would not need any trust funds anyway. But it may be easier politically to avoid this whole controversy and just rely on the sale of new government bonds, leaving the existing Social Security trust funds intact.

Sale of Government Assets

The government could also raise funds for the transition by selling government assets. Over the past decade governments worldwide have sold off more than $500 billion in assets and enterprises, not counting the billions worth of state assets simply given to citizens of former communist countries via privatization voucher programs. The United States has only begun to tap the potential of a serious program to divest federal enterprises and assets.[9]

Table 9.1 lists a small portion of the federal assets available for sale, with a total value of nearly $375 billion. It is also important to note that this list does not include the most environmentally and culturally sensitive lands, parks, and monuments.

Selling government assets has the same immediate economic effect as selling government bonds. Savings are drawn out of the private sector to pay for the asset, and then immediately spent on Social Security benefits. So the effect of the reform in increasing saving would be offset to the extent the transition was financed by the sale of government assets.

But selling government assets has another, beneficial economic effect that selling bonds does not. The assets may be far more productive in the private sector, producing efficiency gains that would increase income and offset the transition financing burden as a result. The assets would also be worth far more, effectively increasing saving. This effect may be quite large, particularly for some government assets like land, which the government may be keeping from productive use.

Politically, it would be easier to see that selling government assets is not creating new debt, as opposed to selling new government

Table 9.1
SALABLE FEDERAL ASSETS

Asset	Potential Sales Revenue ($ Billions)
Tennessee Valley Authority	8.5
Five power marketing administrations	14.0
Dams[a]	10.0
Energy facilities[b]	10.0
U.S. Postal Service	8.1
Air traffic control	3.5
Global Positioning System	7.0
U.S. Enrichment Corporation	1.0
National Weather Service	2.5
U.S. Geological Survey	0.5
Four NASA aeronautics labs	5.6
USDA Agricultural Research Centers	4.0
Department of Energy labs	6.1
Corporation for Public Broadcasting	0.3
Commodity lands (Forest Service, BLM)	160.0
Loan portfolio	108.0
Naval Petroleum Reserve	1.6
Defense stockpile	1.0
Strategic Petroleum Reserve	13.0
Government buildings and land	10.0
TOTAL	374.7 +

[a]Under the Army Corps of Engineers and the Bureau of Reclamation.
[b]Under the General Services Administration, Veterans Administration, and Department of Defense.

bonds. But in most cases, some special interest constituency would oppose the sale of a particular government asset, creating new political controversy.

Elimination of Social Security Deficits

Under intermediate projections, in 2013 Social Security will start running deficits of expenditures over tax revenues, which will grow larger and larger indefinitely into the future. At that point, Social Security will start cashing in trust fund bonds to cover these deficits. The government will then have to come up with the funds to redeem the bonds for Social Security to pay its promised benefits.

Most likely, the government will just issue new bonds to the public to raise the money to cover the Social Security bonds, effectively running a bigger total federal deficit. Issuing these new government bonds will, of course, reduce national saving, as funds are borrowed from the private saving pool and then spent. Indeed, under the intermediate projections Social Security will run sufficient deficits to completely draw down and liquidate the trust fund bonds by 2032. During that time, Social Security will turn in bonds equaling more than $2.9 trillion in today's 1998 dollars, to obtain the cash to pay outstanding benefits. If the government just issues new bonds to the public to obtain the funds to redeem these Social Security bonds, then national saving over this period will be reduced by more than $2.9 trillion.

However, the privatization reform would eliminate the projected Social Security deficits, as workers would be providing for their benefits through the fully funded private system. The projections given in this chapter in fact show a surplus resulting from the reform starting in 2008, even while paying outstanding Social Security benefits. As a result, the massive Social Security trust fund draw-down starting in 2013, and the need to issue new government bonds to finance it, would be avoided. Consequently, saving over this period would be over $2.9 trillion higher than otherwise. This higher saving would produce a still higher revenue feedback from the reform due to the taxation of the full, before-tax tax returns to that saving, as discussed. Those additional revenues could then help cover any remaining transition financing needs.

The government could cover the Social Security deficits by raising taxes or cutting other government spending, rather than issuing new government bonds. This would not have the negative effect on saving we discussed. But in this case, by avoiding these deficits altogether, the privatization reform would free up these resources that would otherwise go to covering the deficits. These freed-up resources could then be used to help finance the transition to the new private system instead.

However, none of these resources—either higher-feedback revenue than otherwise from avoiding the issuance of new government bonds, or freed-up resources from avoiding the need to cover projected Social Security deficits—was counted in the projections of the transition financing. That is because these additional resources

would primarily arise after the net transition deficits had been eliminated due to the other transition financing sources. Nevertheless,
these further resources should be counted as further benefits of the
reform, primarily adding to the net financing surplus the reform
would ultimately produce.

Reduced Social Security Benefit Growth

While Social Security benefits for those retired today would remain
unchanged, the growth in benefits for future retirees could be
reduced, through the proposals discussed in the last chapter or
possibly through other proposals. This would help to reduce the
transition financing gap because the amounts that would have to
be paid in recognition bonds to those who opt out would be substantially less than otherwise, as the Social Security benefits they must
compensate for would be substantially less.

Waiver of Past Tax Payments

As previously discussed, recognition bonds for past tax payments
could be waived for all workers under age 30 or some other cut-off
age. This would reduce transition costs only when workers under
the cut-off age at the time of the reform start to retire (35 to 40 years
from now for workers under age 30 today). As the projections below
show, however, by that time the transition deficits would already
have been long offset by the other transition financing sources discussed, and the reform would be producing large net surpluses.
Consequently, this element was not included in our reform plan
and, therefore, was not counted in the transition projections below.

Enhanced Economic Growth

The privatization reform would increase economic growth in all
the ways discussed in chapter 6. This would produce higher tax
revenues in several ways. We have already discussed the additional
revenues that would result from taxation of the returns on the
increased saving produced by the reform. But the reform would
also produce higher wages and more jobs that would translate into
more productive output and income, which would be taxed and
produce still more revenue. All this increased economic growth and
output should have a multiplier effect, increasing economic growth
still more as the increased income is either saved or spent. This

further growth should produce still more new revenues. All this new revenue would also help to finance the transition.

Reductions in Other Government Spending

Any remaining funds needed to finance the transition should be obtained by cutting other government spending. This would avoid the economically harmful effects of higher taxes or further government borrowing. Indeed, much of this government spending is wasteful and even counterproductive, and reducing it would not be any sacrifice, but a further net gain to society.

Table 9.2 lists potential annual spending reductions of more than $142 billion, far more than would be required to fund the transition plan outlined below. Moreover, this list does not include saving that could be found by reforming major entitlement programs such as Medicare and Medicaid. Nor does it include potential reductions in our bloated defense budget. Cato Institute scholars, for example, have suggested that defense spending could be reduced by $89 billion to $97 billion per year without harming national security.[10]

Individuals may disagree with any of the specific cuts recommended, but it should be possible to put together a package of cuts that provide more than enough revenue to finance the transition.

Some have suggested that the demonstrated inability of Congress to cut federal spending means that substantial spending cuts should not be considered for the transition. However, we believe that considering spending cuts in the context of Social Security reform significantly changes the political equation. Reducing spending for an abstract purpose such as "smaller government" or "reducing the deficit" may be politically problematic. But reducing spending to guarantee Social Security benefits to current recipients should be far more attractive.

In addition, putting the spending cuts up against the potential gains from privatization should frame the debate quite differently. As we have seen, a privatized Social Security system can provide retirement benefits three to five times higher than Social Security. As Stephen Entin of the Institute for Research on the Economics of Taxation has noted, discussing spending cuts in the context of Social Security privatization means people will be forced to ask, "Is the Economic Research Service really doing anything worth more than two-thirds of my potential retirement income?"

Table 9.2
POTENTIAL NONDEFENSE SPENDING REDUCTIONS

Program	Amount ($ Millions)
Department of Agriculture	
Economic Research Service	50
National Agricultural Statistics Service	80
Agricultural Research Service	800
Cooperative State Research, Education and Extension Service	900
Animal and Plant Health Inspection Service	400
Food Safety and Inspection Service	600
Grain Inspection, Packers and Stockyard Administration	20
Agricultural Marketing Service	500
Conservation Reserve Program	1,800
Federal Crop Insurance Corporation	2,000
Agricultural commodity price supports and subsidies	10,000
Natural Resources Conservation Service	1,100
Rural Housing and Community Development Service	1,700
Rural Business and Cooperative Development Service	100
Rural Electrification Administration subsidies	1,000
Foreign Agricultural Service	800
Market Access Program	100
Food Stamp Program	
Children's nutrition subsidies for the nonpoor	1,000
Special Supplemental Food Program for Women, Infants, and Children	3,700
Commodity Credit Corporation export credit	200
Food donations programs for selected groups	200
Export Enhancement Program	400
P.L. 480	300
USDA land acquisition programs	100
Forest Service, renewable resource management	600
Forest Service, road and trail construction	100
Forest Service, forest and rangeland research	200
Forest Service, state and private forestry	150

Program	Amount ($ Millions)
Department of Commerce	
Economic Development Administration	400
Economic and Statistical Analysis	50
International Trade Administration	200
Export Administration	40
Minority Business Development Agency	40
National Ocean Service	200
National Marine Fisheries Service	350
Oceanic and Atmospheric Research	200
Fishery products research, development, and promotion	20
Advanced Technology Program	250
Manufacturing Extension Partnership	100
National Institute of Standards and Technology	300
National Telecommunications and Information Administration	90
Department of Education	
Goals 2000	500
School-to-Work Programs	200
Elementary and Secondary Education Grants	7,100
Impact Aid	800
School Improvement Programs	1,200
Safe and Drug-Free Schools Act	400
Office of Vocational and Adult Education	1,500
Office of Bilingual Education	150
College Work-Study Grants	600
Office of Educational Research and Improvement	500
Direct Student Loan Program	500
Office for Civil Rights	60
Department of Energy	
General Science and Research activities	1,000
Solar and Renewable Energy, research and development	300
Nuclear Fission, research and development	200
Magnetic Fusion, research and development	300
Energy Supply, research and development	3,400
Uranium Supply and Enrichment activities	50

(continued)

Table 9.2
POTENTIAL NONDEFENSE SPENDING REDUCTIONS, *(continued)*

Program	Amount ($ Millions)
Fossil Energy, research and development	400
Naval Petroleum and Oil Shale Reserves	200
Energy conservation programs	400
Strategic Petroleum Reserve	300
Energy Information Administration	70
Economic Regulatory Administration	20
Clean Coal Technology	160
Power Marketing Administration subsidies	200
Departmental administration	300
Department of Health and Human Services	
National Professions Curriculum Assistance	300
National Health Services Corps	100
Maternal and Child Health Block Grants	700
Healthy Start	100
Title X Family Planning Program	200
Indian Health Service	1,900
Substance Abuse Block Grant	1,200
Mental Health Block Grant	300
State Day-Care programs	1,300
State Welfare administrative costs	1,700
State Child Support administrative costs	1,900
Low-Income Home Energy assistance	1,200
Refugee Assistance programs	400
Family Preservation and Support grants	100
Payments to states for Job Training (JOBS)	1,000
Child Care and Development Block Grants	900
Social Services Block Grant	3,200
Head Start	3,300
Child Welfare Services	300
Community Services Block Grants	400
Child Abuse Grants to States	20
NIH overhead cost reimbursements	100
Department of Housing and Urban Development	
Public Housing Program	4,200
College Housing Grants	20

Program	Amount ($ Millions)
Community Development Grants	5,100
HOME Investment Partnerships Program	1,200
Community Planning and Development	500
Low-Income Housing Assistance	10,000
Rental Housing Assistance	600
Fair Housing Activities	20
Federal Housing Administration	300

Department of the Interior

Bureau of Indian Affairs	1,700
Bureau of Reclamation water projects	500
U.S. Geological Survey	600
Helium fund and reserves	20
Migratory Bird Conservation	40
North American Wetlands Conservation	10
Cooperative Endangered Species Conservation	30
National Wildlife Refuge Fund	20
Sport Fish Restoration Fund	200
National Park System, fee collection support	10
Land Acquisition Program	150

Department of Justice

Community Oriented Policing Services	1,800
Violence Against Women Act	120
Byrne Law Enforcement Grants	140
Correctional Facilities Grants	600
Substance Abuse Treatment for State Prisoners	20
State and Local Law Enforcement Assistance	100
Weed and Seed Program	20
Antitrust Division	20
Drug Enforcement Administration	700
Interagency Crime and Drug Enforcement Task Force	200

Department of Labor

The Job Training Partnership Act	1,000
Adult Training Grants	800
Dislocated Worker Assistance	900
Youth Training Grants	100
Summer Youth Employment and Training Program	600

(continued)

Table 9.2
POTENTIAL NONDEFENSE SPENDING REDUCTIONS, (continued)

Program	Amount ($ Millions)
School-to-Work Programs	100
Job Corps	1,100
Migrant and Seasonal Worker Training	60
Community Service Employment for Older Americans	400
Trade Adjustment Assistance	300
Employment Standards Administration	200
Department of State	
United Nations organizations	600
Inter-American organizations	100
North Atlantic Treaty Organization	40
Organization for Economic Cooperation and Development	60
United Nations peacekeeping activities	200
International Fisheries Commissions	20
Migration and Refugee Assistance	700
Foreign aid to Egypt	2,000
Foreign aid to Israel	3,000
Narcotics control assistance to foreign countries	100
Agency for International Development	2,900
Department of Transportation	
Motor Carrier Safety Grants	60
Highway Traffic Safety Grants	200
Federal Railroad Administration	20
Amtrak subsidies	600
Federal Transit Administration	4,500
Grants-in-Aid for Airports	1,500
Payments to air carriers program	20
Maritime Administration	500
Cargo Preference Program	500
Transportation Systems Center	200
Partnership for a New Generation of Vehicles	200
Department of the Treasury	
Presidential Election Campaign Fund	100

Program	Amount ($ Millions)
Customs Service, Air and Marine Interdiction Program	60
Interagency Crime and Drug Enforcement Task Force	60

Department of Veterans Affairs

VA benefits for non-services-related illnesses	200
VA health care facilities construction	600

Other Agencies and Activities

African Development Foundation	20
Appalachian Regional Commission	200
Consumer Product Safety Commission	40
Corporation for National and Community Service	600
Corporation for Public Broadcasting	300
Davis-Bacon Act	1,000
Equal Employment Opportunity Commission	200
EPA Wastewater Treatment Subsidies	2,400
EPA Superfund	1,400
EPA Environmental Technology Initiative	60
EPA Science to Achieve Results grants	80
Export-Import Bank	500
Federal Labor Relations Board	20
Federal Trade Commission	40
High-Performance Computing and Communications	800
Inter-American Foundation	20
International Monetary Fund	40
International Trade Commission	20
Legal Services Corporation	300
NASA International Space Station Program	2,000
NASA New Millennium Initiative	400
NASA Reusable Launch Vehicle Technology Program	100
NASA Aeronautics Initiative Research Partnerships	300
National Endowment for the Arts	200
National Endowment for Democracy	40
National Endowment for the Humanities	200
National Flood Insurance	200
National Labor Relations Board	100

(continued)

Table 9.2
POTENTIAL NONDEFENSE SPENDING REDUCTIONS, *(continued)*

Program	Amount ($ Millions)
National Science Foundation Program to Stimulate Competitive Research	40
Neighborhood Reinvestment Corporation	40
Office of National Drug Control Policy	40
Office of Science and Technology Policy	20
Overseas Private Investment Corporation	40
Peace Corps	200
Securities and Exchange Commission	100
Service Contract Act	600
Small Business Administration	800
Tennessee Valley Authority, development activities	100
Trade and Development Agency	40
U.S. Global Change Research Program	1,700
U.S. Information Agency	1,200
World Bank	40
Total Budget Savings	**142,650**

Taxes

Opponents of Social Security privatization often claim that financing the transition to individual accounts will require a tax increase. Indeed, some supporters of privatization, such as Laurence Kotlikoff, have advocated new taxes.[11] However, given the other possible sources of transition financing discussed, any tax increase is clearly unnecessary. Moreover, Americans are already overtaxed. According to the nonpartisan Tax Foundation, the average American family pays more than 39 percent of its income in taxes, more than it spends on food, clothing, and shelter combined.[12] Tax hikes would also reduce economic growth and undercut other aspects of transition financing.

We, therefore, explicitly reject new or increased taxes as a way to fund the transition. Indeed, because after 10 years our proposal reduces the payroll contribution from 12.4 percent to 10 percent, our plan results in a tax cut for working Americans.

Our Proposal for the Transition

The list of potential transition funding sources discussed above can be thought of as a type of Chinese menu. If you want a little more from column A, take a little less from column B. In the end, any transition plan will be a political decision, with Congress balancing various interests and other factors as it selects from the options.

Table 9.3 shows what the authors believe is a feasible mix of financing methods. These figures are meant to provide a general idea of the likely magnitude of each source over time, not as precise estimates. They are calculated from the Social Security Administration's own projections of the future income of Social Security.

To make these calculations, it was assumed that the reform plan was implemented at the beginning of 1998, and that 50 percent of all workers would choose the private system over Social Security in each of the first three years following implementation. Then 75 percent of all workers were assumed to choose the private option in each of the next three years. Finally, 90 percent of all workers were assumed to choose the private option every year thereafter. All figures in the table are presented in 1998 dollars.

Column 1 shows the amounts that would be invested in the private retirement accounts each year instead of being paid into Social Security. As indicated, workers and employers each pay 5 percent of wages up to the Social Security maximum taxable income into the private system. The transition would have to come up with alternative means of offsetting these shifted payments in order to continue to pay Social Security benefits.

Column 2 shows the additional tax revenues that would be generated from the private investments. While Feldstein estimates that 3.9 percentage points of the full, before-tax return to capital of 9.3 percent is taxed away, we assumed here that only 3 percentage points were taxed away. We assumed as well that the private accounts received a real return of 5 percent on average after these taxes. That leaves 1.3 percentage points of the full 9.3 percent return, which is more than enough for administrative costs, estimated in chapter 4 as less than 50 basis points. In calculating these feedback revenues, we subtracted from the accumulating investment total the survivors, disability, and retirement benefits that would be paid from the private system each system each year. We also subtracted the amount of government bonds issued to finance the transition,

Table 9.3
Financing the Transition
(All Figures in Billions of 1998 Dollars)

Year	Column 1 Revenues Invested in the Private System Instead of S.S.[1]	Column 2 Revenue Feedback from Private Investments[2]	Column 3 Replaced Social Security Benefits for Those Who Opt Out[3]	Column 4 Expenditure Savings Due to Reduced S.S. Benefit Growth[4]	Column 5 Social Security Surpluses	Column 6 General Budget Surpluses	Column 7 Extra Revenue Generated by Higher Economic Growth	Column 8 Revenue Lost Due to Waiver of Continuing Taxes by Those Who Opt Out[5]	Column 9 Reduction in Other Gov't Spending[6]	Column 10 Sale of Gov't Bonds[7]	Column 11 Net Surplus or Deficit Remaining
1998	167	5	4	—	33	—	12	—	60	53	0
1999	169	9	8	—	31	—	13	—	60	48	0
2000	172	15	13	1	31	—	13	—	60	39	0
2001	262	21	21	1	30	10	20	—	60	99	0
2002	266	30	29	2	28	49	20	—	60	48	0
2003	270	39	39	3	27	49	21	—	60	32	0
2004	329	50	50	3	25	70	25	—	60	46	0
2005	335	62	63	5	25	88	26	—	60	6	0
2006	340	74	77	6	23	112	26	—	60	—	0
2007	348	87	87	8	19	148	27	—	22	—	+28
2008	354	99	98	10	16	168	27	47	—	—	+17
2009	359	111	109	13	12	166	28	48	—	—	+32
2010	364	124	117	16	9	163	28	49	—	—	+44
2011	370	136	127	22	4	161	28	74	—	—	+34
2012	374	147	137	25	—	160	29	75	—	—	+49
2013	379	159	146	32	—	154	29	76	—	—	+65
2014	383	171	155	37	—	149	30	92	—	—	+67
2015	387	182	165	45	—	145	30	93	—	—	+87
2016	392	191	176	54	—	139	30	94	—	—	+104

2017	**397**	200	189	63	135	31	95	—	—	+126
2018	**400**	209	202	74	—	31	96	—	—	+20
2019	**404**	216	215	85	—	32	97	—	—	+47
2020	**408**	223	229	97	—	32	98	—	—	+75
2021	**412**	227	237	109	—	32	99	—	—	+94
2022	**416**	230	261	118	—	33	100	—	—	+126
2023	**420**	232	277	127	—	33	101	—	—	+148
2024	**424**	232	293	136	—	33	102	—	—	+168
2025	**427**	231	310	147	—	34	103	—	—	+192
2026	**432**	226	328	157	—	34	104	—	—	+209
2027	**437**	220	346	171	—	35	105	—	—	+230

[1] Assumes that 50 percent of workers opt out in each of the first three years, 75 percent opt out in each of the next three years, and 90 percent opt out after that.

[2] This column presents the new revenues produced from taxation of the full, before-tax real returns earned by the net increase in the private investments, after subtracting the amount of government bonds sold each year.

[3] This column presents the savings arising from replaced Social Security retirement, survivors and disability benefits of those who opt for the private alternatives.

[4] This column presents the savings arising from delaying the retirement age and changing future benefit calculations from wage-indexing to price-indexing.

[5] Includes effect of Social Security surpluses and the continuing 1.2 percent of taxable wages paid by employees and employers each for the first 10 years after the worker opts out of Social Security.

[6] Assumes that projected total federal spending is reduced by the amounts shown to help finance the transition. Does not include approximately $40 billion per year in additional cuts between 1988 and 2012 that will be necessary if the Social Security Trust Fund is not used to finance general operating expenditures.

[7] Assumes the government sells bonds each year to raise money to pay continuing Social Security benefits. These can be either new government bonds or the already existing bonds in the Social Security Trust Fund.

which would offset the net saving increase from the reform, and consequently reduce feedback revenues.

As previously discussed, workers who choose the private option would receive fewer and ultimately no benefits from the old public system, receiving better benefits from the private system instead. Column 3 estimates the saving from this effect that helps to reduce the transition costs. The great majority of the saving shown in the early years results from sharp reductions in disability benefits and preretirement survivors benefits paid by the old system. As previously indicated, workers who opt into the private system would have all such benefits thereafter paid through private life and disability insurance rather than the public system, producing this immediate saving. Over the years, saving from forgone retirement benefits would grow to large amounts, as more and more workers retired who had paid into the private system instead of Social Security for more and more years.

Column 4 shows the saving that would result from delaying the retirement age under Social Security and changing the program's benefit calculation formula from wage-indexing to price-indexing. Since the amount that must be paid in recognition bonds for those who choose the private option will be based on the revised benefit structure, the cost of those bonds will be substantially reduced.

Column 5 shows the projected surpluses in Social Security that would be available to help finance the transition. These are the projected surpluses of taxes over expenditures. Interest on the trust fund bonds is not counted, as that interest is both an expenditure of and income to the federal government, and does not represent funds available to the government to help finance the transition.

Column 6 shows the general budget surpluses that would be available to help finance the transition as well. The Social Security surpluses were subtracted from these general surpluses, so that the Social Security surpluses would not be counted twice. The general budget surpluses were adjusted to a calendar year basis, to be consistent with all of the other data.

Column 7 shows the extra revenue that would be generated from the higher economic growth resulting from the reform. As we saw in chapter 6, most economists agree that, properly done, the reform would produce a large increase in economic growth and national income. Feldstein estimates that just the positive labor impacts from obviating the negative effects of the payroll tax would increase GDP by 1 percent each year.[13] So we assumed that if all workers chose the private option, the reform would increase GDP by 1 percent each year, besides the additional income in returns to the new saving, which was counted in column 2. Following our assumptions about the proportion of workers choosing the private option, we assumed that GDP would increase by an additional 0.5 percent in each of the first 3 years, 0.75 percent in each of the next 3 years, and 0.9 percent thereafter.

Column 8 shows the revenue that would be lost when workers and employers who have opted out of Social Security stop paying the remaining 1.2 percentage points of the payroll tax after 10 years. The revenue from this continuing portion of the tax is not shown separately in the table because we are calculating what is necessary to offset the 10 percentage points of the tax that are withdrawn from Social Security each year, assuming the continued payment of the remaining tax for 10 years. As a result, we must show instead the revenue that would be lost when workers and employers stop paying the tax.

Column 9 shows the amount of other government spending cut each year to help finance the transition. Column 10 shows the amount of government bonds sold each year to raise funds for the transition. These could be either new bonds or already existing Social Security trust fund bonds. The Social Security trust funds hold enough bonds to cover all of the sales shown in column 10. We assume that the bonds sold would be zero coupon bonds that accumulate interest to maturity. The reform would produce more than enough in surpluses in less than 20 years to pay off all these bonds and their accumulated interest in full. Finally, column 11 shows the net surpluses or deficits resulting from the reform after all the prior columns.

The results are truly remarkable. They show that by the 10th year of the reform the transition deficits are eliminated and the reform is leaving net surpluses, even after counting the effective 20 percent payroll tax cut that starts in 2008. Indeed, by 2014, the 16th year of the reform, the general budget surplus is being used only to offset the net tax cut, with the rest of the surplus remaining. Four years later, by the 21st year of the reform, the general budget surplus is no longer needed at all, as the reform produces a net surplus of

$45 billion for the year, even without counting the general budget surplus. Consequently, for the 21st year and the remaining years in the table, the general budget surpluses are not counted in the net surpluses resulting from the reform. These net surpluses are substantial, nearly 2 percent of GDP through 2027.

Government bonds need to be sold to help finance the reform only during the first 7 years, totaling only about $370 billion. These bonds plus interest again could be paid off in full by the reform's surpluses, before the 20th year of the reform. The remaining transition gap can be eliminated by cutting other government spending by about $60 billion for each of the first 8 years of the reform, and $22 billion in the 9th year. This is quite modest spending restraint, less, relative to the total budget, than were Reagan's budget cuts of 1981.

In addition, these projections again show that the reform would eliminate the massive Social Security deficits that would otherwise start in about 2013. Instead, we would have the substantial surpluses during this time that are shown in Table 9.3. As a result, we would save another $2.9 trillion in today's dollars from 2013 through 2032, which would otherwise have to be paid to cover the deficits of Social Security.

Finally, all of this is accomplished without any reductions in Social Security benefits for today's retirees and without tax increases for today's workers. Rather, benefits for today's retires are paid in full without change, and effective payroll tax rates for today's workers are again cut by 20 percent.

Three Caveats

We believe that the plan that has been presented offers a viable option for financing the transition to privatization of Social Security. However, in the interest of full disclosure, we must offer three caveats. There are several second-order effects—actions people may take in response to the reform—that may reduce the benefits flowing from it and make the transition more difficult. While these second-order effects are reasonable and must be considered in any discussion of transition financing, in the end, we do not believe they will substantially undermine the plan we have presented.

The first of these effects is that in seeing their saving in the private retirement system grow so large, workers may reduce their other saving, offsetting the net saving increase resulting from the reform. But the great majority of workers in fact do not have significant liquid saving that they can reduce.[14] To the extent they have any saving at all, it is tied up in homes or held in short-term precautionary balances for which inaccessible long-term retirement saving cannot substitute. Moreover, for the small proportion of the population that may be considered rich, and who hold the bulk of private, discretionary saving, those saving serve broader purposes of investment, ownership, and entrepreneurship that will not be affected by retirement saving. In other words, these people are using their funds to own and run businesses, and that will not be changed by retirement saving.

More plausible is that workers and their employers would reduce their pension saving. But these pensions along with the private system's higher retirement benefits for workers would still be needed. The Social Security benefits these private benefits would replace are quite modest, generally ranging from 28 percent to 42 percent of preretirement income. The higher private benefits would provide retirees with incomes more in line with preretirement income. Moreover, we are not adequately preparing now to finance other major retirement needs, such as health care and long-term nursing home care. The higher private benefits would address these inadequacies, besides providing better retirement income.

In addition, there are other second-order effects that could *increase* saving. The increased income, higher wages, and new jobs and employment resulting from the reform would produce some proportion of new saving out of this new income. Indeed, as people get richer, as they would as a result of privatization of Social Security, they would tend to increase their saving rates. We may well see this effect most prominently in retirees leaving a large proportion of their huge retirement accumulations to their children and grandchildren. If this becomes a major social trend, then it would produce another major increase in saving, as retirees would not consume their retirement saving to the extent expected. Moreover, the economic benefits from privatization of Social Security described in chapter 6 add up to a major economic boom in the United States. That may well draw capital here from around the world, as foreign investors seek to be part of the hottest economy, increasing total U.S. investment. On balance, more net saving than we have assumed, rather than less, may be the result.

Finally, if workers do reduce other saving, that is not necessarily a problem. Workers would then have higher present incomes. Workers would then just be taking more of the net benefits of the reform in present income rather than higher future income. And that higher present income means more resources that could be used to finance the transition for a few years, offsetting any loss of revenue feedback from higher net saving. Such a result would be analogous to having workers invest 8 out of 12.4 percentage points of wages in the private system, and using 4.4 percent to help finance the transition for 10 years, rather than investing 10 points in the private system, and using 2.4 points to help with the transition, as we have proposed.

Another concern is that some of the increased savings may be invested in other countries rather than in the United States. Such foreign investment may well produce an even higher overall return, but the revenue feedback would accrue to foreign governments rather than to the United States. To the extent this occurs, the revenue feedback available to help finance the transition in the United States would be reduced.

But capital investment flows across U.S. borders are not completely random, exogenous events. They are heavily influenced by U.S. economic policy. If the government follows a policy of low taxation and regulation, sound money, and respect for property rights, capital will flow into the United States from abroad. If the government takes the opposite tack, capital will flow out of the United States to foreign opportunities.

Therefore, it would be wise to combine privatization of Social Security with sound overall economic policies. If that were the case, there would be little reason to be concerned about significant losses of U.S. saving resulting from investment in foreign countries. If we follow the right policies, the United States is more likely to be flooded with foreign investment. Indeed, as suggested, privatization of Social Security itself is likely to create an economic and investment boom in the United States that may well attract substantial capital from abroad.

A third concern is that as saving increases, the return to capital will decline. This is standard economic theory. All else being equal, as saving and investment increase, the average return declines, as the most productive investments are made first, and only the less productive investments will be left. But the key questions are how much returns will decline, and to what extent all else will be equal.

Feldstein suggests that reforming Social Security into a fully funded system would have only a modest effect in reducing capital returns, even without considering outside factors.[15] But there are two major factors that suggest sweeping new opportunities for highly productive capital investment that may well offset, if not overwhelm, any reduction in capital returns due to increased supply.

First, we live in an age of rapid and remarkable technological developments. Those developments are opening up whole new vistas of highly productive capital investment. The space exploration, space stations, and space colonies that we have long speculated would be the hallmarks of the next century would consume vast quantities of new capital. But there are broad opportunities here on the ground as well, from new and more widely consumed applications of computer technology, to biotechnology, to ocean mining, farming, and development, and many others. Indeed, recent economic theory suggests that increased capital may accelerate technological development, which tends to increase rather than reduce returns to capital.[16]

Second, all around the world, countries are opening up their economies to free-market development and investment. This opens up broad new opportunities to utilize the world capital supply in highly productive ways. As a result, a major increase in that supply could quite possibly be absorbed without a significant decline in returns.

Finally, a decline in capital returns is again not necessarily a problem. That decline would be largely—if not completely—offset by higher wages for workers, as basic economic theory indicates that more capital makes workers more productive, thereby increasing their wages. Heavy new capital investment, possibly portending a substantial decline in capital returns, suggests as well a substantial increase in wages. In addition, lower capital returns would translate into lower interest rates, which would also greatly benefit working people. Moreover, any significant decline in capital returns would occur well after the initial years of the transition, when the financing problem is nettlesome, so there would likely be no significant effect on transition financing in any event.

Conclusion

Ultimately, the case for Social Security privatization does not stand or fall on any single proposal for financing the transition. Once one decides to travel from New York to San Francisco, there are many routes to get there. All that is required is to show that at least one will allow you to arrive at your destination. The rest is subject to debate and individual preference.

We believe that the plan described in this chapter proves that transition financing is not only possible but also practical. One may disagree with particular aspects of our proposal or one may advocate other approaches. But, clearly, concern over financing the transition should not be an obstacle to privatizing Social Security.

10. Common Questions about a Private Social Security System

We think this book has established an overwhelmingly compelling case for allowing a private option to Social Security. Along the way, we have dealt with the greatest concerns and objections to such reform. Chapter 9 dealt in full detail with how to handle the transition from the current system to the new system, and its effects, probably the greatest concern. In chapters 4 and 5, we discussed the effects of such reform on the poor, showing that they would massively benefit. Chapter 5 dealt also with the effects on blacks, working women, and traditional families, showing that they would all benefit massively as well.

In this chapter, we will deal with other specific concerns and questions that are commonly raised about the privatization of Social Security.[1] We think these objections can all be easily answered and do not provide a credible basis for opposing the proposed reforms.

Why Not Let the Government Do the Investing?

Some defenders of the current Social Security system agree that private capital markets produce much higher returns than Social Security. However, they suggest that the government, rather than individuals, should therefore invest Social Security funds. Generally, they suggest that the government should invest funds from the Social Security trust funds in real capital assets. As former Social Security Commissioner Robert Ball asks, "Why should the trust fund earn just one-third as much as common stocks?"[2] Doing this would increase funding for the program without making radical changes in its structure or shifting risk to individuals.

However, allowing the government to invest the Social Security trust funds in private capital markets would amount to the socialization of at least a large portion of the U.S. economy.[3] It would put ownership rights over much of the American economy in the hands of the U.S. government. To see how this would occur, consider that at its peak, the Social Security trust funds will theoretically contain approximately $2.9 trillion.[4] The total value of all 2,723 stocks traded on the New York Stock Exchange was about $6 trillion at the end of 1995.[5] It is easy to see, therefore, that investing the trust funds would allow the U.S. government to purchase if not a controlling, then at least a commanding, share of virtually every major company in America.

Government decisionmakers would acquire property rights in corporate enterprises. Either they would exercise their rights, thus creating a direct political influence in the management of private enterprises, or they would give up the voting rights and other shareholder privileges, thus indirectly enhancing the power of existing shareholders. In either case, ownership of the enterprises would be powerfully influenced by political agents, and the entire arrangement would be financed by the taxpayers.

Would it make a difference if the government purchased existing index funds from a third party, such as an investment company? Not significantly. In order for the government to purchase shares in an index fund, it would have to do so either through a mutual fund company selling an index fund, which would then purchase actual shares of stocks included in the index, or through some other financial institution creating an index, which would also eventually purchase actual shares. Although the index fund would provide a layer of insulation between the government and the corporations whose stocks were purchased, the problems of control would not be completely avoided.

Consider this scenario: First, the government acquires control over the index fund manager itself and thus indirect control over the corporations. If index fund A controls the majority of shares in company B, and the government controls the management of index fund A, the government can control company B.

However, even if the government does not attempt to exercise corporate control, there is reason to be concerned over allowing index fund managers to use taxpayer money to increase their ownership of corporate America. The huge number of shares purchased with Social Security money will represent powerful voting blocs and, in contrast to most stock purchases, they will be uniformly voted. Yet these powerful new stockholders will not answer to anyone and will derive all of their new powers from the aggregated funds of average American citizens. Never in the history of this country has there been a proposal to hand over this much power to unelected officials with this little responsibility attached to it.

In essence, the arrangement would permit federal government to use tax money to pick corporate winners and losers. Using funds borrowed from Social Security's future beneficiaries, the government would purchase massive blocks of shares, to be controlled either by the government or by financial institutions that are fortunate enough to receive government contracts for such purchases. It is difficult to imagine a more egregious proposal for "corporate welfare."

Allowing the government to own stock in corporate America is an open invitation for the government to interfere with the American economy. After all, what if a company whose stock is purchased by the Social Security trust funds decides to move its operations overseas? Should the administrators of the investments of the trust funds remain indifferent to the plight of the company's workers, who after all will be future beneficiaries of the system? Should not the trustees at least attempt to convince the company to retain its American operations? And if the company moves, would not the ownership of shares represent an indirect subsidy to foreign employees extended by the American workers who are losing their jobs to them? What if the company is convinced by the authorities to keep its operations in the United States and this leads to a consistent stream of losses and subpar share performance?

Moreover, the investment itself provides the opportunity for central planning and control. After all, companies whose stocks are selected will receive a substantial investment boost not available to competitors who are not chosen. This raises a host of questions about what types of investments should be allowed.

For example, cigarette smoking is a major health concern to many people and to the federal and state governments that spend public money to provide health care for those suffering from smoking-related diseases. Should Social Security be allowed to invest in cigarette companies? Is it appropriate for the Social Security system to offer price support to those shares while Medicare and Medicaid spend their resources in treating patients suffering from the long-term consequences of smoking?

Other controversial issues are easy to imagine. Should Social Security invest in nonunion companies? Companies that make nuclear weapons? Companies that pay high executive salaries or do not offer health benefits? Companies that do business in Burma or Cuba? Companies with an insufficient number of women and minorities in executive positions? Companies that produce morally offensive movies? Companies that extend benefits to the partners of gay employees? Companies that do not extend benefits to the partners of gay employees? The list is virtually endless.

Public employee pension funds have long been subject to such controversies.[6] For example, at one time more than 30 states prohibited the investment of pension funds in companies that did business in South Africa. Approximately 11 states restricted investment in companies that failed to meet the "MacBride Principles" for doing business in Northern Ireland. Companies doing business in Libya, other Arab countries, Burma, and communist nations have also been barred from investment. Some states have additional restrictions on investing employee pension funds, including requirements for investing in in-state companies, home mortgages, and alternative energy sources, such as solar power. In some states, investments are prohibited in companies that are accused of polluting, unfair labor practices, or failing to meet equal opportunity guidelines. Some public employee pension funds are prohibited from investing in the alcohol, tobacco, and defense industries. In a recent example, the city of Philadelphia announced it would sell its employee pension fund's Texaco stock because of alleged racist practices by that company.[7]

Use of a passive index—either one created by the government or an existing one—would reduce, but not eliminate, the problem. Questions would remain about what stocks should be included in the index. Almost inevitably there would be a huge temptation to create a better, more socially appealing index of companies friendly to the public policies of the current administration or the current congressional majority.

Those looking for evidence of this temptation need look no further than attempts by the Clinton administration to force private pension plans to invest a portion of their portfolio in "socially redeeming" ways.[8] Actually, the last days of the Bush administration saw the first exploration of the idea of directing private pension investment. In November 1992, the Labor Department released a report discussing a procedure for valuing the "net externalities" of investments as a way of broadening the prevailing rate test permitted under ERISA to allow for politically targeted investments. The Clinton administration jumped on the idea with undisguised enthusiasm. In September 1993, Olena Berg, the Assistant Secretary of Labor for Pensions and Welfare Benefits, announced an expansive interpretation of the prevailing rate test that would "allow collateral benefits to be considered in making investment decisions." She especially urged pension fund investment in "firms that invest in their own workforce."[9]

A year later, in September 1994, Labor Secretary Robert Reich called for investment of a portion of private pension funds in economically targeted investments, which would provide such "collateral benefits" as "affordable housing, infrastructure improvements and jobs.[10] Fortunately, Congress has resisted this dangerous idea. But it is clear that some politicians are anxious to gain control over pension investments.

Moreover, as we saw in chapter 7, those countries that allow the government to control pension investments have a very poor track record of managing those investments. As a result, they have consistently earned a lower rate of return than investments made by the private sector.

We therefore strongly reject any program of government investment. Far better is to allow individuals to own and invest their own funds through individual accounts as discussed below.

Do Average Workers Have Sufficient Knowledge and Sophistication about Private Capital Markets to Handle Private Retirement Investments?

This concern was raised by the *Report of the 1994–1996 Advisory Council on Social Security*, which stated,

> Investors need sophisticated knowledge to invest successfully, a sophistication millions of investors lack. In order to do reasonably well over time—nothing is guaranteed—investors must be able to assess the value of the companies whose stocks and bonds are offered to them. But many, perhaps 100 million participants in Social Security, lack requisite knowledge, such as the market served by individual companies, ways of judging the competence of management, relative changes in technology and whether an individual company is able to keep current, the competitive situation,

both local and sometimes international, the company's unfunded promises to pay deferred compensation to highly paid employees, and many other factors.

Some relevant issues will be included in the accounting statement in the company's annual report, but most retirees do not know how to interpret this information even if provided to them by purveyors of securities. Without adequate knowledge, privatization will leave many who are required to substitute investments for assured Social Security benefits without the ability to protect themselves against potential disaster.[11]

This valid concern was thoroughly addressed by the structure of the proposed reform discussed in chapter 8. Workers would not be expected to manage their own particular retirement investments. They would simply pick among highly sophisticated, knowledgeable, and experienced investment managers, who would then choose the particular investments for them.

Workers could not pick just any investment manager. They could choose only from managers that had applied for and received government approval to offer their services in the private Social Security system. These would be banks, brokerage firms, investment companies, mutual funds, insurance companies, and others with established competence and track records. Moreover, they would be subject to government regulation to prevent irresponsible investments though, as discussed in chapter 8, such regulation must not be excessive or it would unnecessarily reduce returns and benefits for workers.

The track records and past investment performance of each of these companies would be published and readily available. They would be available to every eligible worker by the government near the beginning of each year. Workers could then simply choose among these approved and regulated investment managers.

This system has worked well in Chile and elsewhere, where many workers are quite unknowledgeable and unsophisticated about capital markets.

But we should say, as well, that we think this concern has been overstated. At times, it seems to reflect the typical Washington establishment view that only the wise bureaucrats in Washington know what is best—people outside the Beltway are too stupid to handle their own affairs. Where average people have been allowed the freedom to handle their own retirement investments, they have been quite responsible and intelligent.[12]

Therefore, we think some scope can be allowed for self-direction of investment accounts by those who desire it. As discussed in chapter 8, this can start by allowing self-direction of all funds voluntarily contributed to accounts in excess of the required amounts. Over time, this can be expanded to allow self-direction of funds in excess of the amount needed to cover a minimum required level of benefits.

Such self-direction would operate as it does with IRAs today, where the worker can direct the investment manager to carry out particular investments in his or her account. Workers would still not be able, however, to handle funds without an investment manager serving as a custodian to ensure that the worker complies with still applicable regulations regarding investments and withdrawals.

What Would Happen to People Who Make Investment Mistakes and Suffer Heavy Losses? Will They Still Have Adequate Retirement Incomes?

This concern has also been thoroughly addressed by the structure of the proposed reform discussed in chapter 8. That reform would include a guaranteed minimum benefit. If the benefits that could be financed by the worker's retirement fund fell below this minimum amount, the government would pay supplemental benefits to bring the worker's total benefits up to the minimum.

Indeed, we recommended in chapter 8 that this minimum be generously set at the average benefit under Social Security. Average workers would then be guaranteed at least their Social Security benefits, and lower-income workers would be guaranteed even more. As discussed in chapter 8, this generosity is feasible because the likely private-market benefits are so much higher than Social Security benefits. The government is consequently likely to bear little, if any, costs for such minimum benefits. Indeed, with the reform making everyone so much richer, government assistance for the needy would likely decline substantially overall.

Of course, with any such guarantee there is always a danger of counterproductive moral hazard. Workers assured of minimum benefits may seek to pursue more risky investments, knowing that if they fail the government will back them up. But this risk should be minimal as long as the guaranteed benefit, like Social Security today, is so far below the market benefits that can be achieved by standard investment performance. In that case, workers would still have too much to lose from pursuing overly risky investment strategies. This danger would also be countered by the requirement of investment through a government-approved and -regulated, sophisticated investment manager.

Such a guaranteed minimum benefit has worked quite well in Chile and elsewhere. This policy allows workers to take advantage of the much higher returns and benefits of the private market, with a social safety net assuring them and the general public that some will not be left destitute.

Finally, we think that within the structure of the proposed private system, this concern is also overwrought. With workers choosing among sophisticated, experienced, government-approved and -regulated investment managers, the possibility of an unusual catastrophic loss is minimized. We would not be dealing with unknowledgeable and unsophisticated individual workers mistakenly blowing their retirement nest eggs through foolish investment strategies.

Perhaps President Clinton explained it best. When questioned about fluctuations in the stock market, the president noted:

> . . .most ordinary citizens who are invested in the stock market are invested through their retirement funds and mutual funds and things of that kind. And the people who are managing those funds are managing huge amounts of money, and presumably do have very good judgment about things like that. You know, all markets go up and down at various times. But I think that if you go back over the last 30 years, investments in the stock market held over the long term panned out pretty well. And, you know, I think these mutual funds, these retirement funds, can mix their investments, and they can do it over a longer period of time.[13]

Would a Privatized Social Security System Still Protect Survivors and Disabled Workers?

Somehow, die-hard defenders of the status quo keep making this argument even though it makes no sense in the context of the reform proposals that have been advanced. Nearly all proposals for privatization, including the one in this book, provide for private life and disability insurance to cover the survivors and disability benefits of Social Security. Part of the payments into the private system each year would be used to buy such insurance. The investment managers could, in fact, be held accountable for providing such insurance as part of their services, as a condition of their participation in the private retirement system. In chapter 4, in fact, we discussed how these private survivors and disability benefits would be better than the benefits offered by Social Security.

Would Privatization Benefit the Poor and Low-Wage Workers or Just the Wealthy?

This argument has been thoroughly rebutted by the analysis in chapters 4 and 5. We saw there that not only would average-income workers do far better through the private sector, the poor would do far better as well, despite the special subsidies for them in Social Security.

Indeed, in one example discussed in chapters 4 and 5, a career, low-income couple, each earning the equivalent of today's minimum wage throughout their lives, could expect through the private sector two-and-a-half to five-and-a-half times the benefits promised by Social Security. Quite simply, the superior returns and benefits that can be expected through the increased production created by the private system overwhelm the redistributive subsidies provided by Social Security for the poor.

Since average- and low-income workers would all do so much better through the private system, they would virtually all opt out of Social Security for that system, as would higher-income workers. As discussed under the first objection, average- and low-income workers would not need to be knowledgeable or sophisticated about investment markets to obtain the advantages of the private system. Under a well-structured option, over 90 percent of all workers would likely choose the private system, as occurred in Chile.

Although the Stock Market Rises Over the Long Term, What Happens if It Collapses Right at the End of an Individual's Working Years, Leaving Little or Nothing for Retirement?

This common argument is based on a simple fallacy—that in the private system accumulated funds would all somehow be turned in somewhere at one point just before retirement to finance retirement benefits. Hence, the concern that if markets are way down at that point, the worker would suffer a steep and possibly even catastrophic loss of benefits.

But there is no need to force workers to annuitize their savings at the instant they retire. They can continue to manage their funds, riding out any market slump. So there is no one point under the private system at which the worker is uniquely vulnerable to a market downturn. Retirement investment in the private system is for a worker's entire adult lifetime, a period on average of 60 years or more. During this quite long investment horizon, workers will be able to ride out the ups and downs of private markets. Because investment continues, even when the worker buys an annuity on a certain date, investment firms serving a broad retirement investment market can be expected to offer provisions granting the worker the benefit of a market rebound or good market performance after the annuity purchase date. This has been done in life insurance and other investment products. Indeed, firms in a competitive market would also likely offer provisions to buffer short-term downturns for retirees and make it up over the long run, enabling them to get the highest stable benefits possible.

In addition, Hieger and Shipman reviewed the worst performances of the stock market, as represented by the Standard & Poor's 500, on record for a single day, month, or quarter.[14] Their study shows that over the past 70 years, stocks have fallen by 18 percent or more in a quarter only 10 times, or 3.6 percent of all quarters. They have fallen 14 percent or more in a month only 10 times, or 1.2 percent of all months. And they have fallen 8 percent or more in a day only 10 times, a miniscule portion of all days. The period covered by this analysis includes the Great Depression stock market collapse.

Hieger and Shipman calculate that for all workers of varying income levels entering the workforce today, even if the market suffered the worst of these performances when they entered retirement, the workers would still have enough funds on hand to finance far better benefits than those promised by Social Security. The worst performances on record are declines of 37.68 percent for a quarter, 29.73 percent for a month, and 20.47 percent for a day. But for an average-income worker invested entirely in stocks, the market would have to fall 66 percent at the time the worker entered retirement to leave the worker with only enough funds to finance the same benefits as Social Security. If the worker was invested in a typical mixed fund with 60 percent stocks and 40 percent bonds, stocks would have to fall 89 percent at the time the worker entered retirement to leave the worker with funds sufficient only to match Social Security benefits.

For a low-income worker who invested entirely in stocks, the market would have to fall 57 percent at the time of retirement to leave the worker with no more than Social Security would pay. If the worker had invested in the balanced fund of stocks and bonds, stocks would have to fall 67 percent to leave the worker with no more than Social Security.

Will the Huge Investment Wave into the Stock Market Created by Privatization Cause a Short-Term Speculative Bubble When the Funds Start Flowing In, and a Catastrophic Collapse When Workers Withdraw Their Funds at Retirement?

In their study, Hieger and Shipman show that the markets could easily absorb the new investment from privatization.[15] They calculate that even if everyone chose the private option and invested all of their funds in the New York Stock Exchange, that investment would equal only 6.3 percent of the daily volume in that exchange. That would equal the volume traded in 25 minutes out of the 6-and-a-half hour trading day. Hieger and Shipman conclude, "The actual volume of new investment is unlikely to have a significant short-term impact on stock prices."[16]

Moreover, the concern about a stock market collapse at retirement is based on a simplistic fallacy concerning investment flows under a privatized system. Retirement investments are not all cashed out of the markets on retirement day. As discussed, retirement funds continue to be invested to support benefits during retirement years. To be sure, some funds are effectively withdrawn each year from the markets to finance the benefits for that year. But at the same time, new funds are coming into the market each year from those still working.

Consequently, investment flows into the capital markets would increase rapidly and steadily over the first generation after privatization. Once this generation reaches retirement and starts withdrawing funds to finance annual benefits, these withdrawals would be

Figure 10.1
Investment Flows into Privatized System

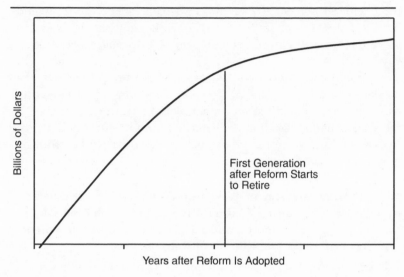

Billions of Dollars

First Generation
after Reform Starts
to Retire

Years after Reform Is Adopted

exceeded by the continuing annual new investments of those still working. So the annual investment flows into the capital markets would still increase, but more slowly. (See Figure 10.1.) There is no point of mad stampede out of the market producing a sudden huge drop in investment flows.

Should Calculations of Private-Market Returns Be Adjusted for Risk?

Calculations of private-market benefits must take into account the risk of private investments. Investment returns can vary over time and among different investors or investment managers. Some investors can suffer catastrophic losses through bad investments. Moreover, different investments offer different risks, with riskier investments offering higher returns. In considering these higher returns, the greater risk must be accounted for as well.

In theory, one way to account for this risk is to "risk adjust" the expected returns. The returns that might be earned on market investments would be adjusted downward by some factor in calculating expected market benefits, to account for the risk of varying returns or losses that may be suffered.

The problem with this theory is that there is no magic formula that calculates how possible returns should be risk adjusted. As a result, advocates of this view are now saying that real stock market returns of about 7.5 percent over the long term should be risk adjusted to the real corporate bond returns of 3 to 4 percent, or maybe even real government bond returns of 2 to 3 percent, because the difference in these investment returns only reflects market risk. Effectively, advocates of this view are saying that private capital market investors on average cannot earn more than the corporate bond or even government bond rate on average, because of the costs of the greater risks of stocks.

In reality, however, if workers opt out of Social Security and into the stock market, and that market earns the same average return over the next 70 years that it earned over the last 70 years, then these investors will receive a 7.5 percent real return on their investments, not the bond market return of 3 percent or 4 percent or 2 percent. To see how far off the mark the concept of risk adjustment is, consider that if it were correct, there would be no reason for rational investors to ever invest in the stock market, because investors could not expect, on a risk-adjusted basis, any greater return than in the less risky bond market.

In chapter 4, we fully account for possible market risk, in a more sound way. The best guess as to what capital markets will earn over the long term in the future is what they have earned over the long term in the past. The emphasis here has to be on the word "guess" because no one knows exactly what market investment returns will be in the future. But, still, this guess is better than any other. We have not heard any reason to think that stock market investors over the next 70 years will earn lower (or higher) returns on average than they did over the last 70 years, let alone half or less of what they earned, as the risk-adjustment advocates insist we must assume.

Indeed, there is good reason to think that long-term returns in the markets are fairly stable. These returns are not arbitrary. They reflect basic, structural factors in our economy, particularly reflecting the productive power of capital. Absent good reasons to think that these fundamental factors will change in the future, past long-run market performance is a workably reasonable expectation of future long-term performance.

Risk can be best accounted for by considering possible variations of market returns around these long-term expected returns. This

217

may be considered a "risk distribution" analysis rather than a "risk adjusted" analysis.

In chapter 4, we discussed first that this possible risk distribution can be greatly narrowed through investment diversification, carried out by highly sophisticated, government-approved and -regulated investment managers. We noted as well that this risk distribution would be further narrowed for long-run retirement investors as compared with shorter-term investors, as performance is more likely to average out over the longer term.

In this context, we argued that our analysis of private-market benefits left plenty of room for possible risk variation around the expected long-term returns. Again, with an average real stock market return over the last 70 years of about 7.5 percent, a real return of 5 to 6 percent, which we used to calculate private benefits, would fully account for the worst long-term periods of stock market performance in recorded history. A real return of 4 percent, which we also used, leaves lots of room for unprecedented poor performance. At that rate, again, average workers can still expect three times or more the benefits of Social Security.

Indeed, any real investment return above the miserable 1 percent or less offered by Social Security, at best, would, of course, provide higher benefits than Social Security. Those who insist on risk adjusting market returns dramatically downward make no adjustment for the higher taxes or lower benefits that we know will be necessary to keep Social Security solvent. Even risk-adjusted real market returns of 3 percent will provide much better benefits than unadjusted Social Security, and even more if Social Security is properly adjusted to account for higher taxes or lower benefits. But the problem is that would seriously and inaccurately underestimate likely market benefits.

We noted as well in chapter 4 what may be considered a sophisticated version of risk adjustment. Feldstein calculated on the basis of past market performance that contributing about 0.75 percent of payroll to an investment fund to cover possible market downturns would ensure payment of promised Social Security benefits through age 100 with a 95 percent probability, with investment by each worker of only an additional 2 percent of payroll.[17] All of the remaining 9.66 percent of Social Security tax, net of a small proportion for private life and disability insurance, would then finance in the private system benefits in excess of Social Security.

Adjusting calculations of private retirement benefits for this small set-aside would be a valid risk adjustment. But, frankly, even this is not necessary given our analysis of the risk distribution of private market returns.

This is especially so given the guaranteed minimum benefit provisions of privatization reform proposals. These provisions lop off the bottom of the possible risk distribution. Indeed, the net risk of a private option with a guaranteed minimum benefit equal to the average Social Security benefit is zero, at least for average- and lower- income workers. In fact, it is less than zero given the financing problems of Social Security.

Finally, we should reiterate here as well a key point made in chapter 4. Effectively precluding working people the freedom to choose the much higher returns and benefits of the private investment market, and in particular the stock market, because of concern over risk is not without costs of its own. It deprives working people of the full economic value of their earnings. Next to the risks of investing in the market we need to consider the risk of *not* investing in the market, and losing the high levels of benefits that would likely result.

Moreover, it is important to remember that Social Security is far from risk free. Indeed, given the system's looming financial crisis, the political risks of Social Security far outweigh those of private investment. The simplistic risk-adjustment advocates have failed to take into account these costs and these risks.

Conclusion

There is an old legal adage: When the facts are on your side, pound the facts. If the facts are against you, pound the law. If both the facts and the law are against you, pound the table. When it comes to the debate over Social Security privatization, opponents have done a lot of table pounding.

A careful examination of the most common objections to privatization shows that they are based on a misunderstanding of financial markets and/or how a privatized Social Security system would work. For example, long-term investment in capital markets is less risky than the current Social Security system and can be handled by even inexperienced investors. A privatized Social Security system will provide better survivors and disability benefits than the current system. A privatized Social Security system will benefit the poor as much as the rich. And, privatizing Social Security will not create a speculative bubble in the stock market.

In the end, the common criticisms of a privatized Social Security system are unfounded and should not stand in the way of providing a better and more secure retirement for today's young workers.

11. Time for Action

In Washington, the motto often seems to be "Why do today what you can put off until tomorrow?" That is particularly true if the issue is controversial or may offend some powerful interest group. But, when it comes to reforming Social Security, the president and Congress must realize that delay would be a serious mistake.

In his 1998 State of the Union address, President Clinton stressed the importance of reforming Social Security and promised to convene congressional leaders in 1999 to craft legislation that would make "Social Security strong in the 21st Century." The president called for the American people to join in the discussion over Social Security's future.[1]

The president is right. Social Security is in need of fundamental reform, and that reform must come sooner rather than later. As we have seen, the system's financial problems are deep and coming much sooner than commonly believed. But even more important, young workers are already being denied the benefits of the much higher returns and benefits that a privately invested Social Security system would bring. Every day that passes without reforming Social Security robs young workers of their future.

The president was also right a few days later when, in a speech at Georgetown University, he called for "bold experimentation" in Social Security reform, saying that we must "be open to new ideas, not to be hidebound and believe that we can see the future through the prism of the past."[2] Given Social Security's underlying flaws, the usual timid reforms—raising taxes and trimming benefits—will not only fail to fix the problem, but will make it worse. In contrast, however, a private, invested Social Security plan would produce enormous benefits for the American people.

Solving Social Security's Long-Term Financing Problems

The reform would eliminate Social Security's long-term financing crisis. Over 90 percent of workers will likely choose the private

221

system, as has been the case in other countries. So there will no longer be an issue of how to pay benefits through a bankrupt Social Security system. In the private system, all future benefits are fully funded by private savings and investments, so there can be no long-term financing crisis for the system. The money to finance retirement benefits is always on hand, in the worker's own account.

Moreover, the program's financing crisis would be eliminated without any tax increases. Indeed, effective taxes would be cut, as required payments for the private system would be 20 percent less than the current taxes for Social Security.

Better Deal for Today's Workers

Through the private system, workers will be able to get much higher returns and benefits. In chapter 4, we examined the case of a husband and wife who both work and earn average incomes each year. At just over half the average return earned in the stock market over the last 70 years, through a private invested system this couple would retire with almost $1 million in today's dollars. That fund would pay more than Social Security out of the interest alone and would allow them to leave the $1 million to their children. Or they could use the entire fund to buy an annuity paying them over three times the benefits promised by Social Security.

Moreover, at a return close to long-term stock market averages, this couple would retire with a fund of $1.6 million in today's dollars. That fund would pay them three times what Social Security promises out of the continuing returns, leaving the $1.6 million to children, or the fund could be used to buy an annuity paying seven times what Social Security promises.

As further shown in chapter 4, the same is true for all other workers. Everyone would get much higher benefits through the private system—low-income workers, high-income workers, married couples, single people, one-earner couples, two-earner couples, families with children, families without children, blacks, whites, Hispanics, indeed, all minority groups.

Moreover, workers would enjoy some of these benefits of the private system well before retirement, through the effective 20 percent payroll tax cut.

Higher Savings and Economic Growth

The private system would likely produce a large increase in national savings, with hundreds of billions of dollars invested in individual retirement accounts each year. This in turn would produce a large increase in national investment, productivity, wages, jobs, and overall economic growth. The effective payroll tax cut through the private option would also increase employment and economic growth.

Martin Feldstein estimates that these changes would increase the U.S. economy (GDP) by at least 5 percent. He estimates the present value of this future economic gain as $10 trillion to $20 trillion. In other words, privatization of Social Security would effectively provide a net gain to America of this magnitude due to improved economic performance. Indeed, our analysis in chapter 6 indicates that the likely gain would be even more, at 6 to 11 percent of GDP.

Helping the Poor

As discussed in chapter 5, lower-income workers would benefit the most from reform. They most need the higher returns and benefits of the private system. Again, we have seen that at just a 4 percent real return even low-income families would receive through the private system about two-and-one-half times the benefits promised by Social Security. At a 6 percent real return, closer to stock market averages, low-income workers would receive over five times the benefits promised by Social Security. Moreover, the private system offers low-income workers their only chance to accumulate some savings over their lives to leave to their children.

African Americans and other minorities who on average live fewer years in retirement to collect benefits would gain even more. Instead of losing a lifetime of contributions after few if any years of benefits, as with Social Security, through the private system they could leave their accumulated funds to their children. They could also use these funds to buy even higher annuity amounts, through innovative group-purchasing arrangements. As a result, the private system would provide minorities even more in benefits relative to Social Security than other workers.

Lower-income workers also most need the increased jobs, wages, and economic growth that would likely result from the private option. These workers are also the most vulnerable to the long-term crisis of the current system, as they cannot afford higher taxes now or reduced benefits in retirement. As a result, they benefit most from avoiding the current system's long-term crisis.

Moreover, through the privatization reform, the distribution of wealth throughout society would become far more equal than it is today, as average- and lower-income workers accumulated substantial assets through their individual retirement accounts. Through the individual private retirement account investments, the socialist dream of the nation's workers owning its business and industry would be effectively achieved. But the policy result would be the opposite of socialism. As the wealth of the nation's workers increased along with their ownership stake in America's business and industry, their support for free-market, pro-growth economic policies would increase dramatically. This social and political effect may ultimately have one of the greatest impacts in increasing economic growth.

Freedom of Choice and Control

Finally, the private option allows American workers much greater freedom of choice and control over their own incomes and financial futures. They would have direct control over the one-eighth of their incomes that is now taken by Social Security each year, and over the huge amounts that income would grow to by retirement. They would have greater freedom to choose their retirement ages. They could tailor their retirement and insurance benefits to their personal needs and preferences.

All of this is accomplished without harming today's retirees. There would be no change in their benefits or in the overall program for them. Indeed, our proposed reform would actually make their benefits more secure.

Other countries around the world are recognizing these enormous benefits and adopting such reforms for their workers. If we cannot change, then in a couple of generations workers in South America, east Asia, and eastern Europe will be retiring as millionaires while Americans will still be paying higher and higher taxes for meager Social Security benefits.

But President Clinton is also right that Social Security reform will not happen without the involvement of the American people. We can expect little leadership from the politicians in Washington. Special interest groups are lined up to defend the status quo. Yet, if average Americans spread the word to their neighbors, organize into local groups, and express their views to their congressional representatives, the demand for change will become a force too powerful for our political leaders to ignore.

We can have a Social Security system that will allow today's young workers to retire with the same dignity that their parents and grandparents did. We can have a Social Security system that is financially solvent, without piling more and more taxes on future generations. We can have a Social Security system that will allow the poor to accumulate real wealth and that will increase economic growth.

The next step is up to the American people.

Notes

Chapter 1

1. "Generation X Believes in UFOs, but Laughs at Social Security," *Washington Times*, September 27, 1994. The poll was conducted by Luntz Research on behalf of Third Millenium.

2. José Piñera, "Empowering Workers: The Privatization of Social Security in Chile," *Cato's Letters* no. 10, 1996.

3. See Luis Larrain, "Pension Reform in Latin American Countries," National Center for Policy Analysis (forthcoming).

4. Louis Enoff and Robert Moffit, "Social Security Privatization in Britain: Key Lessons for American Reformers," Heritage Foundation Backgrounder no. 1133, August 6, 1997.

5. See Peter Ferrara, John Goodman, and Merrill Matthews, "Private Alternatives to Social Security in Other Countries," National Center for Policy Analysis Policy Report no. 200, October 1995.

6. Georges de Menil, "The Momentum Towards Privatizing Public Pensions in Eastern Europe." Paper presented to a conference on "Solving the Global Public Pensions Crisis," London, December 9, 1997.

7. Ian Karleff, "Industrialized Nations Explore Ways to Support Their Aging Populations," *Financial Post*, December 6, 1997.

8. Wu Jie, "China's Social Security System." Paper presented to a conference on "China as a Global Economic Superpower," Shanghai, June 18, 1997.

9. "Bring on Pension Reform," *Wall Street Journal Europe*, December 23, 1997.

10. World Bank, *Averting the Old-Age Crisis* (Oxford: Oxford University Press, 1994).

11. "Solving the Global Public Pensions Crisis: Opportunities for Privatization." Conference cosponsored by the Cato Institute and *The Economist*, London, December 8–9, 1997.

12. Martin Feldstein, "The Missing Piece in Policy Analysis: Social Security Reform," *American Economic Review* 86 (May 1996): 12.

13. Sam Beard, *Restoring Hope in America: The Social Security Solution* (San Francisco: Institute for Contemporary Studies, 1996).

14. Marshall N. Carter and William G. Shipman, *Promises to Keep: Saving Social Security's Dream* (Washington: Regnery Publishing, 1996).

15. Robert Genetski, *A Nation of Millionaires* (Chicago: Heartland Institute, 1996).

16. *Report of the 1994–1995 Advisory Council on Social Security* (Washington: Government Printing Office, 1997).

17. See Randall Pozdena, "The New Oregon Option: Opting Out of Social Security," Cascade Policy Institute Policy Insight no. 103, July 1997.

18. Merrill Matthews, "Some Americans Already Have Privatized Social Security," National Center for Policy Analysis, no. 215, November 4, 1996.

19. Frank Luntz and Mark Seigel, "Social Security: The Credibility Gap," Luntz Research, Rosslyn, Va., September 1994.

20. The poll of 703 adults was conducted by Luntz Research on behalf of 60 Plus Association, August 3–4, 1995.

21. See "Public Opinion and Social Security Privatization," Cato Institute Social Security Paper no. 5, August 6, 1996.

22. The poll of 1,000 adults was conducted by the Gallup Organization on behalf of the Employee Benefit Research Institute in January 1994. Individuals were asked, "Do you think participation in Social Security should be made voluntary?" Fifty-four percent responded "yes"; 44 percent responded "no."

23. The poll of 1,007 adults was conducted by the Gallup Organization on behalf of the Employee Benefit Research Institute in January 1995.

24. The poll of 1,000 registered voters was conducted November 1–8, 1995, by GrassRoots Research of Charlotte, N.C. The margin of error was plus or minus 3 percent.

25. Mark Penn, "Rebuilding the Vital Center: 1996 Post-Election Survey," Democratic Leadership Council, 1997. The poll of 1,200 registered voters was conducted November 9–11, 1996. The margin of error is plus or minus 2.8 percent.

26. The poll of 948 likely voters was conducted by Zogby International of Utica, New York, February 15–17, 1998. The margin of error is plus or minus 3.3 percent.

27. Testimony of Alan Greenspan before the Senate Committee on Finance, November 20, 1997.

28. *1998 Annual Report of the Board of Trustees of the Federal Old-Age and Survivors Insurance and Disability Insurance Trust Fund* (Washington: Government Printing Office, 1998).

29. Ibid.

30. Ibid., Table II.F.17, pp. 121-2.

31. See, for example, William Shipman, "Retiring with Dignity: Social Security vs. Private Markets," Cato Institute Social Security Paper no. 2, August 14, 1995.

32. Martin Feldstein, "Privatizing Social Security: The $10 Trillion Opportunity," Cato Institute Social Security Paper no. 7, January 31, 1997.

33. See Michael Tanner, "Privatizing Social Security: A Big Boost for the Poor," Cato Institute Social Security Paper no. 4, July 26, 1996.

Chapter 2

1. Franklin Waltman, "Roosevelt Signs Security Bill to Benefit 30 Million Citizens," *Washington Post*, August 15, 1935.

2. R. Blanco Fombona, *Simón Bolívar: Compiled Speeches and Proclamations, Notations, Prologues, and Publications* (Paris: Editorial House Garnier Brothers, 1913), p. 49.

3. Marshall Carter and William Shipman, *Promises to Keep: Saving Social Security's Dream* (Washington: Regnery Publishing, 1996), p. 32.

4. See Abraham Ellis, *The Social Security Fraud* (Irvington-on-Hudson, New York: Foundation for Economic Education, 1996), p. 33.

5. Robert J. Myers, *Social Security* (Philadelphia: University of Pennsylvania Press, 1993), p. 7.

6. Barbara Armstrong, *Insuring the Essentials: Minimum Wage Plus Social Insurance — A Living Wage Program* (New York: Macmillan Press, 1932), pp. 399–412.

7. Roy Lubov, *The Struggle for Social Security: 1900–1935* (Pittsburgh: University of Pittsburgh Press, 1986), p. 7.

8. Sheryl Tynes, *Turning Points in Social Security: From "Cruel Hoax" to "Sacred Entitlement"* (Stanford, Calif.: Stanford University Press, 1996), p. 41.

9. Carolyn Weaver, *The Crisis in Social Security: Economic and Political Origins* (Durham, N.C.: Duke Press Policy Studies, 1982), p. 31.

10. "Public Service Retirement Systems in the United States," *Bulletin of the U.S. Bureau of Labor Statistics*, no. 491 (August 1929): 542–9.

11. Weaver, *The Crisis in Social Security*, p. 31.

12. Lubov, *The Struggle for Social Security*, p. 128.

13. William Graebner, *A History of Retirement: The Meaning and Function of an American Institution: 1885–1978* (New Haven, Conn.: Yale University Press, 1980), p. 133.

14. Weaver, *The Crisis in Social Security*, p. 31.

15. Tynes, *Turning Points in Social Security*, p. 42.

16. Lubov, *The Struggle for Social Security*, p. 128.

17. "Congress Faces the Question of Old-Age Pensions," *Congressional Digest* 14 (March 1935): 76.

18. "Efforts Seeking Federal Action on Old-Age Pensions," *Congressional Digest* 14 (March 1935): 72.

19. Weaver, *The Crisis in Social Security*, p. 60.

20. *Old-Age Security: Report of the New York State Commission on Old-Age Security* (Albany, N.Y.: J. B. Lyons, 1930), p. 39.

21. W. Andrew Achenbaum, *Social Security: Visions and Revisions* (Cambridge, Eng.: Cambridge University Press, 1986), p. 14.

22. This is just a rough estimate. The Census Bureau did not begin providing reliable data on poverty until 1947.

23. Weaver, *The Crisis in Social Security* , pp. 41–2.

24. Lubov, *The Struggle for Social Security*, pp. 29–44.

25. Weaver, *The Crisis in Social Security*, p. 36.

26. Abraham Epstein, *Insecurity: A Challenge to America* (New York: Random House, 1936), p. 3, cited in Weaver, *The Crisis in Social Security*, p. 37.

27. Daniel Sanders, *The Impact of Reform Movements on Social Policy Change: The Case of Social Insurance* (Fairlawn, N.J.: R. E. Burdick, 1973), pp. 131–41.

28. Samuel Gompers, "Not Even Compulsory Benevolence Will Do," *American Federationist* 24 (January 1917): 48.

29. Weaver, *The Crisis in Social Security*, p. 40.

30. James Q. Wilson, *Political Organizations* (New York: Basic Books, 1973), pp. 121–2.

31. Tynes, *Turning Points in Social Security*, pp. 42–3.

32. Graebner, *A History of Retirement*, p. 51.

33. Achenbaum, *Social Security*, p. 18.

34. Blanche Coll, *Safety Net: Welfare and Social Security, 1929–1979* (New Brunswick, N.J.: Rutgers University Press, 1995), pp. 1–3.

35. Summer Schlicter, "The Pressing Problem of Old-Age Security," *New York Times Magazine*, October 16, 1949, p. 9.

36. Achenbaum, *Social Security*, p. 17.

37. "Operation of Public Old-Age Pension Systems in the United States in 1931," *Monthly Labor Review* (June 1932): 1260.

38. Paul Douglas, *Social Security in the United States: An Analysis and Appraisal of the Federal Social Security Act* (New York: McGraw-Hill, 1939), p. 9.

39. Weaver, *The Crisis in Social Security*, p. 60.

40. Coll, *Safety Net*, p. 51.

41. Achenbaum, *Social Security*, pp. 17–8.

42. Weaver, *The Crisis in Social Security*, p. 64.

43. Ibid.

44. For a more detailed discussion of the Dill-Connery bill, see Douglas, *Social Security in the United States*, pp. 9–12.

45. These included provisions giving credit to all persons who had ever worked for a railroad, regardless of current employment status, and virtually compulsory retirement at age 65. Myers, *Social Security*, p. 835.

46. Ibid., p. 836.

47. The Railroad Retirement Act was substantially revamped in 1974. See Norman Solomon, "Principal Features of the Railroad Retirement Act of 1974," *Transactions of the Society of Actuaries* XXVII (1975): pp. 167–95.

48. Franklin D. Roosevelt, *The Public Papers and Addresses of Franklin D. Roosevelt*, comp. Samuel Rosenman (New York: Random House, 1939), vol. 3, pp. 287–93.

49. Weaver, *The Crisis in Social Security*, p. 65.

50. The Roosevelt administration was not at all subtle about this. A letter inviting Democratic National Committee vice chairwoman Mary Dewson to serve on the advisory council said, "This Advisory Council will be to some extent representative of the various interests affected but should consist of persons who are in full sympathy with the objectives of the program." Tynes, *Turning Points in Social Security*, p. 46.

51. Cited in Douglas, *Social Security in the United States*, p. 27.

52. Ibid.

53. See, for example, Tynes, *Turning Points in Social Security*, p. 44.

54. Committee on Economic Security, *Report to the President* (Washington: Government Printing Office, 1935). The report also called for the establishment of unemployment insurance and other measures not related to Social Security.

55. Douglas, *Social Security in the United States*, p. 84.

56. The voluntary annuity provision was ultimately killed, while the subsidies for state old-age pensions were significantly watered down.

57. "Is the Administration's Program for Old-Age Pensions Sound?" *Congressional Digest* 14 (1935): 81–3.

58. *Congressional Record*, vol. 79, part 9, 74th Congress (June 17, 1935), p. 9442.

59. *Congressional Record*, vol. 79, part 9, 74th Congress (June 18, 1935), pp. 9532–3.

60. Weaver, *The Crisis in Social Security*, pp. 90–1.

61. Edwin Witte, *The Development of the Social Security Act* (Madison: University of Wisconsin Press, 1962), p. 161.

62. Weaver, *The Crisis in Social Security*, p. 92.

63. Myers, *Social Security*, p. 15.

64. Cited in P. J. O'Brien, *Forward with Roosevelt* (Chicago: John Winston Company, 1936), pp. 92–3.

65. Arthur M. Schlesinger Jr., *The Coming of the New Deal* (Boston: Houghton Mifflin, 1958), pp. 308–9.

66. It is true that original drafts of the CES report and some drafts of the legislation would have included partial general revenue funding to cover shortfalls from the payroll tax in future years. However, Roosevelt explicitly rejected this approach and

the legislation was changed. Peter Ferrara, *Social Security: The Inherent Contradiction* (Washington: Cato Institute, 1980), pp. 21–2.

67. "Is the Administration's Program for Old-Age Pensions Sound?" pp. 83–85.

68. Tynes, *Turning Points in Social Security*, pp. 57–8.

69. Michael Schiltz, *Public Attitudes toward Social Security* (Washington: Social Security Administration, 1970), p. 30.

70. Rosenman, *The Public Papers and Addresses of Franklin D. Roosevelt*, pp. 291–2.

71. Testimony of Henry Morgenthau before the House Committee on Ways and Means, January 22, 1935.

72. Robert Myers suggests that, whatever the intent of its supporters, the program was never really fully funded. Accumulations in the fund would never have been sufficient to finance accrued liabilities without the help of future contributions. Myers argues that Social Security has always been funded on a partial reserve basis supplemented by current taxes. Myers, *Social Security*, pp. 386–7.

73. "Explanation of Federal OASI Under the Social Security Act Amendments of 1939," *Director's Bulletin of Progress* 17 (August 1939).

74. Douglas, *Social Security in the United States*, pp. 69–74.

75. For example, Carolyn Weaver of the American Enterprise Institute suggests, "The success of the Townsend movement may well have been more apparent than real, for a great deal of the literature on the movement was written by affiliates of the CES and other social insurance advocates. The incentive was strong to overstate the popularity of radical plans so as to pose false alternatives to [Social Security]. Indeed, the immediate effect of both the Townsend and Long movements was to smooth the way for the Social Security Act, which could only appear moderate." Weaver, *The Crisis in Social Security*, p. 71.

76. Summarized in ibid., pp. 97–9. The legislation also contained numerous provisions unrelated to old-age pensions, such as the creation of unemployment insurance, and Aid to Dependent Children. However, those programs are beyond the scope of this book.

77. Social Security Administration, *A Brief History of the Social Security Administration* (Washington: Government Printing Office, 1995), p. 4.

78. Republican candidate Alf Landon had made opposition to Social Security an important part of his campaign. Roosevelt therefore interpreted his overwhelming reelection as a mandate for the program. Tynes, *Turning Points in Social Security*, pp. 68–9.

79. Schlessinger, *The Coming of the New Deal*, p. 23.

80. Rosenman, *The Public Papers and Addresses of Franklin D. Roosevelt*, pp. 221–2.

81. Social Security Act of 1935, Preamble.

82. Roger Pilon, "Congress, the Courts, and the Constitution" in *Cato Handbook for Congress*, 105th Congress, eds. Ed Crane and David Boaz, (Washington: Cato Institute, 1997), pp. 26–7.

83. Weaver, *The Crisis in Social Security*, p. 109.

84. Charles Denby, "The Case Against the Constitutionality of the Social Security Act," *Law and Contemporary Problems* 3 (1936): 328–30.

85. Cited in Weaver, *The Crisis in Social Security*, p. 109.

86. Cited in Charles McKinley and Robert Frase, *Launching Social Security: 1935–1937* (Madison: University of Wisconsin Press), p. 453.

87. Cited in Theodore Becker and Malcom Freeley (eds.), *The Impact of Supreme Court Decisions* (Cambridge: Oxford University Press, 1973), pp. 39–41.

88. Ibid.

89. William Eaton, *Who Killed the Constitution: Judges vs. the Law* (Washington: Regnery Gateway, 1988), pp. 190–1.

90. Pilon, "Congress, the Courts, and the Constitution," p. 4.

91. 301 U.S. 609.

92. Ibid., at 641.

93. Ibid., at 619.

94. 363 U.S. 603.

95. In *Fleming v. Nestor* the Court held that "to engraft upon the Social Security system a concept of 'accrued property rights' would deprive it of the flexibility and boldness in adjustment to ever-changing conditions which it demands." Ibid., at 616.

96. Weaver, *The Crisis in Social Security*, p. 110.

97. Arthur J. Altmeyer, "Progress and Prospects Under the Social Security Act." Address to the National Conference of Social Workers, Washington, May 25, 1937.

98. *Congressional Record* vol. 81, part 2, 75th Congress (March 17, 1937), p. 2324.

99. Weaver, *The Crisis in Social Security*, pp. 120–1. Interestingly, this issue would resurface with the report of the 1994–1995 Advisory Council on Social Security. A plurality of the panel, led by former Social Security commissioner Robert Ball, proposed investing the Social Security trust funds in private securities. *Report of the 1994–1995 Advisory Council on Social Security* (Washington: Government Printing Office, 1997), pp. 25–6. Allowing such investment would be disastrous for the American economy. Krzystof Ostaszewski, "Privatizing the Social Security Trust Fund? Don't Let the Government Invest," Cato Institute Social Security Paper no. 6, January 14, 1997.

100. Carter and Shipman, *Promises to Keep*, p. 37.

101. Weaver, *The Crisis in Social Security*, pp. 115–6.

102. Ibid, pp. 123–4.

103. *Annual Budget Message to Congress*, January 10, 1949.

104. Summarized in Weaver, *The Crisis in Social Security*, pp. 132–3.

105. Ibid., pp. 133–40.

106. U.S. Advisory Council on Financing Social Security, *Financing OASDI* (Washington, U.S. Department of Health, Education, and Welfare, 1959).

107. Weaver, *The Crisis in Social Security*, p. 140.

108. Ibid., p. 154.

109. Ibid.

110. See Doug Bandow and Michael Tanner, "The Wrong and Right Ways to Reform Medicare," Cato Institute Policy Analysis no. 230, June 8, 1995.

111. Weaver, *The Crisis in Social Security*, p. 156.

112. Ibid., 160–1.

113. Carter and Shipman, *Promises to Keep*, pp. 57–8.

114. Tynes, *Turning Points in Social Security*, pp. 139–40.

115. Weaver, *The Crisis in Social Security*, p. 170. C. Eugene Steurle and Jon Bakija of the Urban Institute suggest that given Congress's history in the early 1970s, they may well have voted benefit increases at least as large as those brought about by COLAs. C. Eugene Steurle and Jon Bakija, *Retooling Social Security for the 21st Century: Right and Wrong Approaches to Reform* (Washington: Urban Institute Press, 1994), pp. 178–81. However, at least it would have been possible, in that case, to hold Congress politically responsible. COLAs removed any such accountability.

116. Michael Tanner, "Social Security: 60 Years of Tinkering," *World & I*, November, 1995.

117. Congress essentially indexed both the past wages on which Social Security benefits were based, and the benefits themselves. Paul Crag Roberts, "Social Security: Myths and Realities," *Cato Journal*, vol. 3, no. 2 (Fall 1983): 394–5.

118. *1980 Annual Report of the Board of Trustees of the Federal Old-Age, Survivors Insurance and Disability Insurance Trust Funds* cited in Ferrara, pp. 180–1.

119. Weaver, *The Crisis in Social Security*, p. 179.

120. William Simon, "How to Rescue Social Security," *Wall Street Journal*, November 3, 1976.

121. Carter and Shipman, *Promises to Keep*, p. 99.

122. Geoffrey Kollmann, "Summary of Major Changes in the Social Security Cash Benefits Program: 1935–1996," *Congressional Research Service Report for Congress* no. 94-36, December 20, 1996, p. 14.

123. Tynes, *Turning Points in Social Security*, Table 9, p. 165.

124. Kollmann, "Summary of Major Changes in the Social Security Cash Benefits Program," p. 14.

125. Ironically, it was repealing this double indexing provision that created the so-called "notch babies," one of the most fanatic of all Social Security lobbying groups. Notch babies are individuals born between January 2, 1917, and January 1, 1922, who reached age 65 between 1982 and 1986. The 1977 change to the benefit formula took away from this group some of the unintended benefits of double indexing that were received by people born just previously. Although this group was still among Social Security's big winners—receiving more in benefits than they paid in taxes—they have been extremely well organized and vocal in demanding a return of their lost benefits. Steuerle and Bakija, *Retooling Social Security*, p. 126.

126. "Carter Signs Social Security Tax Rise for 10 Million," *New York Times*, December 21, 1977.

127. Kollmann, "Summary of Major Changes in the Social Security Cash Benefits Program," p. 16.

128. For an interesting account of the Reagan proposals and the politics surrounding them, see William Niskanen, *Reaganomics: An Insider's Account of the Policies and the People* (New York: Oxford University Press, 1988), pp. 36–40.

129. "Coalition Plans Drive Against Move to Trim Social Security Benefits," *New York Times*, May 14, 1981.

130. Ibid.

131. "Reagan Urges Pension Negotiations," *New York Times*, May 22, 1981.

132. Merton Bernstein and John Brodshaug Bernstein, *Social Security: The System that Works*, (New York: Basic Books, 1988) p. 36.

133. In addition to Greenspan, the commission included Robert Beck, CEO of Prudential Insurance; Mary Fuller, a management consultant; Alexander Trowbridge, president of the National Association of Manufacturers; Joe Waggonner, a former congressman and a consultant to Bossier Bank and Trust Company; Sens. William Armstrong (R-Colo.), Robert Dole (R-Kans.), John Heinz (R-Pa.), and Daniel Patrick Moynihan (D-N.Y.); Reps. William Archer (R-Tex.), Barber Conable (R-N.Y.), and Claude Pepper (D-Fla.); and Lane Kirkland, president of the AFL-CIO; Martha Keyes, director of education programs for the Association of Former Members of Congress; and former Social Security commissioner Robert Ball.

134. Achenbaum, *Social Security*, p. 84.

135. Tynes, *Turning Points in Social Security*, p. 81.

136. For a discussion of the deliberations of the Greenspan Commission, see Paul Light, *Artful Work: The Politics of Social Security Reform* (New York: Random House, 1985).

137. Achenbaum, *Social Security*, p. 85.

138. Bernstein and Bernstein, *Social Security*, pp. 47–9.

139. Cited in Dorcas Hardy and C. Colburn Hardy, *Social Insecurity: The Crisis in America's Social Security System and How to Plan Now for Your Own Financial Survival* (New York: Villard Books, 1991), p. 14.

140. Spencer Rich, "Hill Passes Aged Aid Rescue Bill," *Washington Post*, March 25, 1983.

141. "Reagan Signs Social Security Rescue Plan," *Los Angeles Times*, April 21, 1983, p. 1.

142. Josh Weston et al., *Fixing Social Security* (New York: Committee for Economic Development, 1997), p. 29.

143. Martin Feldstein, "Privatizing Social Security: The $10 Trillion Opportunity," Cato Institute Social Security Paper no. 7, May 29, 1997, p. 2.

144. *1997 Trustees Report*, p. 4.

145. Mark Weinberger, "Social Security: Facing the Facts," Cato Institute Social Security Paper no. 3, April 10, 1997, p. 2.

146. "Statement of Celia Silverman, Employee Benefit Research Institute, to the 1994–1995 Advisory Council on Social Security," *Report of the 1994–1995 Advisory Council on Social Security*, vol. II (Washington: Government Printing Office, 1997), p. 304.

147. Josh Weston et al., "Who Will Pay for Your Retirement?" Committee for Economic Development, Washington, 1995.

148. U.S. House of Representatives Committee on Ways and Means, *1994 Green Book: Overview of Entitlement Programs* (Washington: Government Printing Office, 1994), pp. 10–2.

149. Ibid., pp. 12–3.

150. Ibid., p. 13.

151. The monthly benefit cap formula is 150 percent of the first $544 of PIA, plus 272 percent of PIA between $545 and $785 per month, 134 percent of PIA between $786 and $1,024, and 175 percent of PIA above $1,024. *1995 Annual Report of the Board of Trustees of the Federal Old-Age and Survivors Insurance and Disability Insurance Trust Funds* (Washington: Government Printing Office, 1995), p. 68.

152. Social Security Administration, *Understanding Social Security*, January 1993, p. 18.

153. Myers, *Social Security*, p. 55.

154. Ibid., p. 54.

Chapter 3

1. Under intermediate projections. *1998 Annual Report of the Board of Trustees of the Federal Old-Age and Survivors Insurance and Disability Insurance Trust Funds* (Washington: Government Printing Office, 1998), pp. 28–30.

2. This does not include the combined 2.9 percent payroll tax used to fund Medicare.

3. Elizabeth Bogan and Joseph Kiernan, *Macroeconomics: Theories and Application* (St. Paul, Minn.: West Publishing Company, 1987), p. 46.

4. Cited in P.J. O'Brien, *Forward with Roosevelt,* (Chicago: John C. Winston Company, 1936), p. 92.

5. Jay Robert Nash, *Bloodletters and Badmen* (New York: M. Evans and Co., 1995).

6. Paul A. Samuelson, "Paul A. Samuleson on Social Security," *Newsweek,* February 13, 1967, p. 88.

7. General Accounting Office, *Retirement Income: Implications of Demographic Trends for Social Security and Pension Reform* (Washington: Government Printing Office, GAO/HEHS-97-81, July 1997), p. 15.

8. Mark Weinberger, "Social Security: Facing the Facts," Cato Institute Social Security Paper no. 3, April 10, 1996, p. 5.

9. *1997 Trustees Report,* p. 63.

10. General Accounting Office, *Retirement Income,* p. 16.

11. Calculated from data in *1997 Trustees Report,* p. 63.

12. Charles Mullen and Tomas Philipson, "The Future of Old-Age Longevity: Competitive Pricing of Mortality Contingent Claims," University of Chicago, George J. Stigler Center for the Study of the Economy and the State, Working Paper no. 134, May 1, 1997.

13. Cited in James Smalhout, "Mortality Sins," *Barron's,* December 1, 1997.

14. Ibid.

15. Cited in "New Views on Life Spans Alter Forecasts on Elderly," *New York Times,* November 16, 1992.

16. Ansley Coale and Marin Zelnik, *New Estimates of Fertility and Population in the United States* (Princeton, N.J.: Princeton University Press, 1989); National Center for Health Statistics; *Annual Report of the Board of Trustees of the Federal Old-Age and Survivors Insurance and Disability Insurance Trust Funds,* various years.

17. Stephen Entin, "The Future of Social Security Benefits," in *Report of the Task Force on Social Security,* ed. Tom Miller, Citizens Against Government Waste, Washington, August 1994, p. 11.

18. *1998 Trustees Report,* p. 22.

19. See, for example, Richard Posner, "Why Not to Worry about the Aging of the Population." Paper presented to the American Enterprise Institute, Washington, March 11, 1996.

20. *Retirement Income,* General Accounting Office, p. 18.

21. David Altig and Jagadeesh Gokhale, "Social Security Privatization: One Proposal," Cato Institute Social Security Paper no. 9, May 29, 1997, p. 6.

22. Lawrence Mead, *The New Politics of Poverty: The Nonworking Poor in America* (New York: Basic Books, 1992), p. 89.

23. Council of Economic Advisors, *Economic Report of the President* (Washington: Government Printing Office, 1997), Table B-47, p. 354.

24. *Report of the 1994–1995 Advisory Council on Social Security,* vol. II (Washington: Government Printing Office, 1997), p. 161.

25. J. Bradford DeLong and Lawrence Summers, "Equipment Investment and Economic Growth," *Quarterly Journal of Economics* 106, vol. 2 (1991): 445–502.

26. *1998 Trustees Report,* Table I.D.1, p. 8.

27. Ibid., p. 10.

28. Ibid.

29. Robert Myers, *Social Security* (Philadelphia: University of Pennsylvania Press, 1993), p. 142.

30. Weinberger, "Social Security: Facing the Facts," p. 5.

31. Myers, *Social Security*, p. 142.

32. David Wise, "Six Initiatives to Promote Private Savings," *Challenge*, November–December 1992, p. 23.

33. Weinberger, "Social Security: Facing the Facts," p. 5.

34. Monetizing the debt would likely invite higher inflation. An increase in consumer prices would result in larger increases in cost of living adjustments (COLAs), which in part determine the level of Social Security benefits paid out. Accordingly, such action would likely cause a vicious cycle of increased benefit payments that would exacerbate the problem.

35. *1997 Trustees Report*, Table II.B.1, p. 33.

36. William Shipman, "Retiring with Dignity: Social Security vs. Private Markets," Cato Institute Social Security Paper no. 2, August 14, 1995, p. 4.

37. Young workers entering the workforce today will retire in about 2045. Under intermediate projections, promised benefits in that year will equal 17.78 percent of taxable payroll. *1997 Trustees Report*, Table III.A.2, pp. 172–3. While taxation of Social Security benefits will provide revenue equal to approximately 0.78 percent of payroll, payroll taxes would inevitably have to be raised above 17 percent to allow some cash flow cushion during the time taxes are collected each month. Ibid., Table II.F.17, pp.121–2. By 2060, when most of those workers will still be drawing benefits, benefit expenditures will equal 18.72 percent of payroll. Even with revenue from the taxation of Social Security benefits, the payroll tax will have to be increased to more than 18 percent.

38. Medicare Part A is the portion of the Medicare program that pays for hospital care. Medicare Part B pays for physician care and is mostly funded out of general revenues rather than through payroll taxes.

39. Doug Bandow and Michael Tanner, "The Wrong and Right Ways to Reform Medicare," Cato Institute Policy Analysis no. 230.

40. By 2045, when those entering the workforce today will be retiring, total Social Security and Medicare Part A benefits will equal 27.95 percent of payroll, under intermediate projections. *1997 Trustees Report*, Table III.A.2, pp. 172–3. Counting income equal to 0.78 percent of payroll as a result of taxing Social Security benefits still leaves a required payroll tax of more than 27 percent. Ibid., Table II.F.17, pp. 121–2. By 2060, when most of those workers will still be alive and drawing benefits, obligations under both Social Security and Medicare Part A will equal 29.53 percent of payroll. Even counting revenue from the taxation of Social Security benefits, a payroll tax of nearly 29 percent will be required.

41. A. Haeworth Robertson, *Social Security: What Every Taxpayer Should Know* (Washington: Retirement Policy Institute, 1992), pp. 53–4.

42. Ibid.

43. *1997 Trustees Report*, p. 138.

44. *1994–95 Advisory Council*, vol. II, p. 148.

45. Quoted in Smalhout, "Mortality Sins," *Barron's*, December 1, 1997.

46. Robertson, *Social Security*, p. 59.

47. *1997 Trustees Report*, p. 138.

48. Under pessimistic projections, by 2045, when those entering the workforce today will be retiring, total Social Security benefits will equal 23.15 percent of payroll. *1997 Trustees Report*, Table III.A.2, pp. 172–3. With income from taxation of benefits equal to 1.04 percent of payroll, the payroll tax would still have to be hiked to more than 22 percent. Table II.F.17, pp. 121–2. By 2060, when most of those workers will

still be drawing benefits, benefit expenditures will equal 26.55 percent of payroll. Even with revenue from the taxation of Social Security benefits, the payroll tax will have to be increased to nearly 26 percent. And, by 2070, with some of those workers still alive, the payroll tax would have to be raised to approximately 27.5 percent.

49. Ibid. By 2045, those benefits would equal 42.77 percent of payroll under pessimistic projections. Counting revenue from the taxation of benefits, the payroll tax would still have to be raised to nearly 42 percent. By 2060, benefits would equal 47.31 percent of payroll, with a required payroll tax of approximately 46 percent. By 2070, the payroll tax would have to be 49 percent.

50. Laurence Kotlikoff and Jagadeesh Gokhale, "An Economic Burden Is Being Placed on Future Generations," ed. Charles Cozic, *An Aging Population: Opposing Viewpoints* (San Diego: Greenhausen Press, 1996), p. 35. For a more detailed discussion see Lawrence Kotlikoff, *Generational Accounting*, (New York: Free Press, 1992).

51. U.S. House of Representatives Committee on Ways and Means, "Background Materials on the Federal Budget and Tax Policy for the Fiscal Year 1991 and Beyond," February 6, 1990, p. 24.

52. Michael Tanner, "Privatizing Social Security: A Big Boost for the Poor," Cato Institute Social Security Paper no. 4, July 26, 1996, pp. 8–9.

53. Congressional Budget Office, "Aggregate Income Effects of Changes in Social Security Taxes," August 1982, p. 30.

54. Aldona Robbins and Gary Robbins, "Effects of the 1988 and 1990 Social Security Tax Increases," Institute for Research on the Economics of Taxation, Washington, D.C., 1991, pp. 14–5.

55. See speech by Sen. Edward Kennedy (D-Mass.) to the National Press Club, December 11, 1997.

56. *1997 Trustees Report*, Table II.F.14.

57. Neil Howe and Richard Jackson, "The Myth of the 2.2% Solution," Cato Institute Social Security Paper no. 11, June 15, 1998.

58. George Buck, "Actuarial Soundness in Trusteed and Government Retirement Plans," *Proceedings of Panel Meeting: What Is Actuarial Soundness in a Pension Plan?* American Statistical Association, American Association of University Teachers of Insurance, and Industrial Relations Research Association, Chicago, December 19, 1952.

59. Testimony of Lawrence Summers before the Senate Budget Committee, Social Security Task Force, January 29, 1998.

60. *1997 Trustees Report*, Figure III.B.1, p. 181.

61. Ibid.

62. David Koitz and Geoffrey Kollmann, "Current Social Security Issues," Congressional Research Service Report for Congress no. 96-43 EPW, May 14, 1997, pp. 8–9.

63. Martin Feldstein, "The Right Way to Adjust for Inflation," *Wall Street Journal*, February 26, 1997.

64. Advisory Commission to Study the Consumer Price Index, "Toward a More Accurate Measure of the Cost of Living: Final Report to the Senate Finance Committee," December 4, 1996, p. ii.

65. Dennis Fixler, "The Consumer Price Index: Underlying Concepts and Caveats, Anatomy of Price Change," *Monthly Labor Review*, December 1993, pp. 3–11.

66. James Storey, "Adjusting Benefits for Inflation: Impacts of Policy Change," Congressional Research Service Report for Congress no. 95-670 EPW, 1997.

67. Cited in Koitz and Kollmann, *Current Social Security Issues*, p. 9.

68. Nathan Amble and Kenneth Stewart, "Experimental Price Index for Elderly Consumers," *Monthly Labor Review*, May 1994, p. 11–5.

69. Laurel Beedon and Lee Cohen, "The Consumer Price Index," AARP Fact Sheet no. 42, April 1995.

70. The poorest 20 percent of the elderly depend on Social Security for 81 percent of their income. Neil Gilbert and Neung-Hoo Park, "Privatization, Provision, and Targeting: Trends and Policy Implications for Social Security in the United States," *International Social Security Review* 49 (January 1996): 22.

71. Donna Clemments and Suzanne Barbour, "1997 Guide to Social Security and Medicare," William Mercer Company, Louisville, Ky., November 1996, p. 16.

72. Bureau of the Census, *The American Almanac: Statistical Abstract of the United States, 1995* (Austin: Reference Press, 1995), Table 114, p. 86.

73. Daniel Garett, "The Effects of Different Mortality Rates on the Progressivity of Social Security," *Economic Inquiry* 33 (July 1995): 458.

74. Del Jones, "Pushing Back Retirement," *USA Today*, December 11, 1997.

75. Peter Peterson, *Will America Grow Up before It Grows Old?* (New York: Random House, 1996), pp. 167–8.

76. Bipartisan Commission on Entitlement and Tax Reform, *Final Report to the President* (Washington: Government Printing Office, 1995), p. 167.

77. The authors acknowledge that in many ways Social Security *is* a welfare program. However, that is clearly not the public perception.

78. See for example, David Neumark and Elizabeth Powers, "Consequences of Means Testing Social Security: Evidence from the SSI Program," Federal Reserve Bank of Cleveland Working Paper no. 96-18, March 10, 1997; Martin Feldstein, "Should Social Security be Means Tested?" *Journal of Political Economy* 95, no. 3 (1987): 468–84.

79. Bipartisan Commission on Entitlement and Tax Reform, pp. 112–4.

80. Neumark and Powers, "Consequences of Means Testing Social Security," p. 3.

81. General Accounting Office, *Retirement Income*, pp. 40–1.

82. Congressional Budget Office, "Monthly Treasury Statement of Receipts and Outlays of the United States Government, FY1997," November 30, 1997.

83. Congressional Budget Office, "CBO Revised Baseline Projections for Fiscal Years 1999–2008," March 3, 1998.

84. James Buchanan, "The Budgetary Politics of Social Security," in *Social Security's Looming Surpluses: Prospects and Implications,* ed. Carolyn Weaver (Washington: American Enterprise Institute, 1990), pp. 50–1.

85. Peterson, *Will America Grow Up?* p. 32.

86. Martin Feldstein and Andrew Samwick, "The Transition Path to Privatizing Social Security," National Bureau of Economic Research Working Paper no. 5761, September 1996.

87. http://www.pu.bicdebt.treas.gov/opedpenny.htm.

88. Bipartisan Commission on Entitlement and Tax Reform, pp. 8–9.

Chapter 4

1. *Congressional Record*, June 12, 1935, cited in Warren Shore, *Social Security: The Fraud in Your Future* (New York: Macmillan, 1975), p. 2.

2. Dorcas Hardy and C. Colburn Hardy, *Social Insecurity: The Crisis in America's Social Security System and How to Plan Now for Your Own Financial Survival* (New York: Villard Books, 1991), p. 10.

3. Martin Feldstein, Louis Dicks-Mireaux, and James Porterba, "The Effective Tax Rate and Pretax Rate of Return," *Journal of Public Economics* 21 (July 1993): 12–58.

4. Peter J. Ferrara, "Social Security Rates of Return for Today's Young Workers," National Chamber Foundation, Washington, 1986.

5. *1986 Report of the Board of Trustees of the Federal Old-Age and Survivors Insurance and Disability Insurance Trust Funds* (Washington: Government Printing Office, 1986).

6. Jonathan Berry Forman, "Why Treat Today's Women As If This Were the 1930s?" *Los Angeles Times*, May 4, 1997.

7. This provision discriminates against working spouses as discussed in detail in chapter 5.

8. Arthur Hall, "Forcing a Bad Investment on Retiring Americans," Tax Foundation Special Report no. 55, November 1995.

9. *Report of the 1994–1995 Advisory Council on Social Security*, (Washington: Government Printing Office, 1997), pp. 206–18.

10. William Beach and Gareth Davis, "Social Security's Rate of Return," Report of the Heritage Foundation Center for Data Analysis no. 98-01, January 15, 1998.

11. Jeremy Siegel, *Stocks for the Long Run* (Chicago: Irwin Professional Publishing, 1994), pp. 5–7.

12. *Stocks, Bonds, Bills, and Inflation 1997 Yearbook* (Chicago: Ibbotson Associates), pp. 266–75.

13. Calculated from Moody's Investor Service, Moody's Industrial Manual, Moody's Bond Survey, 1920–1996.

14. It is interesting to note, however, that while bonds are often considered a "safer" investment than stocks, they are in fact more volatile and there are 20-year periods during which individuals would lose money by investing solely in bonds. Siegel, *Stocks for the Long Run*, pp. 28–39.

15. Ferrara, "Social Security Rates of Return for Today's Young Workers."

16. Peter Ferrara and John Lott, "Social Security Rates of Return for Today's Young Workers," ed. Peter Ferrara, *Social Security: Prospects for Real Reform* (Washington: Cato Institute, 1983), pp. 13–36.

17. William G. Shipman, "Retiring with Dignity: Social Security vs. Private Markets," Cato Institute Social Security Paper no. 2, August 14, 1995.

18. Melissa Hieger and William Shipman, "Common Objections to a Market-Based Social Security System: A Response," Cato Institute Social Security Paper no. 10, July 22, 1997.

19. Readers who wish to find out how Social Security compares to what they could earn from private investment can contact the Cato Institute's Social Security website at www.socialsecurity.org. In addition to materials on Social Security privatization, the site contains an interactive calculator designed by the accounting firm of KPMG Peat Marwick. Readers can enter personal data (age, income, etc.) to see what their future Social Security benefits would be and how they compare to what they could earn in a privately invested system.

20. *1997 Annual Report of the Board of Trustees of the Federal Old-Age and Survivors Insurance and Disability Insurance Trust Funds*, Table II.C.7, p. 52.

21. Hieger and Shipman, "Common Objections to a Market-Based Social Security System," p. 14.

22. Social Security Administration, "Social Security Update 1998," SSA Publication no. 05-10003, January 1998.

23. Hieger and Shipman, "Common Objections to a Market-Based Social Security System," p. 13.

24. Olivia Mitchell, "Administrative Costs in Public and Private Retirement Systems," Privatizing Social Security Conference, National Bureau of Economic Research, Cambridge, Mass., August 1–2, 1996.

25. For example, critics of privatization often point to the stock market crash of 1929 and the Great Depression as a warning of what could happen under a privatized Social Security system. Yet, unemployment reached 37 percent during the Depression. How would the government continue to fund the current system, based on a payroll tax, given such levels of unemployment?

26. Hieger and Shipman, "Common Objections to a Market-Based Social Security System," p. 8.

27. Seigel, *Stocks for the Long Run.*

28. Hieger and Shipman, "Common Objections to a Market-Based Social Security System," p. 9.

29. Martin Feldstein and Andrew Samwick, "The Transition Path in Privatizing Social Security," National Bureau of Economic Research Working Paper no. 5761, Cambridge, Mass., September 1996, p. 41.

30. 363 U.S. at 616.

31. 363 U.S. at 610.

Chapter 5

1. Josh Weston et al., "Who Will Pay for Your Retirement?" Committee for Economic Development, Washington, 1995, p. 32.

2. Neil Gilbert and Neung-Hoo Park, "Privatization, Provision, and Targeting: Trends and Policy Implications for Social Security in the United States," *International Social Security Review* 49 (January 1996): 22.

3. U.S. House of Representatives Committee on Ways and Means, *1994 Green Book: Overview of Entitlement Programs* (Washington: Government Printing Office, 1994), Table 1.7, p. 16.

4. Ibid.

5. A. Haeworth Robertson, *Social Security: What Every Taxpayer Should Know* (Washington: Retirement Policy Institute, 1992), p. 218.

6. *1994 Green Book*, Chart H-1, p. 1159.

7. Stephen Entin, "Social Security: Problems and Opportunity," Institute for Research on Economics of Taxation, Washington, June 19, 1995, p. 3.

8. See, for example, Harriet Duleep, "Measuring the Effect of Income on Adult Mortality Using Longitudinal Administrative Record Data," *Journal of Human Resources* 21 (Spring 1986): 238–51; Evelyn Kitagawa and Philip Hauser, *Differences in Mortality in the United States: A Study in Socioeconomic Epidemiology* (Cambridge, Mass.: Harvard University Press, 1973); Eugene Roget, Paul Sorlie, and Norman Johnson, "Life Expectancy by Employment Status, Income, and Education in the National Longitudinal Mortality Study," *Public Health Reports* 107 (July–August 1992): 457–61; and Howard Iams and John McCoy, "Predictors of Mortality among Newly Retired Workers," *Social Security Bulletin* 54 (March 1991): 2–10.

9. Henry Aaron, *Demographic Effects on the Equity of Social Security Benefits* (Washington: Brookings Institution, 1979).

10. Personal note to Michael Tanner, May 14, 1997.

11. C. Eugene Steuerle and Jon Bakija, *Retooling Social Security for the 21st Century: Right & Wrong Approaches to Reform* (Washington: Urban Institute, 1994), pp. 115–9.

12. James Duggan, Robert Gillingham, and John Greenlees, "Progressive Returns to Social Security? An Answer from Social Security Records," Research Paper no. 9501, U.S. Department of the Treasury, November 1995.

13. Daniel Garrett, "The Effects of Differential Mortality Rates on the Progressivity of Social Security," *Economic Inquiry* 33 (July 1995): 457–75.

14. Quoted in ibid., p. 457.

15. Steuerle and Bakija, *Retooling Social Security for the 21st Century*, p. 119; Garrett, "Effects of Differential Mortality Rates," p. 458.

16. One of the earliest to write about this problem was Milton Friedman. See Milton Friedman and Wilbur Cohen, *Social Security: Universal or Selective?* (Washington: American Enterprise Institute, 1972).

17. W. Constantijn, A. Panis and Lee Lillard, "Socioeconomic Differentials in the Return to Social Security," RAND Corporation Working Paper Series no. 96-05, February 1996, p. 20.

18. Ibid.

19. See, for example, testimony of Alicia Munnell before the Senate Budget Committee Task Force on Social Security, January 21, 1998.

20. Testimony of Sylvester Schieber before the Senate Budget Committee Task Force on Social Security, January 21, 1998.

21. Peter Ferrara, *Social Security: The Inherent Contradiction* (Washington: Cato Institute, 1980), pp. 229–30.

22. Bureau of the Census, *Poverty in the United States, 1996*, Current Population Reports (Washington: Government Printing Office, 1996), Table 6, p. 18.

23. Bureau of the Census, *Statistical Abstract of the United States, 1995* (Washington: Government Printing Office, 1996), Table B-1.

24. Ibid., Table B-2.

25. Pannis and Lillard, "Socioeconomic Differentials in the Return to Social Security," p. 14.

26. William Beach and Gareth Davis, "Social Security's Rate of Return," Report of the Heritage Center for Data Analysis no. 98-01, January 15, 1998.

27. Testimony of Alicia Munnell, January 21, 1998.

28. The provisions apply to both men and women. However, because there are relatively few families in which the husband does not work at all, and few families in which the husband earns less than 50 percent of his wife's wages, the provision in question affects women almost exclusively.

29. Because of the progressive annual benefits formula, a woman actually needs to earn only about one-third of her husband's wages to earn benefits equal to 50 percent of her husband's.

30. Jane Ross, *Social Security Reform: Implications for the Financial Well-Being of Women*, General Accounting Office, GAO/T-HEHS-97-112, April 10, 1997, p. 5.

31. Cited in W. Andrew Achenbaum, *Social Security: Visions and Revisions* (Cambridge: Cambridge University Press, 1986), p. 132.

32. Extrapolated from Steven Sandell, "Adequacy and Equity of Social Security," *Report of the 1994–1996 Advisory Council on Social Security* (Washington: Government Printing Office, 1997), vol. II, chart 8, p. 329.

33. Ibid. "What Can Be Done about Marriage Penalties?" *Family Law Quarterly* 30 (1996):1–22.

34. U.S. Bureau of the Census, *Marital and Family Characteristics of the Labor Force*, Current Population Reports, March 1997, Table 15.

35. Sandell, "Adequacy and Equity of Social Security," p. 328–9.

36. Extrapolated from ibid., charts 7 and 8, pp. 328–9.

37. Ross, *Social Security Reform*, p. 2.

38. Testimony of Deborah Briceland-Betts, executive director, Older Women's League, before the 1994–1996 Advisory Council on Social Security, March 8, 1995.

39. "Women Fret More Than Men About Retirement Savings," *Investors Business Daily*, April 9, 1997.

40. Judith Burns, "Women Are Faulted on Retirement Funds," *Wall Street Journal*, June 20, 1997.

41. "When It Comes to Investing, Women Are Paying More Attention," Oppenheimer Funds, press release, January 14, 1998.

42. Ibid. The poll was conducted by the Richard Wirthlin Company. The margin of error is plus or minus 6.2 percent.

43. William Shipman, "Retiring with Dignity: Social Security vs. Private Markets," Cato Institute Social Security Paper no. 2, August 14, 1995, p. 4.

44. In fact, if federal tax rates—as a percentage of family income—were restored to 1948 levels, the average employed mother could leave the labor force entirely, and the family would experience little or no decline in after-tax income. Robert Rector, "Uncle Sam and the Kids: Parents, Politics, and Child Care," *The World & I*, September 1981, p. 497.

45. See Michael Tanner, *The End of Welfare: Fighting Poverty in the Civil Society*, (Washington: Cato Institute, 1996), pp. 69–85.

46. Allan Carlson, "Is Social Security Pro-Family?" *Policy Review* (Fall 1987): 49.

47. Ibid., p. 50.

48. Darcy Olsen, "The Advancing Nanny State: Why Government Should Stay Out of Child Care," Cato Institute Policy Analysis no. 285, October 23, 1997.

49. See, for example, Richard Burkhauser, Douglas Holtz-Eakin, and Stephin Rhody, "Labor Earnings Mobility and Inequality in the United States and Germany in the Growth Years of the 1980's," accepted for publication in a forthcoming issue of *International Economic Review*, and W. Michael Cox and Richard Alm, "By Our Own Bootstraps: Economic Opportunity and the Dynamics of Income Distribution," Federal Reserve Bank of Dallas, 1995.

50. James Smith, "Unequal Wealth and Incentives to Save," Rand Corporation, 1995.

51. "Remodeling Social Security," Economic Security 2000, 1997.

52. Quoted in Sam Beard, *Restoring Hope in America: The Social Security Solution* (San Francisco: Institute for Contemporary Studies, 1996), p. 160.

53. Internal Revenue Service Code, Federal Insurance Contributions Act, Secs. 3101 and 3102.

54. Many economists also argue that Social Security *benefits* reduce savings. Since Social Security provides beneficiaries with retirement income, people feel less need to save for retirement. Martin Feldstein, "Social Security, Induced Retirement, and Aggregate Capital Accumulation," *Journal of Political Economy* 82, no. 5 (September–October 1974); Martin Feldstein, "Inflation, Tax Rules and Investment: Some Econometric Evidence," *Econometrica* 50, no. 4 (July 1982): 825–62; and Peter Diamond and J. A. Hausman, "Individual Retirement and Savings Behavior," *Journal of Public*

Economics 23, no. 1–2 (February–March 1984): 81–114. This would apply equally to a privatized system.

55. U.S. House of Representatives Committee on Ways and Means, "Background Materials on the Federal Budget and Tax Policy for Fiscal Year 1991 and Beyond," February 6, 1990, p. 30.

56. Peter Elinsky and James Buckley, "Retirement Benefits in the 1990's: 1997 Survey Data," KPMG Peat Marwick, 1997, p. 32.

57. Ibid., p. 34.

58. Ibid., pp. 28–31.

59. Martin Feldstein, "Social Insurance," Harvard Institute of Economic Research Discussion Paper no. 477, May 1976.

60. "Black-White Income Inequalities," *New York Times*, February 17, 1998.

61. Speech by Sen. Robert Kerrey to the National Press Club, Washington, September 17, 1997.

62. Quoted in *Restoring Hope in America*, p. 143.

63. José Piñera, "Empowering Workers: The Privatization of Social Security in Chile," Cato's Letters no. 10, April 1996.

64. Martin Feldstein, "Social Security and the Distribution of Wealth," *Journal of the American Statistical Association* (December 1976): 90–3.

65. Testimony of Alan Greenspan before the House Budget Committee, October 8, 1997.

Chapter 6

1. Martin Feldstein, "Toward a Reform of Social Security," *The Public Interest* (Summer 1975): 75.

2. Martin Feldstein, "Privatizing Social Security: The $10 Trillion Opportunity," Cato Institute Social Security Paper no. 7, January 31, 1997.

3. Organization for Economic Cooperation and Development, *National Accounts, Main Aggregates* 1960–1992, vol. I (Paris: OECD, 1993).

4. Congressional Budget Office, "Assessing the Decline in the National Savings Rate," April 1993, p. 2.

5. Ibid., p. 8.

6. This is a systemwide estimate. Individual savings decisions will vary from worker to worker. Martin Feldstein, "Social Security, Induced Retirement, and Aggregate Capital Accumulation," *Journal of Political Economy* 82, no. 5 (September–October 1974): 905–26.

7. U.S. Bureau of the Census, *Statistical Abstract of the United States* (Washington: Government Printing Office, 1997), Table 704, p. 455.

8. Martin Feldstein, "The Missing Piece in Policy Analysis: Social Security Reform," *American Economic Review* 86, 1–2 (May 1996): 1.

9. Ibid.

10. Feldstein, "Privatizing Social Security: The $10 Trillion Opportunity."

11. U.S. Bureau of the Census, *Statistical Abstract of the United States*, Table 750, p. 455.

12. Albert Ando and Franco Modigliani, "The 'Life Cycle' Hypothesis of Saving: Aggregate Implications and Tests," *American Economic Review* 53 (March 1963): 55–84.

13. Alicia Munnell, "The Impact of Social Security on Personal Savings," *National Tax Journal* 27 (December 1974): 553–67.

14. Robert J. Barro, "Are Government Bonds Net Wealth?" *Journal of Political Economy* 82 (November–December 1974), pp. 1095–117.

15. The average monthly benefit was less than $50 until 1954, and was less than $75 until 1965. Peter Ferrara, *Social Security: The Inherent Contradiction* (Washington: Cato Institute, 1980), Table 15, p. 415.

16. Council of Economic Advisors, *Economic Report of the President*, (Washington: Government Printing Office, 1997), Table B-28, p. 332.

17. Feldstein's response is published in Robert Barro, *The Impact of Social Security on Private Saving* (Washington: American Enterprise Institute, 1977).

18. Ibid., p. 40.

19. Barro, *The Impact of Social Security on Private Savings*.

20. Ibid., p. 41.

21. Martin Feldstein, "Social Security, Induced Retirement, and Aggregate Capital Accumulation," *Journal of Political Economy* 82 (September–October 1974): 905–26.

22. Martin Feldstein and Anthony Pellechio, "Social Security and Household Wealth Accumulation: New Microeconomic Evidence," *Review of Economics and Statistics* 61 (August 1979): 361–8.

23. Martin Feldstein, "Social Security and Private Savings: International Evidence in an Extended Life-Cycle Model," Harvard Institute of Economic Research Discussion Paper no. 361, 1974.

24. N. Bulent Gultekin and Dennis Logue, "Social Security and Personal Savings: Survey and New Evidence," ed. Robert Barro, *Social Security and Private Saving — Evidence from the U.S. Time Series* (Washington: American Enterprise Institute, 1978), p. 97.

25. Dean Leimer and David Richardson, "Social Security, Uncertainty Adjustments, and the Consumption Decision," *Economica* 59 (August 1992): 24.

26. Josh Weston, "Who Will Pay for Your Retirement? The Looming Crisis," Committee for Economic Development, New York, 1995.

27. Peter Diamond, "A Framework for Social Security Analysis," *Journal of Public Economics* 8 (December 1977): 275–98.

28. "Social Security Reform and U.S. Economic Growth," *Capital Formation*, U.S. Council on Capital Formation, January–February 1996.

29. Paul Samuelson and William Nordhaus, *Economics* (New York: McGraw Hill, 1985), p. 800.

30. See, for example, Louis Esposito, "The Impact of Social Security on Private Saving: Review of Studies Using Time Series Data," *Social Security Bulletin* 41 (May 1978): 9–17; Dean Leimer and Selig Lesnoy, "Social Security and Private Saving: New Time Series Evidence," *Journal of Political Economy* 90 (June 1982): 606–29; Peter Diamond and Jerry Hausman, "Individual Retirement and Saving Behavior," *Journal of Public Economics* 23 (February–March 1984): 81–114; and Alan Blinder, R. Gordon, and David Wise, "Social Security, Bequests, and Life-Cycle Theory of Savings: Cross-Sectional Tests," ed. Blinder, *Inventory Theory and Consumer Behavior* (Ann Arbor: University of Michigan Press, 1990), pp. 229–56.

31. Feldstein, "The Missing Piece in Policy Analysis."

32. Daniel Hammermesh, *Labor Demand* (Princeton: Princeton University Press, 1993).

33. Elizabeth Bogan and Joseph Kiernan, *Macroeconomics: Theories and Application* (St. Paul, Minn.: West Publishing Company, 1987), p. 46.

34. It should be noted that if any part of the tax were borne by the employer, that would just change, not eliminate, the negative effects of the tax. In that case, the tax would cause the employer to reduce employment.

35. Martin Feldstein and Andrew Samwick, "The Transition Path in Privatizing Social Security," National Bureau of Economic Research Working Paper no. 5761, September 1996.

36. Feldstein, "The Missing Piece in Policy Analysis," p. 5.

37. Peter Diamond and Jonathan Gruber, "Social Security and Retirement in the United States," National Bureau of Economic Research Working Paper no. 6097, July 1, 1997.

38. Gary Becker, "The Economic Impact of Privatizing Social Security." Paper presented to a conference on "Solving the Global Public Pensions Crisis: Opportunities for Privatization," London, December 8, 1997.

39. Feldstein, "Privatizing Social Security: The $10 Trillion Opportunity," p. 4. The present value gain is the present value of annual gains of 5 percent of GDP. Since the current level of GDP is approximately $7.5 trillion, a gain of 5 percent of that would be $375 billion. The annual gain would increase in proportion to the GDP and would therefore grow at about 3 percent per year in real terms. Discounting this at a rate of 5 percent (approximately the rate of return net of tax that an individual investor received on the Standard & Poor's portfolio over the period since 1970) implies a present value of $18.75 trillion.

40. Daniel Mitchell, "A Brief Guide to Social Security Reform," Heritage Foundation Talking Points no. 22, August 7, 1997.

41. Michael Darby, "The Effects of Social Security on Income and the Capital Stock," (Washington: American Enterprise Institute, 1979), p. 79.

42. Laurence Kotlikoff, "Simulating the Privatization of Social Security in General Equilibrium." Paper presented to a conference on "Privatizing Social Security," National Bureau of Economic Research, Cambridge, Mass., August 1, 1996.

43. Mike McNamee and Paul Magnusson, "Let's Get Growing," *Business Week,* July 8, 1996.

Chapter 7

1. World Bank, *Averting the Old-Age Crisis* (Oxford: Oxford University Press, 1994), p. 7.

2. John Silva, "World Economic Outlook," Zurich Kemper Investments, August 28, 1996.

3. William Poortvliet and Thomas Laine, "Privatization and Reform of Social Security Pension Plans as a Global Trend: Part 1: The Underlying Problem," *Journal of the American Society of CLU & ChFC* (July1997): 55.

4. Yusuke Matsunaga, "Preparing for Old-Age: The Challenge of Japan's Aging Society," *Nomura Research Institute Quarterly* (Spring 1997), pp. 22–35.

5. Testimony of Estelle James before the U.S. Senate Special Committee on Aging, September 10, 1996.

6. Poortvleit and Laine, "Privatization and Reform of Social Security Pension Plans as a Global Trend," p. 59.

7. Stephen Meyer, "Savings and Demographics: Some International Comparisons," *Business Review* (March–April 1992): 15.

8. *Aging Populations: The Social Policy Implications* (Paris: OECD, 1988).

9. Paul Van der Noord and Richard Heard, *Pension Liabilities in Seven Major Economies*, (Paris: OECD, 1993).

10. World Bank, *Averting the Old-Age Crisis*, pp. 280–1.

11. See Constance Holden, "New Populations of Old Add to Poor Nations' Burden," *Science*, July 5, 1996.

12. World Bank, *Averting the Old-Age Crisis*, p. xiii.

13. See Robert Myers, "Privatization of Chile's Social Security Program," *Benefits Quarterly* 1, no. 3 (Fall 1985): 26–35.

14. The description of the Chilean social security system that follows is drawn from José Piñera, "Empowering Workers: The Privatization of Social Security in Chile," Cato's Letters no. 10, July 1996. For a detailed discussion of Chile's system, see José Piñera, *El Cascabel al Gato* (Santiago: Editorial Zig Zag, 1991).

15. The number of AFPs varies over time as some companies merge or go out of business and new companies enter the system. There is free entry to the market for any company meeting the basic requirements for participation.

16. The value of the bond was derived by taking 80 percent of the worker's average salary in the 12 months leading to mid-1979 (indexed for inflation), multiplied by the number of years the employee contributed to the system (up to a maximum of 35 years), and multiplied by an annuity factor of 10.35 for men and 11.36 for women. Myers, "Privatization of Chile's Social Security Program," p. 30.

17. This represents the gross return. The net return, after deducting commissions, has been somewhat lower, but still substantial.

18. Augusto Palau, "Chile: Results and Lessons after 15 Years of Reform." Paper presented to a conference on "The Pension Fund Revolution in Latin America," Miami, September 19, 1996.

19. Sergio Baeza, *Quince Años Despues: Una Miranda al Sistema Privado de Pensiones* (Santiago: Centro de Estudios Publicos, 1995).

20. Marco Santamaría, "Privatizing Social Security: The Chilean Case," Federal Reserve Bank of New York Research Paper no. 9127, November 1991, p. 9.

21. Palau, "Chile: Results and Lessons after 15 Years of Reform."

22. Jim Barrineau, "Analyzing the Effect of Pension Reform on Local Stock Markets." Paper presented to a conference on The Pension Fund Revolution in Latin America, Miami, September 19, 1996. Of course there is disagreement about the degree to which Chile's social security system is responsible for those economic developments, as opposed to other economic reforms that took place at the same time. See, for example, Peter Diamond and Salvador Valdes-Prieto, *Social Security Reforms* (Washington: Brookings Institution, 1994); Santamaría, "Privatizing Social Security," pp. 9–18. But the general consensus is that the new pension system has made a significant contribution to the reduction of poverty by increasing the size and certainty of old-age, survivors, and disability pensions and by the indirect, but very powerful, effect of promoting economic growth and employment. See, for example, Monika Queisser, "Chile and Beyond: The Second Generation of Pension Reform in Latin America," *International Social Security Review* 48 (March–April 1995): 23–39.

23. Quoted in Peter Ferrara, "The Social Security Mess: A Way Out," *Readers Digest*, December 1995.

24. See, for example, testimony of Stephen Kaye before the House Committee on Ways and Means, Subcommittee on Social Security, September 18, 1997.

25. Palau, "Chile: Results and Lessons after 15 Years of Reform."

246

26. Queisser, "Chile and Beyond," p. 28.

27. Olivia Mitchell, "Administrative Costs in Public and Private Retirement Systems," National Bureau of Economic Research Working Paper no. 5734, 1996.

28. Letter from José Piñera to Martin Feldstein, dated February 10, 1998, citing Chilean government statistics.

29. Mitchell, "Administrative Costs in Public and Private Retirement Systems."

30. Rob Wright, "Social Security Reform: Is the Chilean Option Really the Answer?" *Plan Sponsor*, October 1996.

31. Queisser, "Chile and Beyond," p. 28.

32. Ibid., p. 28.

33. See, for example, Frank Wright, "Chile Is a Model: But Is It a Good One?" *Minneapolis Star-Tribune*, February 10, 1997.

34. Alberto Arenas de Mesa and Fabio Bertranou, "Learning from Social Security Reforms: Two Different Cases, Chile and Argentina," *World Development* 25, no. 3 (1997): 335.

35. Osvaldo Macías Muñoz, *The Chilean Pension System* (Santiago: Superintendence of Pension Funds Administrators, 1996), Table IV.2, p. 92.

36. Ibid., p. 164.

37. Ibid., p. 166.

38. Ibid.

39. For a discussion of the underground economy in Latin America, see Hernando de Soto, *The Other Path: The Invisible Revolution in the Third World* (New York: Harper and Row, 1989).

40. Macías, *The Chilean Pension System*, p. 91.

41. Collins and Lear, *Chile's Free-Market Miracle*, p. 173.

42. Wright, "Social Security Reform."

43. Sharon Schmickle, "Is Chile's Pension Plan a Model for Everyone?" *Minneapolis Star-Tribune*, December 21, 1997.

44. José Piñera and Mark Klugman, *The Chilean Private Pension System* (Santiago: International Center for Pension Reform, 1995), p. 9.

45. See, for example, Roger Beattie and Warren McGillivray, "A Risky Strategy: Reflections on the World Bank's *Averting the Old-Age Crisis*," *International Social Security Review* 48 (March–April 1995): 13.

46. As of 1995, the average AFP portfolio consisted of 39.4 percent government bonds; 5.3 percent corporate bond; 15.8 percent mortgage bonds; 29.4 percent stocks; and 10.1 percent other investments. Macías, *The Chilean Pension System*, p. 181.

47. Cited in Arenas and Bertranou, *Learning from Social Security Reforms*, pp. 329–48.

48. For white-collar workers, the replacement rate was targetted at 100 percent of wages.

49. Santamaría, "Privatizing Social Security," p. 5.

50. Queisser, "Chile and Beyond," p. 25.

51. Raúl Bustos Castillo, "Analysis of a National Private Pension Scheme: The Case of Chile—A Response," *International Labor Review* 123, no. 3 (1993).

52. Testimony of José Piñera before the House Committee on the Budget, September 30, 1997.

53. G. A. MacKenzie, "Reforming Latin America's Old-Age Pension Systems," *Finance and Development* (March 1995): 10–3.

54. Santamaría, "Privatizing Social Security," p. 5.

55. Walter Schultless and G. Demarco, *Argentina: Evolucion del Sistema Nacional de Prevision Social y Propuesta de Reforma* (Santiago: CEPAL/PNUD, 1993).

56. The description of Argentina's system is largely drawn from Arenas and Bertranou, pp. 331–3.

57. Queisser, "Chile and Beyond," p. 32.

58. Arenas and Bertranou, "Learning From Social Security Reforms," p. 335.

59. Ignacio Krueger and Felipe Rodolfo Murolo, "Examining Reform Issues of the Argentinean Pension Fund System." Paper presented to a conference on The Pension Fund Revolution in Latin America, Miami, September 19, 1996.

60. Steve Bergsman, "Argentina's Private Parts," *Global Custodian* (Spring 1997), pp. 92–8.

61. James Smalhout, "Rethinking Retirement: Looking Back on Pension Reform," *Emerging Markets IMF/World Bank Daily*, September 25, 1997.

62. Queisser, "Chile and Beyond," p. 30.

63. Rudolf Hommes, "Colombia's Social Security Reforms: A Case Study of Political and Financial Viability." Paper presented to the Second Hemispheric Conference on Social Security, Pension Reforms, and Capital Market Development, Inter-American Development Bank, Washington, June 13, 1995.

64. Ibid.

65. Queisser, "Chile and Beyond," p. 34.

66. Ibid.

67. Ibid.

68. Hommes, "Colombia's Social Security Reforms," p. 15.

69. Queisser, "Chile and Beyond," p. 32.

70. Ibid., p. 35.

71. Barineau, "Analyzing the Effect of Pension Reform on Local Stock Markets."

72. See, for example, John Williamson, ed. *Latin American Adjustment: How Much Has Happened?* (Washington: Institute for International Economics, 1990).

73. Queisser, "Chile and Beyond," p. 32.

74. Social Security Administration, *Social Security Programs throughout the World — 1997* (Washington: Government Printing Office, 1997), pp. 280–3.

75. Queisser, "Chile and Beyond," pp. 33–4.

76. Mark Alloway, "Private Pension Reform in Peru." Paper presented to a conference on The Pension Fund Revolution in Latin America, Miami, September 19, 1996.

77. Ibid.

78. Gabriel Martínez, "A New Social Security Law for Mexico." Paper presented to a conference on the Pension Fund Revolution in Latin America, Miami, September 19, 1996.

79. Ibid.

80. Ian Vasquez, "Two Cheers for Mexico's Pension Reform," *Wall Street Journal*, June 27, 1997.

81. "El Salvador's New Pension Fund System: A Radical Change and a Reason to Come Home," *Washington Times*, March 26, 1998.

82. Smalhout, "Rethinking Retirement."

83. Georges de Menil, "National Private Pension Systems: The Movement of Reform in Eastern Europe and the Newly Independent States." Paper presented to a Cato Institute conference on Solving the Global Public Pensions Crisis, December 8, 1997.

84. Matthew Kaminski, "Hungary Braces for Pension Privatization," *Wall Street Journal*, October 21, 1997.

85. De Menil, "National Private Pension Systems."

86. Marek Belka, "Social Security Reform in Poland." Paper presented to a Cato Institute conference on Solving the Global Public Pensions Crisis, December 8, 1997.

87. "Bring on Pension Reform," *Wall Street Journal Europe*, December 23, 1997.

88. De Menil, "National Private Pension Systems."

89. John Dixon, "Social Security and the Ghosts Who Haunt It," eds. John Dixon and Robert Scheurell, *Social Security Programs: A Cross-Cultural Comparative Perspective* (Westport, Conn.: Greenwood Press, 1990), pp. 8–9.

90. Malaysia was actually the first nation to institute a mandatory savings program with a Central Provident Fund in 1951. India and Indonesia also established such systems, albeit with limited coverage, in the early 1950s. However, the system has largely come to be identified with Singapore.

91. Mukal Asher, *The Singapore Central Provident Fund* (Singapore: National University of Singapore, 1992).

92. Ibid.

93. Eamonn Butler, Mukul Asher, and Karl Borden, *Singapore vs. Chile: Competing Models for Welfare Reform* (London: Adam Smith Institute, 1996), pp. 20–1.

94. Michael McLindon, *Privatization & Capital Market Development* (Washington: Institute for Public-Private Partnerships, 1996), p. 144.

95. World Bank, *Averting the Old-Age Crisis*, pp. 94–5.

96. Singapore's public assistance program is so limited that only 2,008 individuals were receiving government benefits as of 1996. Mukal Asher, "Singapore's Social Security System: How Well Does It Address the Central Issues in Social Security Reform?" Paper presented to a conference on Solving the Global Pension Crisis: Opportunities for Privatization, London, England, December 8, 1997.

97. Ibid.

98. Much of the discussion of the British system is drawn from Louis Enoff and Robert Moffit, "Social Security Privatization in Britain: Key Lessons for American Reformers," Heritage Foundation Backgrounder no. 1133, August 6, 1997.

99. Andrew Dilnot, Richard Disney et al., *Pensions Policy in the UK: An Economic Analysis* (London: Institute for Fiscal Studies, 1994), p. 9.

100. Paul Johnson, "The Reform of Pensions in the UK," Institute for Fiscal Studies, London, 1996, p. 12.

101. Robert Preston, James Blitz, and William Lewis, "Tories Plan to Privatize Pensions," *Financial Times*, March 6, 1997.

102. *New Labour: Because Britain Deserves Better* (London: Labour Party, 1997).

103. See, for example, Frank Field, *Private Pensions for All: Squaring the Circle* (London: Fabian Society, 1993).

104. Australia does allow states to levy a payroll tax on employers, but such taxes are unrelated to the old-age pension system. Daniel Mitchell and Robert O'Quinn, "Australia's Privatized Retirement System: Lessons for the United States," Heritage Foundation Backgrounder no. 1149, December 8, 1997, p. 3.

105. Ibid, p. 5.

106. Mitchell and O'Quinn, "Australia's Privatized Retirement System," pp. 14–15.

107. "Superannuation Investment Performance," Insurance and Superannuation Bulletin, Insurance and Superannuation Commission, Canberra, Australia, September 1996, p. 19.

108. Mitchell and O'Quinn, "Australia's Privatized Retirement System," p. 8.

109. For an analysis of the impact of Australian pension reform's impact on savings, investment, and growth, see www.treasury.gov.au/organizations/rimtf.

110. U. S. Congress, Joint Economic Committee, *China's Economic Future: Challenges to U.S. Policy* (Washington: Government Printing Office, 1996).

111. Interestingly, when China rejected Hong Kong governor Chris Patten's attempt to implement a pay-as-you-go system for the island, China's Hong Kong representative Zhou Nan dismissed it as a "costly Euro-Socialist" proposal, clearly differentiating such welfare-statism from the Chinese goal of a "socialist market economy." "Is Welfare UnAsian?" *Economist*, February 11, 1995, pp. 16–7.

112. Wu Jie, "China's Social Security System." Paper presented to a Cato Institute conference on China as a Global Economic Power: Market Reforms in the New Millennium, Shanghai, China, June 15, 1997.

113. Gao Shangquan and Chi Fulin, *China's Social Security System* (Beijing: Foreign Language Press, 1996).

114. The mandated savings rate for individual accounts and the rate of employer contributions to both the individual accounts and social insurance pools vary from province to province, as do administrative rules. Wu, "China's Social Security System."

115. Gao and Chi, *China's Social Security System*.

116. World Bank, "China Pension System Reform," World Bank Resident Mission in China and Mongolia, August 22, 1996.

117. William Even and David McPherson, *Freed from FICA: How Seven States & Localities Exempt a Million Employees from Social Security and Provide Higher Pension Benefits to Retirees* (New York: Third Millennium, 1997).

118. Merrill Matthews, "Some Americans Already Have Privatized Social Security," National Center for Policy Analysis Brief Analysis no. 215, November 4, 1996.

119. Ibid.

120. Ibid, p. 2.

121. Testimony of Don Kibbideaux before the Senate Committee on Finance, Subcommittee on Securities, April 30, 1996.

122. Ibid.

123. Evan and MacPherson, *Freed from FICA*, p. 9.

124. Ibid., p. 40.

Chapter 8

1. The private accounts should be exempt from the estate tax. The government should not be seizing funds already taxed that can serve as the economic foundation for the next generation.

2. For a more detailed discussion of this issue, see Melissa Hieger and William Shipman, "Common Objections to a Market-Based Social Security System: A Response," Cato Institute Social Security Paper no. 10, July 22, 1997, p. 12.

3. World Bank, *Averting the Old-Age Crisis* (Oxford: Oxford University Press, 1994), pp. 21–2, 261–4.

4. Details of the commission's findings can be found in Bipartisan Commission on Tax and Entitlement Reform, *Final Report: Bipartisan Commission on Tax and Entitlement Reform* (Washington: Government Printing Office, 1995).

5. Milton Friedman, *Capitalism and Freedom* (Chicago: University of Chicago Press, 1962), p. 188.

6. Ibid., p. 187.

7. Michael Tanner, *The End of Welfare: Fighting Poverty in the Civil Society* (Washington: Cato Institute, 1996).

8. John Stuart Mill, "Objections to Government Interference," reprinted in David Boaz, ed., *The Libertarian Reader* (New York: Free Press, 1997), p. 26.

9. The poll of 1,000 adults was conducted by the Gallup Organization on behalf of the Employee Benefits Research Institute in January 1994. Individuals were asked, "Do you think participation in Social Security should be made voluntary?" Fifty-four percent responded "yes"; 44 percent responded "no." The margin of error was plus or minus 3.5 percent.

10. Friedman, *Capitalism and Freedom*, p. 183.

11. Peter Ferrara, *Social Security: Averting the Crisis* (Washington: Cato Institute, 1982), pp. 86–7.

12. The authors disagree about whether future workers should be required to enter the new private system. Michael Tanner believes that future entrants into the labor force should automatically be enrolled in the privatized system. As a result, once all current workers have left the system, the old pay-as-you-go Social Security system will cease to exist. Peter Ferrara believes that since virtually all new workers will voluntarily choose the new system, it is unnecessary and politically unwise to abolish the old system.

Chapter 9

1. There are several different ways to measure Social Security's unfunded liability. The Social Security Administration projects unfunded liabilities at $3 trillion, basically the cash-flow deficit over the next 75 years. The Social Security Administration refers to this as the "open-group deficiency." It includes all future benefit obligations (over the next 75 years) to both current and future beneficiaries and all future tax revenue from both current and future workers, including unborn workers, less assets on hand. The figure is small because we get the benefit of assuming that taxes will be paid by young and unborn workers without having to account for the benefits that will be due to them beyond the truncated 75-year window. We believe it is more accurate to use the "closed-group deficiency" model, including all obligations incurred during the 75-year window, even if they will be paid beyond the window. That figure is approximately $8.9 trillion. It is also important to understand that beyond the 75-year window, the unfunded liabilities of the system rise significantly. The House Budget Committee estimates that if the window were extended to 2078, the unfunded liabilities would total $14.6 trillion.

2. We presume that markets have already fully discounted the current implicit debt. The actual impact on existing markets of explicitly recognizing that debt has not been fully studied. As Alan Greenspan notes, "If markets perceive that this liability has the same status as explicit federal debt, then one must presume that interest rates have already fully adjusted to the implicit contingent liability. However, if markets have not fully accounted for this implicit liability, then making it explicit could lead to higher interest rates for the U.S. government." Testimony of Alan Greenspan before the U.S. Senate Committee on Budget, Task Force on Social Security, November 20, 1997. Greenspan's personal view is that "There is reason to suspect,

however, that if a liability is made explicit in a manner similar to the transition procedure in Chile, each dollar of new liability will weigh far less on financial markets than a dollar of current public debt." Ibid.

3. If some workers choose to continue in Social Security for some reason, their benefits would continue to be financed through the steady-state Social Security system. With Social Security benefits considerably reduced, as suggested in the last chapter, payroll tax revenues at current rates should be sufficient to finance those benefits. Of course, workers who make this choice would then be left with the abysmally low return that Social Security's pay-as-you-go system can pay.

4. Martin Feldstein, "The Missing Piece in Policy Analysis: Social Security Reform," *American Economic Review* 86 (May 1996): 3. See also Richard Rippe, "Further Gains in Corporate Profitability," *American Economic Review* 95 (August 1995); Martin Feldstein, Louis Dicks-Mireaux, and James Poterba, "The Effective Tax Rate and the Pre-Tax Rate of Return," *Journal of Public Economics* 21 (July 1983): 129–58.

5. James Buchanan, "Comment on Browning's Paper," ed. Colin Campbell, *Proceedings of an American Enterprise Institute Conference on Social Security* (Washington, American Enterprise Institute, 1979), pp. 208–12; Milton Friedman and Rose Friedman, *Free to Choose* (New York: Avon Books, 1980), p. 114.

6. World Bank, *Averting the Old-Age Crisis*, pp. 182–9.

7. The authors are grateful to George H. O'Neill Jr. for this suggestion.

8. Indeed, if a balanced budget amendment is adopted that applies to Social Security, and the program is not taken fully off budget, then the sale of new bonds may not be allowed without the required supermajority approval under the balanced budget amendment. But the sale of an existing asset like Social Security trust fund bonds would not run into this requirement.

9. See Robert Poole, "A Federal Privatization Agenda," eds. Ed Crane and David Boaz, *Cato Handbook for Congress*, 105th Congress (Washington: Cato Institute, 1997), pp. 291–301.

10. See Earl Ravenal, "The 1988 Defense Budget," in Ibid., pp. 101–15.

11. Kotlikoff, for example, advocates a temporary 7 percent national sales tax. Laurence Kotlikoff, "Privatizing Social Security at Home and Abroad," *American Economic Review* 86 (1996): 368–72.

12. Clair Hintz, "Tax Burden on American Families Rises Again," Tax Foundation Special Report no. 74, November 1997.

13. Feldstein, "The Missing Piece in Policy Analysis," p. 5

14. See, for example, Sanford Grossman, "An Analysis of the Effects of Removing the Deductibility of IRA Contributions on the Incentive to Save," Princeton University, June 16, 1986; James Long, "Taxation and IRA Participation: Re-Examination and Confirmation," *National Tax Journal* 4 (December 1988): 585–93; R. Glenn Hubbard, "Do IRAs and Keoghs Increase Saving?" *National Tax Journal* 37 (March 1984): 43–54; Lawrence Summers, "IRAs Really Do Spark New Savings," *New York Times*, May 25, 1986; Daniel Feenberg and Jonathan Skinner, "Sources of IRA Saving," National Bureau of Economic Research Working Paper no. 2845, February 1989; and Steven Venti and David Wise, National Bureau of Economic Research Working Paper no. 1879, April 1986.

15. Feldstein calculated that if everyone saved and invested enough to replace Social Security benefits, the real rate of return to capital would decline by about 15 percent or less. See Martin Feldstein, "National Savings in the United States," Harvard

Institute of Economic Research Discussion Paper no. 506, October 1976; Martin Feldstein, "The Optimal Financing of Social Security," Harvard Institute of Economic Research Discussion Paper no. 388, May 1974. However, this decline would not be complete until sufficient investment had been accumulated to replace Social Security, which would take decades, well after the transition had been financed in any event.

16. See, for example, W. Michael Cox and Richard Alm, "Technology and Growth in the Information Age—And Beyond," Federal Reserve Bank of Dallas, *1997 Annual Report*, January 1, 1997.

Chapter 10

1. The authors are grateful to Melissa Hieger and William Shipman for their work in addressing these issues. Much of the discussion herein was first raised in their paper, "Common Objections to a Market-Based Social Security System: A Response," Cato Institute Social Security Paper no. 10, July 22, 1997.

2. Quoted in Peter Passell, "Can Retirees' Safety Net Be Saved?" *New York Times*, February 18, 1996.

3. Much of this section is drawn from Krzystof Ostaszewski, "Privatizing the Social Security Trust Fund? Don't Let the Government Invest," Cato Institute Social Security Paper no. 6, January 14, 1997.

4. *1997 Annual Report of the Board of Trustees of the Federal Old-Age and Survivors Insurance and Disability Insurance Trust Funds* (Washington: Government Printing Office), Table III.B 3, p. 180. (Intermediate Assumptions, Year 2020).

5. *1995 Annual Report of the New York Stock Exchange* (New York: New York Stock Exchange, Inc., 1995).

6. For a thorough discussion of state employee pension systems and their investment policies, see Carolyn Peterson, *State Employee Retirement Systems: A Decade of Change* (Washington: American Legislative Exchange Council, 1987).

7. Del Jones, "City Pension Fund to Sell Texaco Stock," *USA Today*, November 22, 1996.

8. Cassandra Chrones Moore, "Whose Pension Is It Anyway? Economically Targeted Investments and the Pension Funds," Cato Institute Policy Analysis no. 236, September 1, 1995.

9. See, for example, Thomas Jones, "Social Security: Invaluable, Irreplaceable, and Fixable," *Participant*, February 1996.

10. Robert Reich, "Pension Fund Raid Just Ain't So." Letter to the editor, *Wall Street Journal*, October 26, 1994.

11. Report of the 1994–1995 Advisory Council on Social Security (Washington: Government Printing Office, 1997), p. 146.

12. David Green, "Pensions: The Case against Compulsion," Institute for Economic Affairs, London, December 1997.

13. "Excerpts from President Clinton's News Conference," *Washington Post*, November 11, 1997.

14. Hieger and Shipman, "Common Objections to a Market-Based Social Security System," pp. 8–10.

15. Ibid, pp. 10–1.

16. Ibid., p. 10.

17. Martin Feldstein and Andrew Samwick, "The Transition Path in Privatizing Social Security," National Bureau of Economic Research Working Paper no. 5761, Cambridge, Mass., September 1996.

Chapter 11

1. "1998 State of the Union Address," January 27, 1998.
2. "Remarks by the President on Social Security," Georgetown University, Washington, February 9, 1998.

Index

About the Authors

Peter J. Ferrara is the general counsel and chief economist for Americans for Tax Reform, the nation's largest grassroots advocacy group. Considered one of the foremost experts on Social Security privatization, Ferrara has published numerous books and articles fo a large number of journals and newspapers, including the *Wall Street Journal*, *Human Events*, the *Washington Times*, and *National Review*. He served as associate deputy attorney general of the United States from 1992 to 1993 and served in the Reagan Administration from 1981 to 1983.

Michael Tanner is director of health and welfare studies at the Cato Institute in Washington, D.C. Before joining Cato, he served as director of research for the Georgia Public Policy Foundation in Atlanta. Tanner also spent five years as legislative director with the American Legislative Exchange Council. He is the author of six previous books on health and welfare reform.

His work has appeared in such publications as the *Wall Street Journal*, the *Baltimore Sun*, the *Washington Times*, the *Indianapolis Star*, the *Cleveland Plain Dealer*, the *Detroit News*, the *Portland Oregonian*, *USA Today*, and the *National Review*. A frequent media guest, he has appeared on *ABC World News Tonight*, *CBS Evening News*, *NBC Dateline*, and *Good Morning America*, among other programs.

Cato Institute

Founded in 1977, the Cato Institute is a public policy research foundation dedicated to broadening the parameters of policy debate to allow consideration of more options that are consistent with the traditional American principles of limited government, individual liberty, and peace. To that end, the Institute strives to achieve greater involvement of the intelligent, concerned lay public in questions of policy and the proper role of government.

The Institute is named for *Cato's Letters*, libertarian pamphlets that were widely read in the American Colonies in the early 18th century and played a major role in laying the philosophical foundation for the American Revolution.

Despite the achievement of the nation's Founders, today virtually no aspect of life is free from government encroachment. A pervasive intolerance for individual rights is shown by government's arbitrary intrusions into private economic transactions and its disregard for civil liberties.

To counter that trend, the Cato Institute undertakes an extensive publications program that addresses the complete spectrum of policy issues. Books, monographs, and shorter studies are commissioned to examine the federal budget, Social Security, regulation, military spending, international trade, and myriad other issues. Major policy conferences are held throughout the year, from which papers are published thrice yearly in the *Cato Journal*. The Institute also publishes the quarterly magazine *Regulation.*

In order to maintain its independence, the Cato Institute accepts no government funding. Contributions are received from foundations, corporations, and individuals, and other revenue is generated from the sale of publications. The Institute is a nonprofit, tax-exempt, educational foundation under Section 501(c)3 of the Internal Revenue Code.

CATO INSTITUTE
1000 Massachusetts Ave., N.W.
Washington, D.C. 20001